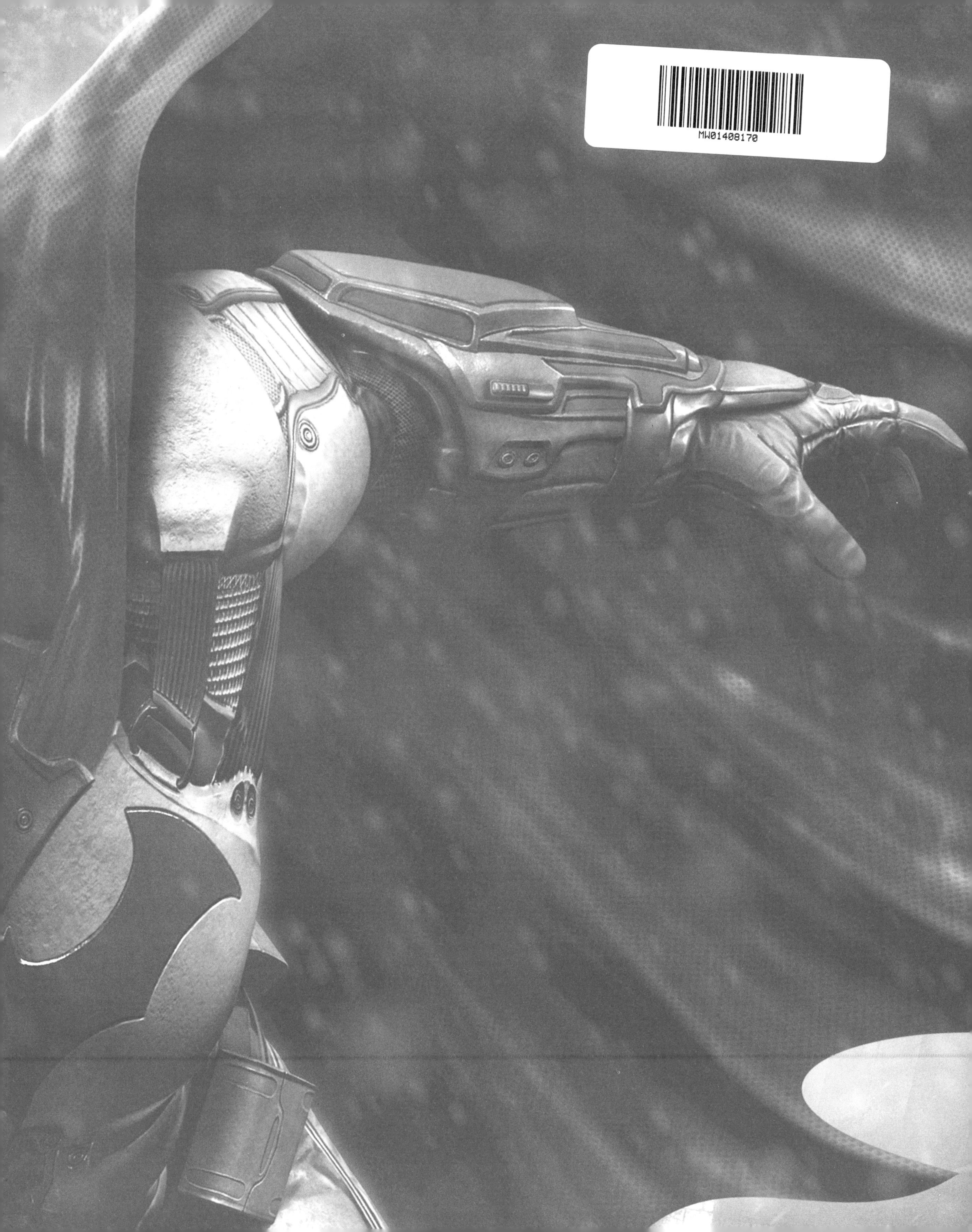

ARKHAM UNIVERSE
THE ULTIMATE VISUAL GUIDE

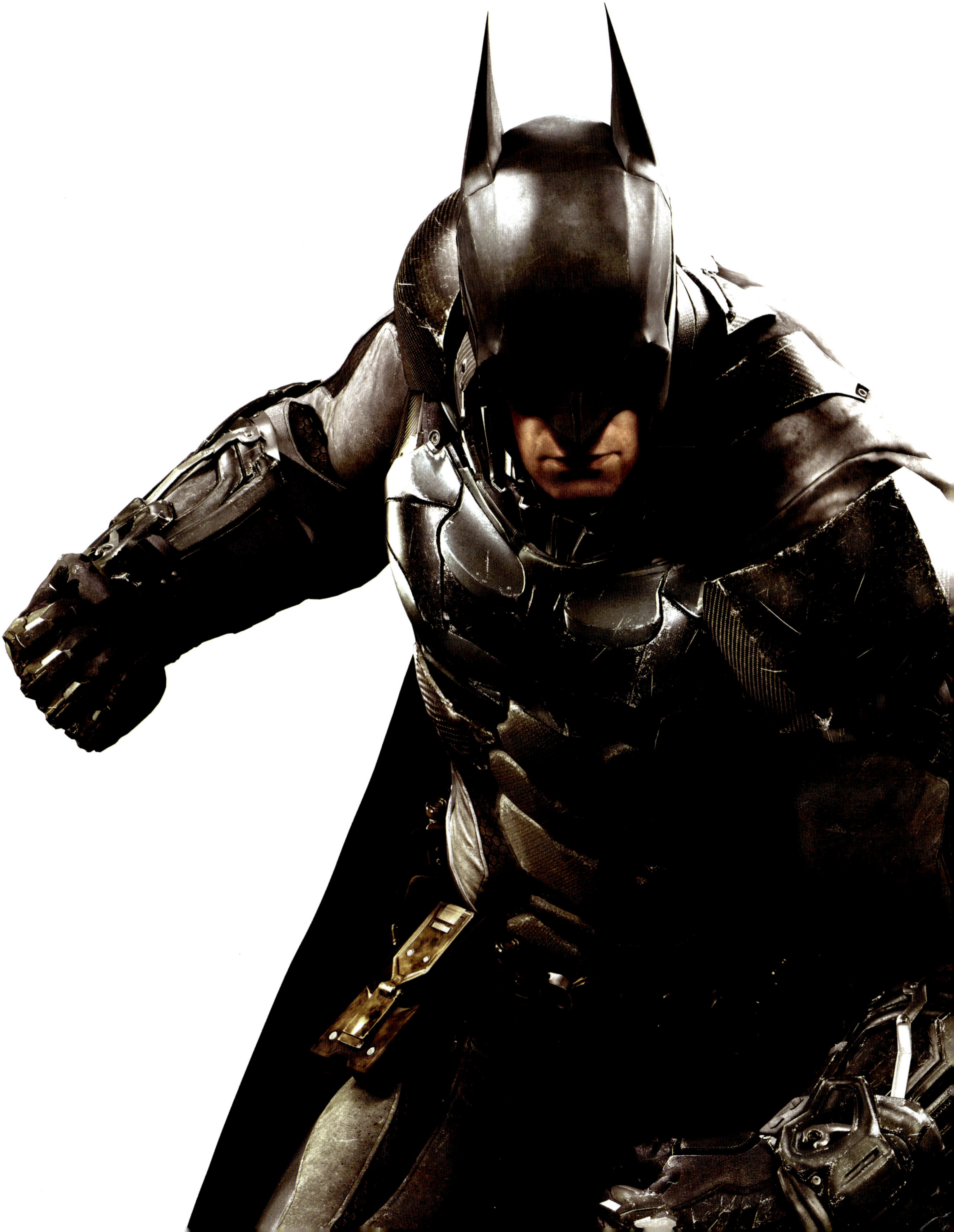

ARKHAM UNIVERSE
THE ULTIMATE VISUAL GUIDE

WRITTEN BY
MATTHEW K. MANNING

CONTENTS

Foreword by Kevin Conroy	6
Introduction	8
Timeline	12

Batman	**18**
The Dark Knight	20
Bruce Wayne	24
Wayne Manor	26
The Batcave	28
The Batsuits	30
Other Suits	32
Fighting Techniques	38
The Batmobile	40
Up Close	42
Under the Hood	44
The Batwing	48
The Batarang	50
Smoke Pellets	51
Grenades	54
Remote Claw	55
Disruptor	56
Batclaw	57
Explosive Gel	60
Shock Gloves	61
Cryptographic Sequencer	62
Remote Electrical Charge	63
Detective Mode	64
Cold Cases	66
Gotham City	68
Gotham Locations	70
City Society	78

Allies	**80**

Arkham Staff	106

Enemies	**108**
The Joker	110
Harley Quinn	114
Arkham Takeover	116
The Penguin	118
The Riddler	120
Black Mask	122
The Bounty	124
Killer Croc	126
Copperhead	128
Deathstroke	130
Electrocutioner	134
Bane	136
Blackgate Break-In	138
Firefly	140
Deadshot	142
Mr. Freeze	144
Cold, Cold Heart	146
Lady Shiva	148
Anarky	150
The Mad Hatter	154
Scarecrow	156
Ace in the Hole	158
Catwoman	160
Poison Ivy	162
Professor Hugo Strange	164
Arkham City	166
Strange City	168
Rā's al Ghūl	170
Talia al Ghūl	172
Two-Face	174

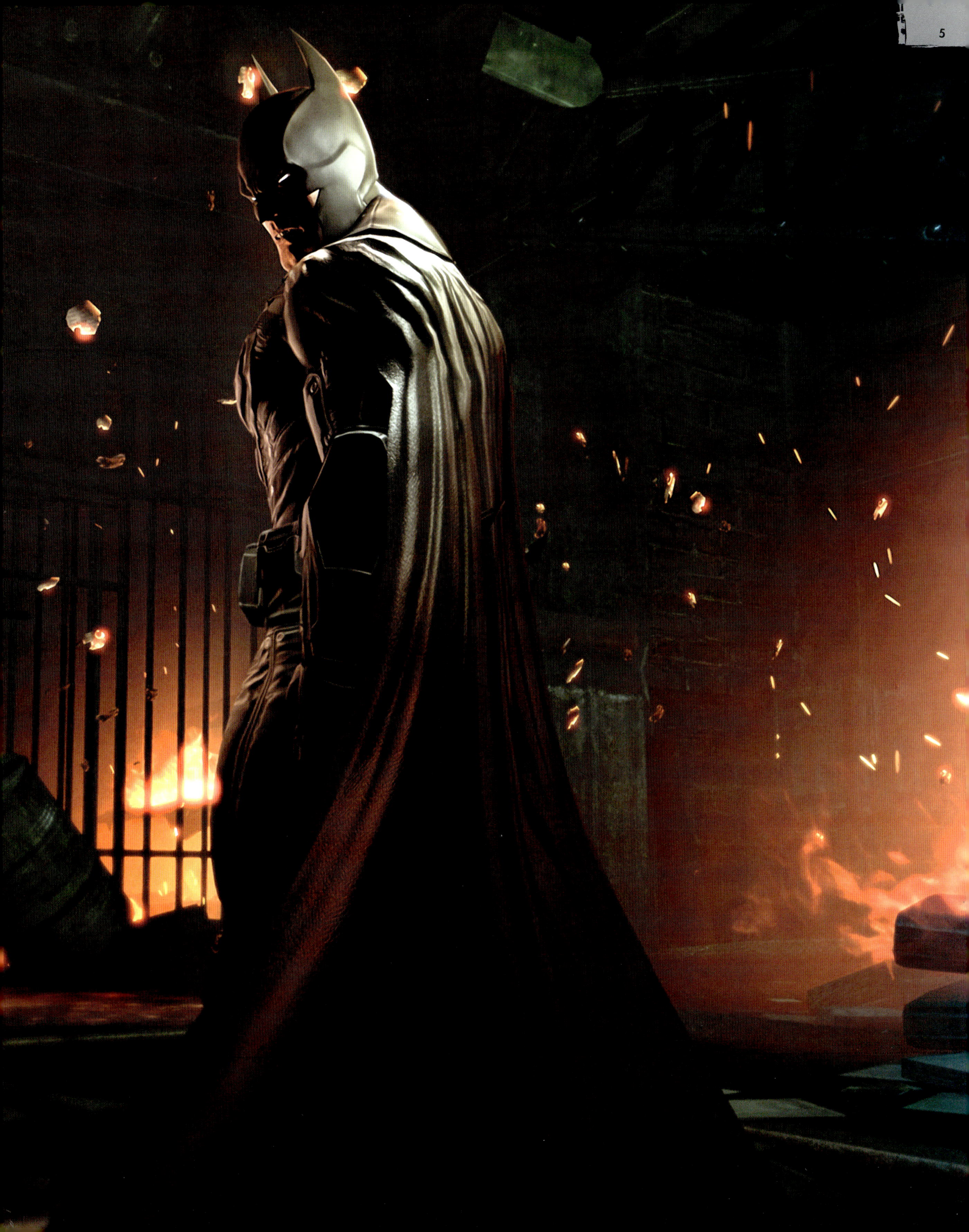

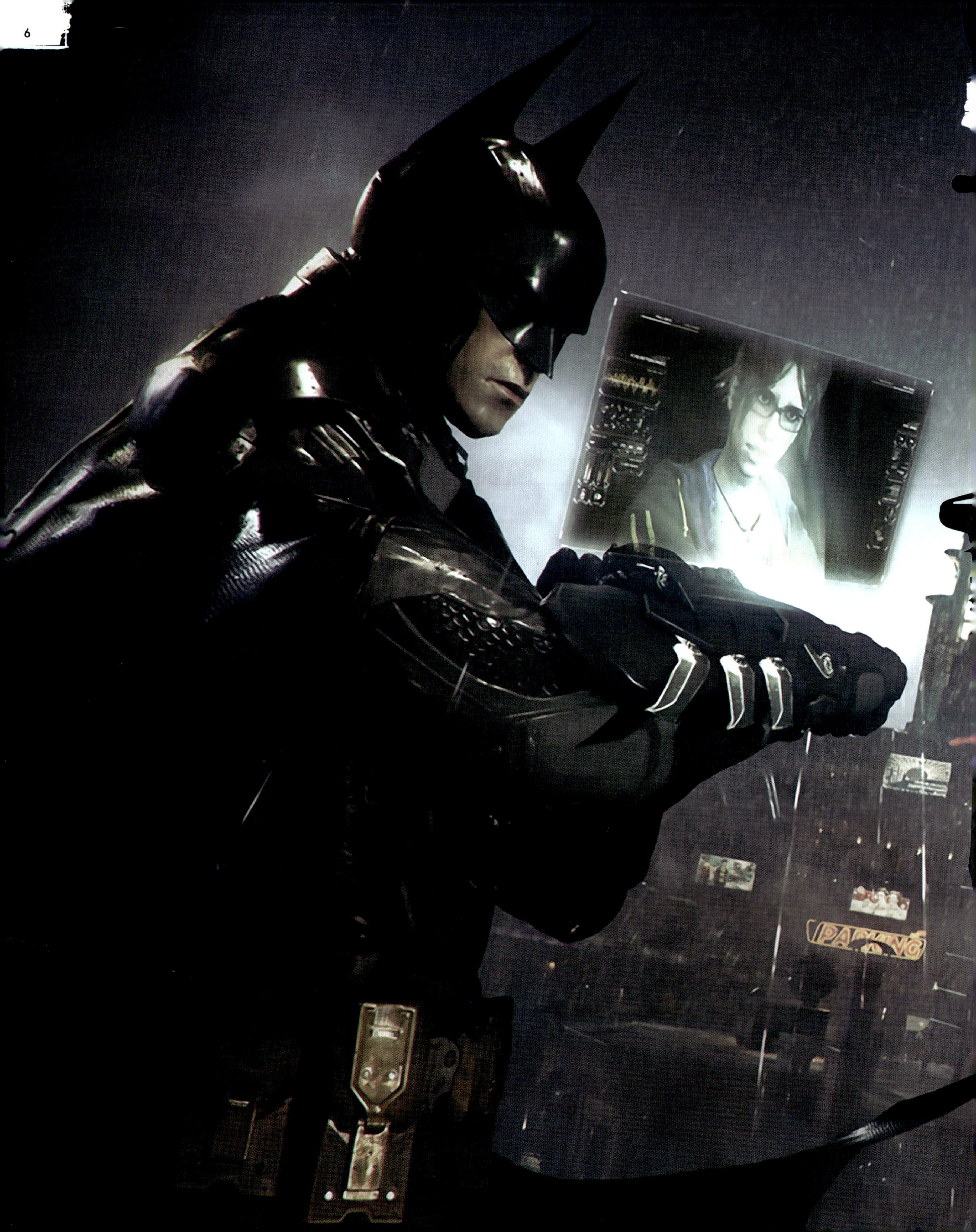

FOREWORD BY KEVIN CONROY

"HEY, BUDDY, YOU GOT ANY CHANGE?" THE VOICE CAME FROM A PILE OF RAGS AND DEBRIS IN THE SHADOWY CORNER OF THE VACANT PARKING LOT OF THE HOLLYWOOD POST OFFICE.

It was 5:00 a.m. The early morning dark in a vacant parking lot is not where I'm my most comfortable. I didn't even have my wallet—I'd just jumped out of my car to toss some bills in the mail on my way to a 5:30 call at the studio. "Sorry man, I don't even have my wallet, just my mail." A ruddy, filthy face emerged from the pile. "Oh man! You're Kevin Conroy, aren't you?" What?! How did he know me? Had he read my mail? Impossible. Was he some actor who'd fallen on hard times? Someone from my past I hadn't recognized? I had to admit the truth. I cautiously replied "Yes." "Oh man, you're Batman!" This was getting really weird. The role I'd been recording for just a few years I considered a completely anonymous job. *I'd* never even heard of me, how could he have? "How do you know that?" "Oh man, this is so cool! Batman! I watch your show every day at the Circuit City on Hollywood! They have all the TVs set to your show! This is so cool! Oh man, would you just say it? You know what I want you to say? Please?" This can't be happening, I thought. "Oh come on, you know." Okay, here goes, the iconic Batman line. I let her rip: "I am Batman!" "Oh man, this is so awesome!" I built the energy: "I am the night!" "Awesome! Now bring it home, bring it on home, Batman!" I built to a crescendo: "I am Batman!!"

It echoed through the parking lot and beyond to the vacant streets and up to the hills, echoing back to us." Thank you, Jesus! I got Batman in my parking lot!" I realized I couldn't leave this guy empty handed. "Just wait here a second, let me get you something." I started back to my car to get my wallet. "Oh no! Man, I can't take Batman's money. This has been cool enough!" I was having none of that: "You'll take Batman's money, or you'll tell everyone Batman is cheap!"

Later that day I called Andrea Romano, the director of the Batman shows and a close friend. I told her of my 5:00 a.m. encounter. She roared with laughter. "I love the idea of you bellowing in the dark with someone you met in a parking lot!" "Well, at least we know the show is getting popular," I said.

I like to tell about that encounter, because I think it illustrates how Batman has permeated our culture on so many levels. Children get swept up in the fantasy of it, adolescents in the action-adventure, adults in the complex psychodrama of Batman/Bruce Wayne and the cast of extraordinarily complex psychotics that make up the villains. It appeals on so many levels because Batman is an ordinary man doing extraordinary things and always on the side of Justice. He's an icon, a role model, and I feel incredibly lucky to have been able to contribute to the Batman legacy.

When I first auditioned for the role, my only exposure had been the Adam West series of the late 60s. It was great entertainment with an exceptional cast, but Bruce Timm and Paul Dini, the creators of the animated series, wanted to go back to the roots of the Dark Knight in the Bob Kane comics. So their focus was away from the broad brushstrokes of the TV series and toward a darker, grittier, film noir Gotham City, where danger and epic battles between good and evil were fought. I found the voice spontaneously during the audition, I had very little background in animation or Batman. I was just an actor using his imagination to create an effect, a mood, that reflected the darkness of the man's life and the cave of despair he worked from. It brought me to a deep, husky, brooding sound that just felt right for the background of the character. What I never anticipated was how iconic the character would become and in how many different incarnations he would appear: *Batman: the Animated Series*, *The Adventures of Batman and Robin*, *The Justice League*, *Batman Beyond*, and now the Arkham games.

The unifying theme of all these incarnations is, of course, the character of Batman and the amazing crew of eccentric villains, but another, just as important aspect, is the artwork.

From the beginning of the Batman animated series, when Bruce Timm decided to paint on a black background to emphasize the noir aspect of the Gotham City world, the artwork has been an integral character in the episodes. That emphasis on a rich visual experience with elegant artwork has now been fully translated to the Batman Arkham universe. So much of what makes the games so absorbing and exciting to play is the visual thrill of inhabiting the artwork that creates the world of Gotham City.

As well as celebrating the flair and dynamism of Rocksteady's crew of artists, the book you have in your hands, *Batman Arkham Universe: The Ultimate Visual Guide*, provides Batman Arkham fans with all the information they'll ever need on the games' storylines, characters, locations, weapons, and equipment. It'll not only massively enrich the game-playing experience for long-time aficionados, it's also a great introduction for anyone venturing down those dark and dangerous Gotham City streets for the first time, streets whose one true guardian announces himself with the immortal words: "I am Batman!"

I hope the player finds these gritty Gotham City streets as exciting as I have.

Kevin Conroy

INTRODUCTION

I was in 5th grade when I first played a Batman video game. It was 1989, and the game was a Nintendo cartridge titled, appropriately enough, *Batman: The Video Game*. As a tie-in to the blockbuster movie of the same year, there was something about that little, purple, 8-bit Batman that caught my interest. The Dark Knight was at my control. I was in charge of his adventures.

A lifelong comic book fan, I continued collecting Batman games on various devices. As I grew up and became a comic book writer and historian, any time for video games was slowly replaced with time for reading, and I fell out of the gamer loop entirely. Then I heard about *Batman: Arkham Asylum*, a video game written by Paul Dini, of *Batman: The Animated Series* fame, that starred the voices of Kevin Conroy and Mark Hamill, reprising their roles as Batman and the Joker from that same cartoon. I was interested. Those were very impressive feathers for any cap.

So I searched out a gameplay video on YouTube. And then another. And then another. Before I knew it, it had become my daily habit to take my lunches in front of Arkham Asylum. I was completely engrossed in the story, the graphics, and the world that Rocksteady Studios had created. Some of the character designs were different, but there was no doubt. This was Batman. This was Arkham Asylum. They'd captured an element that hadn't been as pronounced in every other Batman video game to date: atmosphere.

The choice was pretty much made for me. I bought a PlayStation, and tried the game out until I'd finished it. Then came *Batman: Arkham City*, and finally, *Batman: Arkham Origins*. Each game built on the rich mood of its predecessor, and each was an extremely rewarding experience. So much so, that when I was asked to write this book and given a chance to read the script for *Batman: Arkham Knight*, I didn't have much choice in that decision, either.

I'd like to thank the many people at DK, DC Entertainment, Warner Bros., and Rocksteady for their invaluable assistance on this book. I'd also like to thank my wife, Dorothy, and my two daughters, Lilly and Gwen, who somehow accepted the fact that playing video games during the day was part of my "work." I'm still not quite sure how I tricked them so easily.

When I first mashed those few buttons on a rectangular controller back in 1989, I had no idea I'd still be playing and enjoying Batman video games over 25 years later. And I certainly had no idea that I'd be doing it for a living.

Matthew K. Manning
Asheville, North Carolina

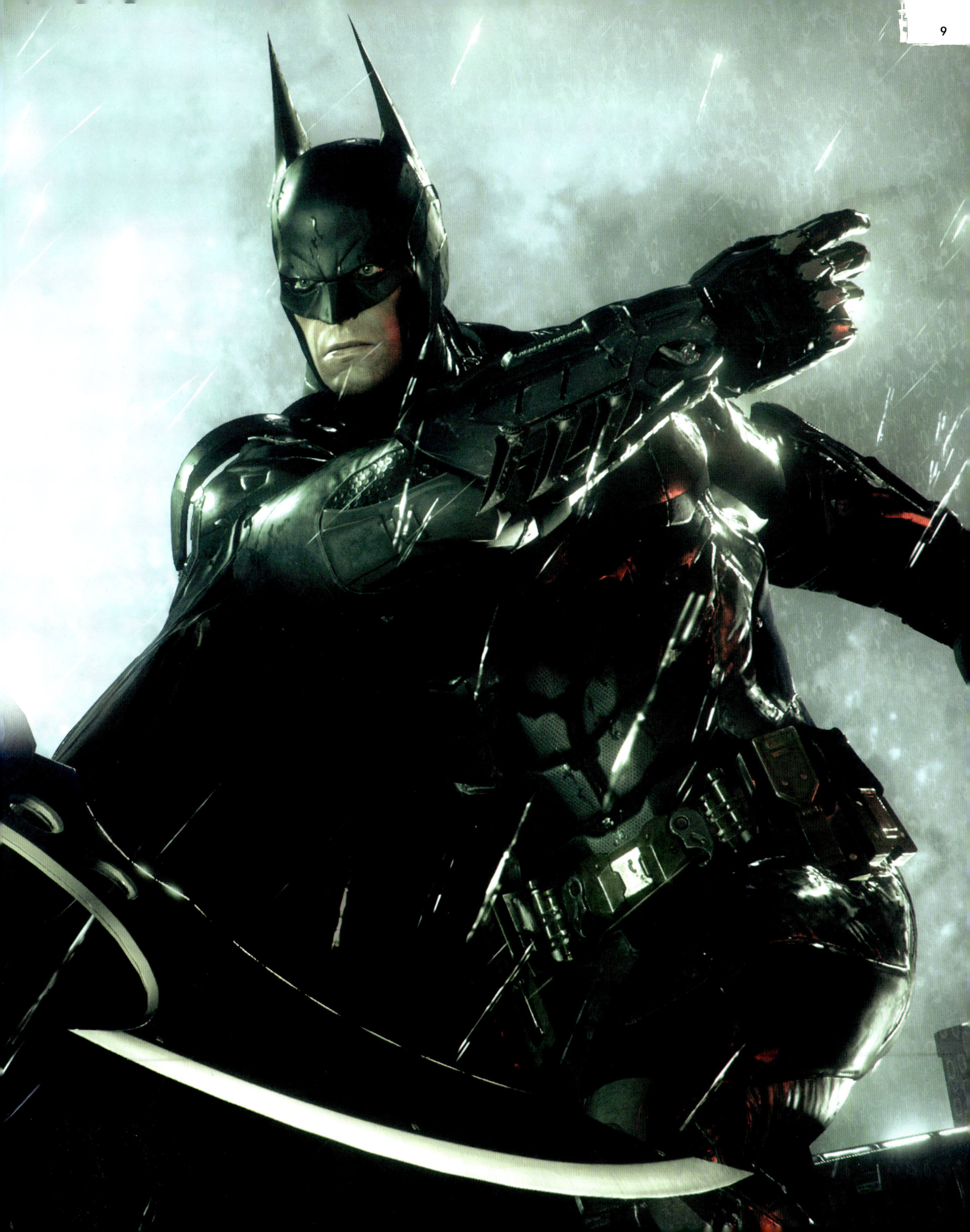

Knight Moves
When Scarecrow causes a citywide panic by introducing a new strain of his fear toxin, Batman breaks out his Batmobile. With the streets mostly evacuated, Batman is free to travel the city without fear of traffic barring his way. And should enemies oppose him, this new Batmobile model comes equipped with the latest in non-lethal weaponry.

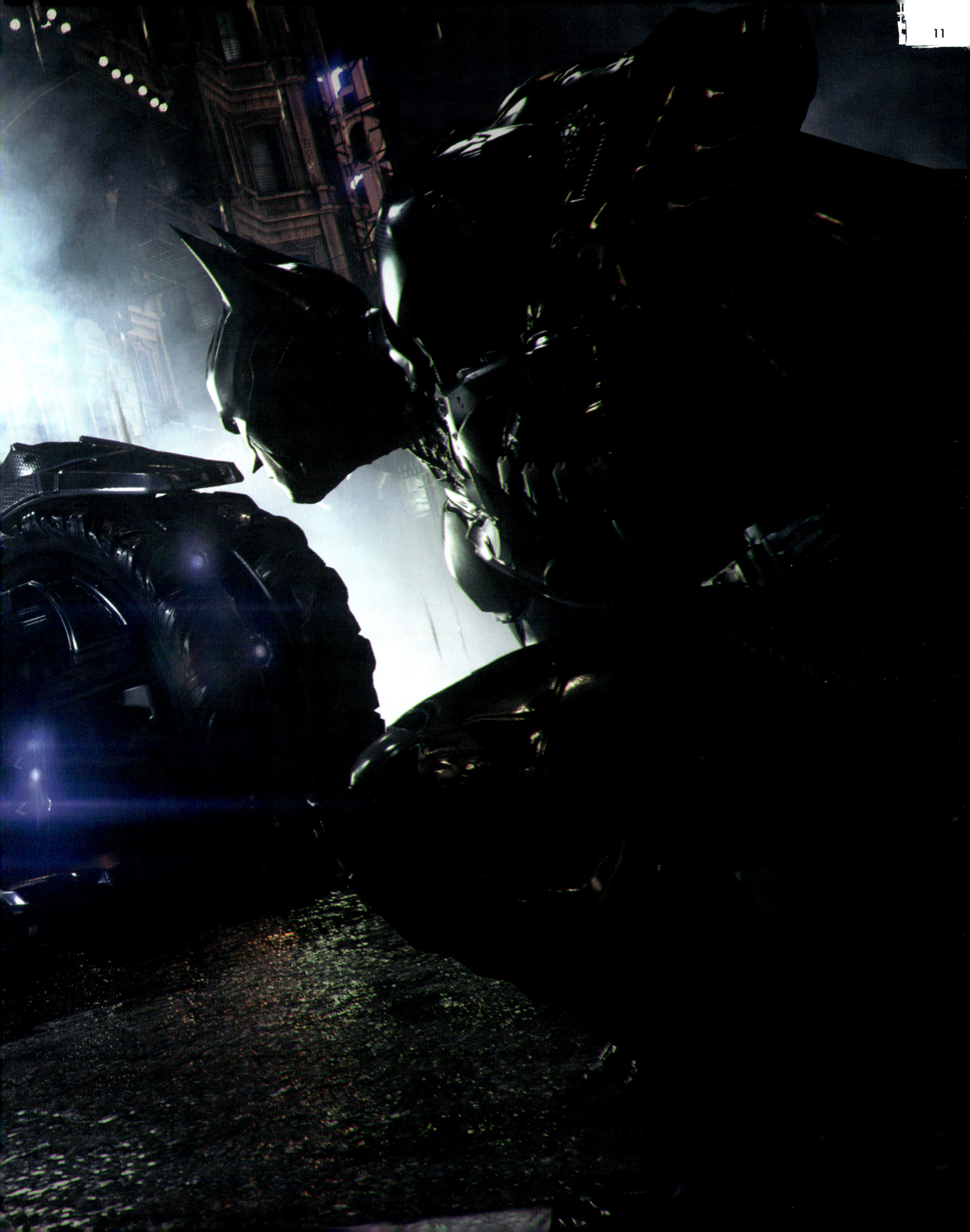

TIMELINE

IN THE FINAL DAYS OF HIS TRAINING FOR LIFE AS BATMAN, BRUCE WAYNE HEADS TO A SECRET MONASTERY IN THE MOUNTAINOUS REGION OF NORTH KOREA TO LEARN THE WAYS OF TOGAKURE-RYU UNDER MASTER KIRIGI. AFTER A LONG ABSENCE, BRUCE RETURNS TO GOTHAM CITY. BATMAN SIGHTINGS BEGIN AND HE SOON BECOMES AN URBAN LEGEND. MEANWHILE, A FAILED COMEDIAN TURNED PETTY CRIMINAL HIRED BY THE MOB FALLS INTO A VAT OF CHEMICALS AND EMERGES AS THE JOKER.

A PRICE ON BATMAN'S HEAD

- Black Mask breaks into Blackgate Prison. Batman saves Warden Joseph and discovers that Commissioner Loeb was working with Black Mask just as the villain kills the Commissioner. Black Mask escapes, but Killer Croc remains behind to face Batman, who defeats him. Batman learns that there is a bounty on his head.

- Back in the Batcave, Batman discovers that eight assassins intend to collect the bounty: Killer Croc, Bane, Copperhead, Deathstroke, Electrocutioner, Deadshot, Lady Shiva, and Firefly.

- The control towers Batman uses for his Batwing's auto-nav system are emitting jamming signals. Batman discovers that a criminal calling himself Enigma is responsible.

- Batman interrupts a gang deal involving Ricky "Loose Lips" Leblanc and tracks his employer, a gangster called the Penguin, to a cargo ship named *The Final Offer*. There, he defeats the Electrocutioner and Penguin's employee, Tracey Buxton.

- Batman stops Penguin and his employee Candy from torturing crime rival Alberto Falcone. Batman then faces Deathstroke, only just defeating the assassin. Batman takes Deathstroke's Remote Claw before heading to Lacey Towers in pursuit of the Penguin.

- The villain Anarky plants bombs around Gotham. Batman tracks down and defuses the bombs, and then defeats Anarky in the Solomon Wayne Courthouse.

- At Lacey Towers, Batman finds a body that may be Black Mask. To verify this, Batman infiltrates the G.C.P.D.'s National Criminal Database. Batman is aided by Captain Gordon's daughter Barbara.

- Leaving the G.C.P.D., Batman runs into Captain Gordon who attempts to arrest him. Batman takes out S.W.A.T. team leader Branden, and escapes into the sewers.

ENTER THE JOKER

- Batman deduces that Black Mask was not murdered by the Penguin, as authorities believe. In his place, Black Mask sent a decoy, who was murdered by a new player in town, the Joker.

- The Mad Hatter kidnaps an innocent woman he calls Alice. Batman confronts the villain for the first time and rescues her.

- At Gotham Merchants Bank, Batman meets the Joker, who admits to placing the bounty on Batman's head. The Joker escapes with Black Mask's cash and heads to Sionis' Steel Mill, his new headquarters.

- Batman is lured into a meeting with Lady Shiva. She forces the Dark Knight to participate in a test at Wonder Tower. Batman passes this test, and Shiva claims that a mysterious master is out to destroy Gotham City before evading the Dark Knight.

- After tracking down the real Black Mask, Batman is attacked and poisoned by Copperhead. He manages to fight through hallucinations and gain a cure from Alfred, but Black Mask escapes. Batman traps Copperhead in a shipping container.

- Batman triumphs over Black Mask after destroying his various chemical stashes in Gotham City.

- Batman learns that Deadshot has caused a helicopter crash and heads to Gotham Merchants Bank to apprehend him.

- Batman discovers a meeting between the Joker and the remaining assassins at the Gotham Royal Hotel.

- When the Joker kills the Electrocutioner for doubting him, Batman commandeers the villain's Shock Gloves.

- The Joker causes an explosion at the Gotham Royal Hotel. Batman is caught on camera by Vicki Vale's GCTV news crew.

- Batman is attacked by Bane. The two fight on a balcony of the Royal Hotel until police intervene. Bane escapes via helicopter, but Batman tags him with a homing device.

- As Bane departs, he fires a bazooka at the Joker, causing the villain to plummet off the side of the building. Batman leaps after his enemy and saves his life. The Joker kills two of his own men and then tries to kill himself, but is stopped by Batman. The Joker becomes fascinated with Batman.

- In Blackgate prison, the Joker is evaluated by psychiatrist Dr. Harleen Quinzel, who falls in love with him.

THE THREAT OF BANE

- Batman heads to the G.C.P.D. to inspect a body he believes is Bane's. He then learns that Bane knows his secret identity.

- Firefly places bombs on Pioneers Bridge and takes hostages. Captain Gordon refuses Batman's warning, leaving Batman to disarm the bombs. Batman eventually defeats Firefly and, in the aftermath, forms an uneasy alliance with Captain Gordon.

- Bane breaks into the Batcave and nearly kills Batman's butler, Alfred Pennyworth. The Dark Knight restarts Alfred's heart using the Electrocutioner's Shock Gloves.

- The Joker takes over Blackgate Prison. Batman arrives and defeats Bane despite the villain having TN-1 in his system. The drug turns Bane into a hulking monster and erases his knowledge of Batman's secret identity. Batman then defeats the Joker in the prison chapel, ending his reign of terror.

- The Dark Knight hunts down Bane's right-hand man Bird at the My Alibi nightclub and stops him dealing the drug Venom.

- Batman stops Enigma from releasing his files on the citizens of Gotham City. He learns that Enigma's real name is Edward Nashton.

- Victor Fries is betrayed by his employer, Ferris Boyle, when trying to cure his wife's Huntington's disease. A scuffle in his lab at GothCorp turns Fries into Mr. Freeze.

- Mr. Freeze and the Penguin's men crash a New Year's Eve party at Wayne Manor. Freeze kidnaps Ferris Boyle. Batman tracks the Penguin to GothCorp. and prevents Mr. Freeze from offering the Penguin a weapons deal.

- At Fries's old lab, Batman discovers the truth about Boyle and Mr. Freeze. He ends up taking them both down.

THE BAT AND THE CAT

- Batman first meets Catwoman—an encounter that leads to her arrest by police.

- Batman investigates an explosion at Blackgate to discover that the prison has been divided up into territories by some of Gotham City's worst rogues.

- In Blackgate, Batman rescues Catwoman from the Penguin's goons, and the two team up. Batman is unaware that Catwoman has been hired by Justice Department agent Amanda Waller to break Bane out of the prison.

- In the prison exercise yard, Batman faces Bronze Tiger, a criminal who refused to join Penguin's gang. Bronze Tiger helps Batman to escape Penguin's men.

- Batman defeats Deadshot, before fighting his way through the Joker's carnival game to save the life of Warden Joseph.

- When Black Mask overloads the Blackgate generators, Batman is forced to battle the monstrous Solomon Grundy, before stabilizing the generators and defeating Black Mask.

- In the Arkham Wing of Blackgate, Batman learns Catwoman's true motives. Catwoman forces Batman to defuse the Joker's bombs while she makes off with Bane.

- With the bombs deactivated, Batman defeats Catwoman and meets a Federal agent named Captain Rick Flag who has captured Bane.

THE JOKER ON THE LOOSE

- Captain Gordon uses the Bat-Signal for the first time.

- The Joker escapes Blackgate, as do the Penguin and Black Mask.

- Mayor Hill resigns as Gotham City's mayor. Captain Gordon is promoted to Commissioner of Police.

- Arkham Asylum reopens following a campaign by Quincy Sharp.

- Barbara Gordon is shot and paralyzed by the Joker. She later adopts the identity of Oracle.

- While on Arkham Island, Batman discovers a cave and sets up a satellite Batcave under Arkham North.

- The Joker's doctor at Arkham Island, Dr. Penelope Young is bribed to create an army for the Joker using a more powerful version of Bane's drug Venom, called Titan. She then has a change of heart and refuses to work with the Joker.

- A fire at Blackgate results in inmates, including hundreds of the Joker's crew, being shipped to Arkham Island.

- The Joker takes the Gotham City Mayor hostage.

- Batman apprehends the Joker who accompanies him willingly back to Arkham Island. There they are greeted by Officer Frank Boles and Warden Quincy Sharp.

- The Joker eludes his guards with the help of Harley Quinn and his crew. He takes over Arkham, effectively locking in Batman, Commissioner Gordon, and the staff.

- Batman confronts and defeats serial killer Mr. Zsasz, one of the many Arkham inmates freed by the Joker's coup.

- Harley Quinn kidnaps Quincy Sharp just as Oracle informs Batman that the Joker is threatening to detonate bombs in Gotham City if anyone sets foot on Arkham Island.

FEAR ON ARKHAM ISLAND

- Officer Boles reveals himself as one of the Joker's employees as he helps the villain kidnap Commissioner Gordon. Batman tracks down Boles, only to find him murdered.

- The Riddler hacks into Batman's cowl and inundates him with a variety of riddles.

- Batman rescues Arkham's doctors, including Dr. Penelope Young, from the Joker's thugs. He also saves guard Aaron Cash.

- Batman finds Commissioner Gordon's body, only to learn that Gordon is alive and under the influence of Scarecrow's fear toxin. Batman fights through the toxin and Scarecrow flees the scene.

- After rescuing Commissioner Gordon, Batman battles Bane. Batman bests his foe thanks to the timely arrival of his Batmobile.

- Oracle and Batman discover Dr. Young's secret and Batman attempts to rescue the corrupt doctor, who has been kidnapped by Mr. Zsasz.

- Batman locates Mr. Zsasz and frees Dr. Young, only to watch helplessly as Young is killed in an explosion rigged by the Joker.

- After rescuing Warden Sharp, Batman defeats Harley Quinn and then follows her fingerprint trail to the Joker's secret lab in the Botanical Gardens.

THE TITAN STRAIN

- Batman destroys the Joker's Titan production facility after discovering the Titan strain was created via a Venom plant hybrid. He then tracks down Poison Ivy.

- Batman learns of a plant growing in Killer Croc's underground lair that can counter the Titan strain.

- The Joker injects Poison Ivy with the Titan strain, causing Arkham Island to be overrun by plant life.

- Batman fights off another powerful hallucination caused by Scarecrow, and chases the villain down to the sewers. There, Scarecrow is viciously attacked by Killer Croc.

- While in the sewers, Batman collects the plant spores he needs and defeats Killer Croc.

- Back in his Arkham Batcave, Batman concocts an antidote to the Titan strain and collects his Ultra Batclaw.

- The Joker attempts to release Titan into the Gotham River, but is foiled by Batman.

- Batman defeats the Titan-charged Poison Ivy in the Elizabeth Arkham Glasshouse.

- Summoning Batman to his makeshift funhouse in the Arkham Asylum Visitor Center using fireworks, the Joker injects Batman and himself with the Titan strain.

- Cameras from *The Jack Ryder Show* capture the climactic battle between the hulking Titan Joker and Batman, with the newly recaptured Commissioner Gordon's life hanging in the balance. Batman injects himself with the antidote, and then defeats the Joker with the help of his Ultra-Batclaw, freeing Gordon and restoring order to Arkham Island.

ARKHAM CITY CHAOS

- Quincy Sharp is elected Mayor of Gotham City, advised by his psychiatrist, Hugo Strange.

- Mayor Sharp declares martial law, hires a private military force called TYGER, and proposes the establishment of Arkham City, a walled-off, open-air prison comprising half of Gotham City.

- A number of Arkham Asylum inmates escape. Batman locates and defeats Two-Face, a group of the Penguin's thugs, Solomon Grundy, Deathstroke, and the Joker.

- Arkham City is erected, and prisoners from Arkham and Blackgate are shipped inside.

- Catwoman is taken prisoner by Two-Face when she tries to steal a key card for the TYGER confiscated goods vault.

- Bruce Wayne holds a press conference to announce his campaign to close Arkham City. At the conference, Wayne is ambushed by TYGER guards and taken into captivity inside the prison.

- Confronting his prisoner, Hugo Strange admits to knowing Batman's double identity. He also mentions initiating the start of "Protocol 10."

- Bruce Wayne is incarcerated alongside political prisoners and investigative reporter Jack Ryder only to be greeted violently by the Penguin. Wayne escapes the Penguin's clutches and heads to the rooftop to retrieve his Batsuit at a Batwing drop point.

- Batman rescues Catwoman from Two-Face at the Courthouse. Catwoman takes Two-Face's TYGER card as she leaves, after the Joker attempts to kill her via sniper.

- Batman confronts Harley Quinn in the makeshift medical center of Gotham Cathedral, but Harley escapes.

- Batman discovers Bane at Krank Co. Toys. The two form an uneasy alliance in order to destroy the remaining Titan canisters the Joker has smuggled into Arkham City. Bane double-crosses Batman, but the Dark Knight cages him.

- Batman encounters Azrael on a rooftop in Park Row, the first of many mysterious meetings that eventually lead Batman to a church inside Arkham City. There, Azrael warns Batman of an ancient prophecy that states Gotham City will burn alongside Batman.

- Batman answers a pay phone call by Mr. Zsasz, and is then forced to travel across the city quickly to save victims from the killer. Batman soon locates the killer's position and imprisons him.

- After tracking the Joker back to the Sionis Steel Mill, Batman bests the Joker's thug Mr. Hammer.

THE SEARCH FOR A CURE

- The Joker gets the drop on Batman, faking his own death with a "corpse" that looks like him. The Joker reveals to Batman that he is sick and dying, and has sent his diseased blood to various Gotham City hospitals. He then injects Batman with his blood, forcing the Dark Knight to seek a cure for himself as well as his arch foe. Batman then learns that the Joker has hired Mr. Freeze to develop a cure for him.

- Catwoman heads to the Baudelaire shop inside Arkham City to meet with Poison Ivy. After a brief fight, Poison Ivy agrees to help Catwoman break into the TYGER vault in exchange for a rare flower held there.

- Batman learns that Deadshot has been hired by Hugo Strange to assassinate all the political prisoners in Arkham City. Batman eventually captures the killer.

- Batman tracks Mr. Freeze to the Penguin's headquarters at the Cyrus Pinkney's Institute for Natural History, and battles and defeats a Penguin thug named Sickle.

- Batman fights off one of the Penguin's pets, a large shark, on his way to confront the crime boss at the Iceberg Lounge. Although he beats Penguin by deactivating his stolen freeze gun, the villain destroys the floor under Batman's feet.

- Penguin unleashes Solomon Grundy, forcing Batman to battle the giant undead monster before taking down the Penguin as well.

- Freeze informs Batman that his cure for the Joker's disease is missing an important enzyme. Batman realizes that the enzyme can only be found in the villain Rā's al Ghūl's bloodstream.

• Hearing Batman discuss Rā's al Ghūl, a League of Assassins member escapes Penguin's custody. Batman catches up to the League of Assassins ninja and tags her with a tracking device.

• After investigating the murders of several Arkham City inmates, Batman learns that the killer looks exactly like Bruce Wayne. Batman discovers that the real perpertrator is the villain Hush, but the killer eludes him.

• Following his tracking device's signal, Batman heads through the collapsed streets under Arkham City, fighting the effects of the sickness in his bloodstream.

• Batman arrives in Wonder City, an abandoned template for a futuristic city that is fueled by the energies of a nearby Lazarus Pit. Near death's door, Batman meets Talia al Ghūl and convinces her that he wants to join the League of Assassins and become her father's heir.

• Talia has Batman take part in the hallucinatory Demon Trials. Batman bests them and then defeats Rā's al Ghūl himself, after admitting his application to the League was a ploy. Batman then takes a sample of Rā's al Ghūl's blood.

• Batman interrogates the newly imprisoned Quincy Sharp, discovering that Strange has mysterious "friends" that have funded Arkham City.

• Returning to Mr. Freeze with Rā's al Ghūl's blood sample, Batman defeats the villain when Mr. Freeze refuses to hold up his end of the deal.

• Batman discovers that Harley Quinn has stolen two cure samples from Mr. Freeze's safe. He heads back to the Steel Mill to confront the Joker.

• Vicki Vale's news helicopter is shot down in Arkham City. Batman rescues her from a group of the Joker's men.

• Alfred informs Batman that Lucius Fox has found a cure for his condition. But when Batman uses the concoction, he finds out that the Mad Hatter has tricked and drugged him. He is outfitted in a bizarre mask and fights his way out of his drugged state, defeating the Mad Hatter in the process.

• Batman heads to the Steel Mill and tracks down the Joker. The seemingly cured Joker gains the upper hand against Batman, but before he can kill him, is interrupted by Talia, who offers the Joker immortality in exchange for sparing Batman's life. She leaves, but not before activating a tracking device on her uniform for Batman to follow.

PROTOCOL 10—AND 11

• When Poison Ivy uses her control of plant life to make an underground entrance for Catwoman, the feline thief uses her key cards to open the TYGER vault.

• Hugo Strange activates Protocol 10, a devastating barrage of missiles on Arkham City from Wonder Tower and from various TYGER helicopters.

• Catwoman breaks into the vault and destroys the very plant that she had agreed to steal for Poison Ivy. As she's about to depart, Catwoman hears about Protocol 10. Given the choice between escape and saving the injured Batman, she leaves her loot behind and heads off to the Steel Mill to rescue the Dark Knight.

• Freed from the rubble, Batman ascends Wonder Tower, takes down Strange's men and then Strange himself. Batman then deactivates Protocol 10 with the help of Oracle.

• Rā's al Ghūl stabs Hugo Strange, revealing that he has been bankrolling the demented professor after Strange revealed Batman's double identity to him.

• Strange activates Protocol 11, causing Wonder Tower to explode. Batman leaps out the window with Rā's al Ghūl, and the two fight as they plummet to the ground. Only Batman survives the fall.

THE JOKER'S DEATH CARD

- Batman follows the Joker's trail to the Monarch Theatre where Talia stabs the Joker in the chest.

- Batman deduces that this "cured" Joker is not the Joker at all, but Clayface. The Joker had hired Clayface to keep up appearances as his health deteriorated.

- Talia is shot by the true Joker. Meanwhile, Clayface attacks Batman, who defeats Clayface with his freeze blasts. He then takes the cure and drinks half of it. But before he can cure the Joker, the villain shatters the vial.

- The Joker dies and Batman carries his deceased foe out into the night, as police arrive in Arkham City.

- Catwoman decides to leave Arkham City for good. However, a bomb set by Two-Face in her apartment prompts her to head to the museum and confront the villain.

- Batman tracks down hostages captured by the Riddler and imprisons the villain in one of his own traps.

- Nightwing hunts Black Mask and brings him to justice after a fight on the subway.

- Arkham City is officially condemned.

- Harley Quinn ambushes a few police officers and holds them captive in the Steel Mill. Batman goes in to the mill to investigate and is promptly captured by Harley.

- Two days later, Oracle sends Robin to the Steel Mill. He discovers Batman trapped in a bizarre monument to the Joker. He tracks down Harley and he and the Batman defeat her.

- The Joker's body is cremated. Nine months of relative calm fall across Gotham City.

FEAR SCARECROW

- Scarecrow meets with the Penguin, the Riddler, Two-Face, Poison Ivy, and Harley Quinn in a plot to take over Gotham City and kill Batman. Ivy refuses to comply, and is imprisoned in Scarecrow's penthouse.

- On the eve of Halloween, Scarecrow unleashes his newest fear gas in Pauli's Diner, causing havoc. He threatens to do the same to the rest of Gotham City the following day. Millions flee, leaving only criminals, action-seekers, and police behind.

- Batman chases a suspicious military vehicle in hopes of finding Scarecrow.

- The Dark Knight discovers Poison Ivy in Scarecrow's penthouse and brings her to the G.C.P.D.'s WayneTech isolation chamber. On the way, they are surrounded by drone tanks that Batman defeats with his new Batmobile.

- Working with Oracle in her Clocktower, Batman tracks Scarecrow to the ACE Chemical plant where he is confronted by a new mysterious villain called the Arkham Knight. The new villain escapes Batman's Batmobile attack.

- Batman confronts Scarecrow only to be infected by Scarecrow's fear toxin.

- The Riddler abducts Catwoman, forcing the Dark Knight to once again engage in a battle of wits with the villain.

- Nightwing meets Batman at the ferry terminal to inform him that the Penguin is smuggling weapons out of Blüdhaven using North Refrigeration trucks. Nightwing gives Batman the Disrupter in order to keep tabs on the trucks, eventually leading to Batman ending the Penguin's smuggling operation.

- Discovering that businessman Simon Stagg is working with Scarecrow, Batman confronts the villain in a zeppelin. The Arkham Knight fires a rocket at Batman and the Dark Knight narrowly escapes with his life.

- Alfred informs Batman that Simon Stagg's Cloudburst device can disperse Scarecrow's fear gas across the entire city.

- Back at G.C.P.D. headquarters, Batman retrieves Poison Ivy from her cell, teaming up with her to save the citizens (and plants) of Gotham City. They head to the Botanical Gardens to find trees capable of purifying the air.

- Firefly embarks on another arson spree, before Batman takes him down with the help of the Batmobile.

- Two-Face attempts a bank heist, forcing Batman to defeat the villain and his lackeys.

- The villainous Deacon Blackfire captures Jack Ryder near the Lady of Gotham statue until Batman puts the criminal's campaign to an end.

- Batman discovers the true secret of the Arkham Knight.

- Batman confronts Scarecrow once and for all in a battle that changes everything…

BATMAN

BORN OF TRAGEDY, RAISED BY SHEER WILL AND DETERMINATION, AND REBORN AS SOMETHING ELSE ENTIRELY, BATMAN IS GOTHAM CITY'S BRUTAL HOPE COME ALIVE AND ITS ONLY CHANCE AGAINST THE CITY'S ROGUES GALLERY OF MADMEN AND CRIMINALS.

It's night time in Gotham City. A man and his wife are walking home from a late movie. The street appears to be empty but they hear footsteps behind them, mixed with hushed whispers and perhaps a sinister laugh. They increase their pace, but the footsteps come closer and closer. Suddenly there is a thump and a scream. They turn to discover three would-be muggers lying unconscious on the ground. From the rooftops above they hear the faint rustling of a leather cape until the sound is drowned out by police sirens. They have just encountered Batman.

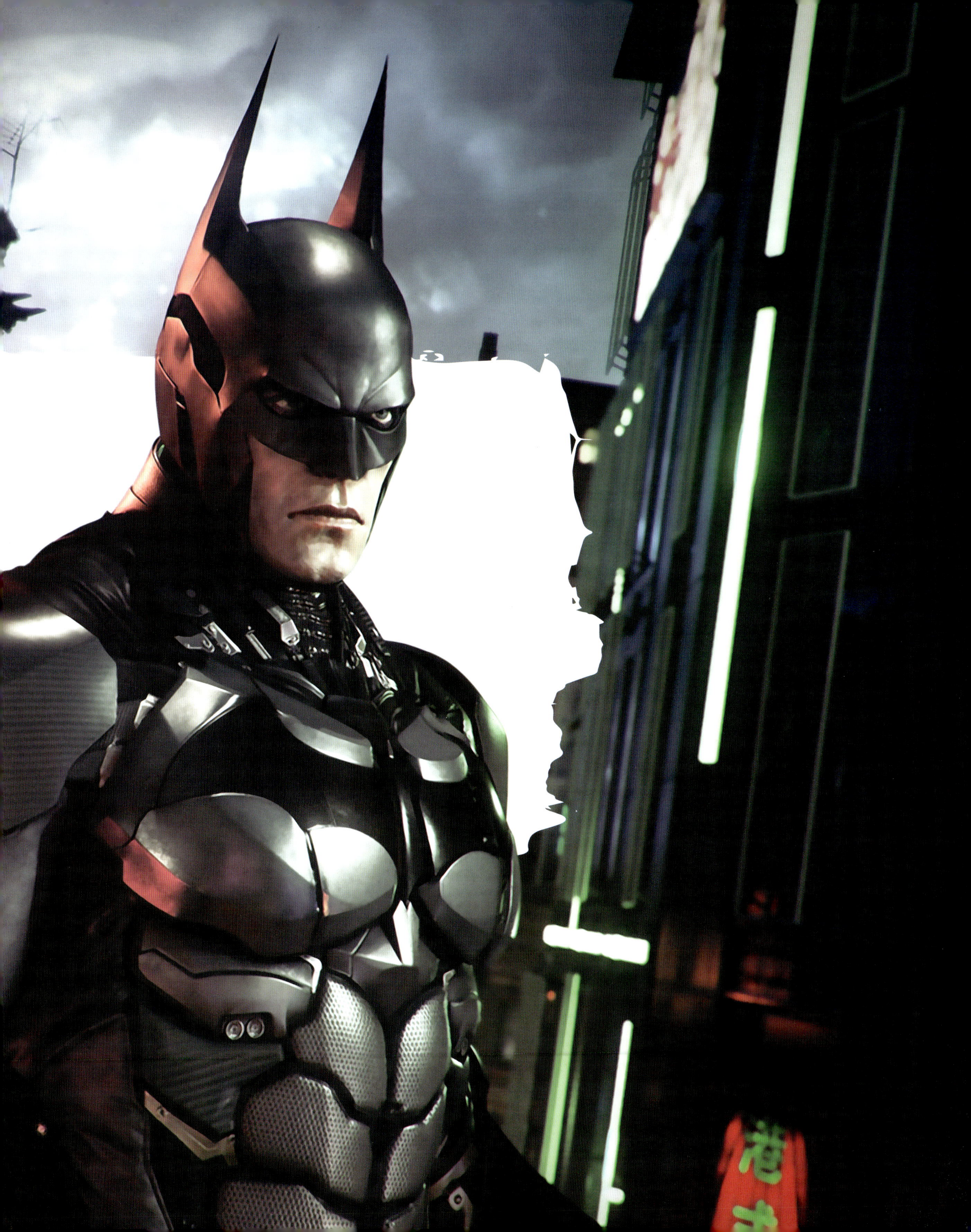
港

THE DARK KNIGHT

CRIMINALS ARE A COWARDLY AND SUPERSTITIOUS LOT. TO COMBAT THEM, BRUCE WAYNE BECAME SOMETHING THEY WOULD FEAR. HE BECAME A SYMBOL, AN URBAN LEGEND—BATMAN.

Bruce Wayne's life changed forever when his parents were gunned down in the street by a thug. He dedicated his every waking moment to understanding the criminal mind and training himself to physical and mental perfection. He studied criminology and fighting techniques that few had mastered, hoping that no one else would ever have to experience what he and his parents had gone through on that tragic night.

MAKING A DIFFERENCE

Bruce Wayne decided to dedicate his life to protecting the innocent. However, he was well aware that corruption in Gotham City ran deep and that the police force participated in nearly as many crimes as the gangs. Instead of pursuing a conventional career in law enforcement, Wayne resolved to wage a private war on crime. He believed that to be truly effective, he had to operate on the outside. With the massive technological resources of WayneTech to draw upon, he knew he could make a difference.

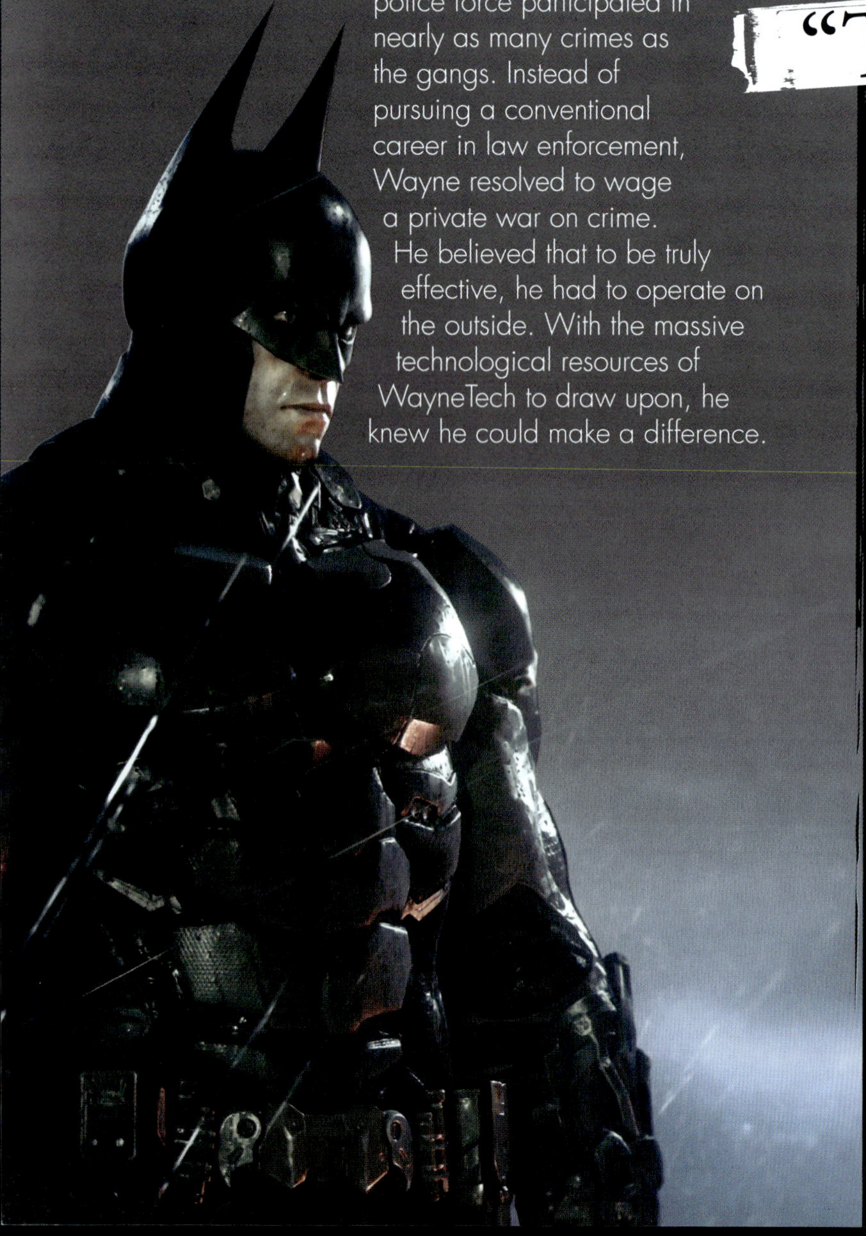

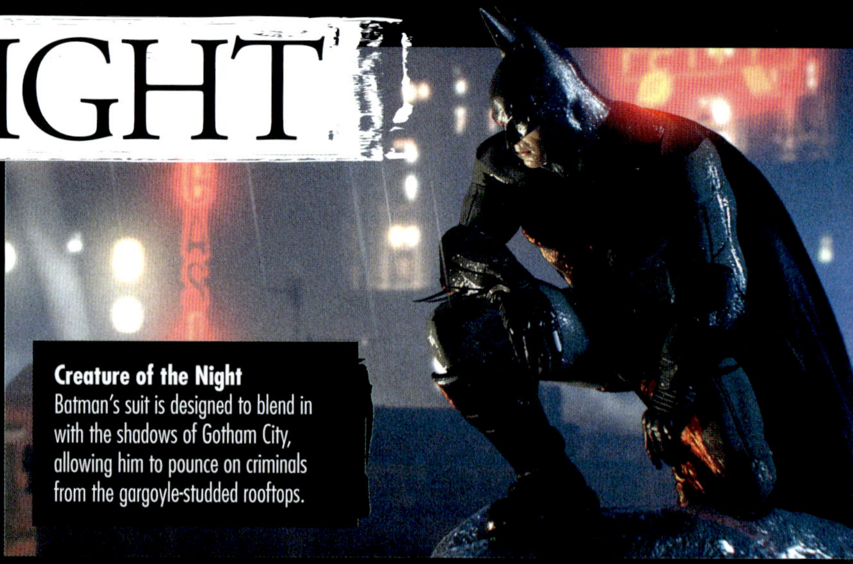

Creature of the Night
Batman's suit is designed to blend in with the shadows of Gotham City, allowing him to pounce on criminals from the gargoyle-studded rooftops.

I SHALL BECOME A BAT

When Bruce Wayne began his crusade against crime, he knew he had to do so anonymously, or risk attacks on his associates, friends, and charitable business efforts. If exposed, he could even face time in jail. Gotham City was a dark place, and needed someone equally dark to fight for it. Bruce adopted the mantle of Batman both to strike fear in Gotham City's villains and keep his identity well hidden.

> "THERE'S ALWAYS A CHOICE."
>
> **Batman**

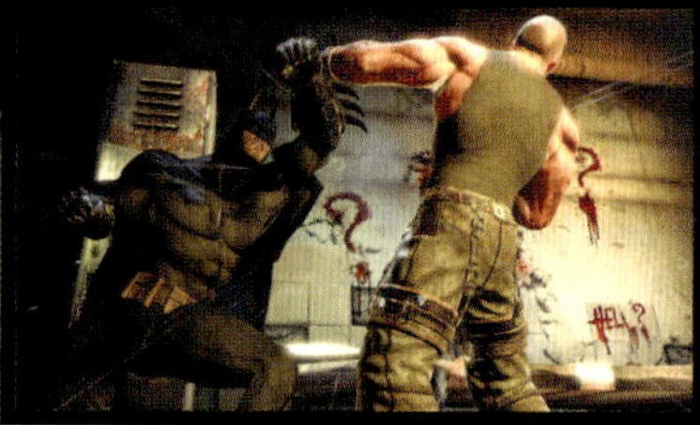

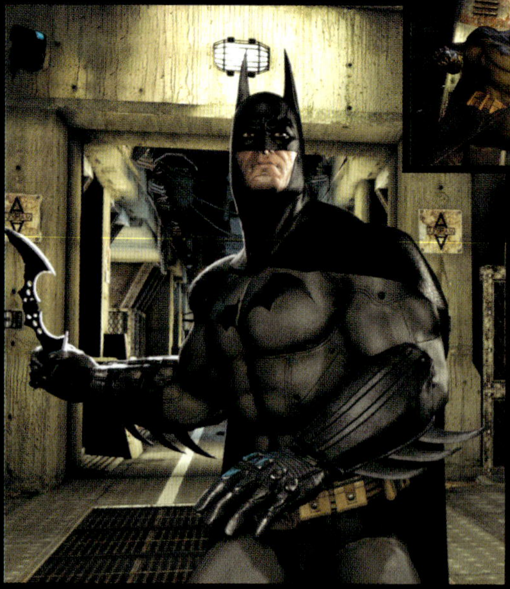

▲ The Ultimate Fighter
A master of martial arts as well as common street-fighting techniques, Batman can take on a variety of attackers at once and emerge victorious.

◀ Tool Belt
The Batarang is one of Batman's most trusted weapons, and just one of the many tools stored in his Utility Belt.

A DIFFERENT KIND OF CRIME-FIGHTER

Batman is an extremely versatile fighter. He has trained himself for any situation imaginable—and has a Utility Belt full of tools to confront the unimaginable. Whether facing opponents in cramped quarters or in the open air, whether confronted with brain teasers or by a heavyweight fighter, the Dark Knight is equipped to battle all comers and come out on top.

BATMAN THE DARK KNIGHT   21

DATA FILE

- **REAL NAME:** Bruce Wayne
- **OCCUPATION:** Crime-Fighter
- **HEIGHT:** 6 ft. 2 in.
- **WEIGHT:** 210 lbs.
- **EYES:** Blue
- **HAIR:** Black

The Cowl
Batman's cowl is crafted to conceal Batman's identity as well as to protect his skull with reinforced armor.

Braintrust
Batman is incredibly intelligent, possessing a keen deductive mind that he has honed since childhood.

Bat-Symbol
The bat is not just an iconic warning. Heavily armored, it's designed to draw gunfire to his suit's strongest point.

Utility Belt
Batman's Utility Belt is ever-changing, hosting compact devices needed for his war on crime.

Fighting Fit
Batman is a master fighter, possessing amazing skill and muscle reflex.

Crime Crusader
Dubbed the Dark Knight, and the World's Greatest Detective, the Batman has gained a formidable crime-fighting reputation over the years.

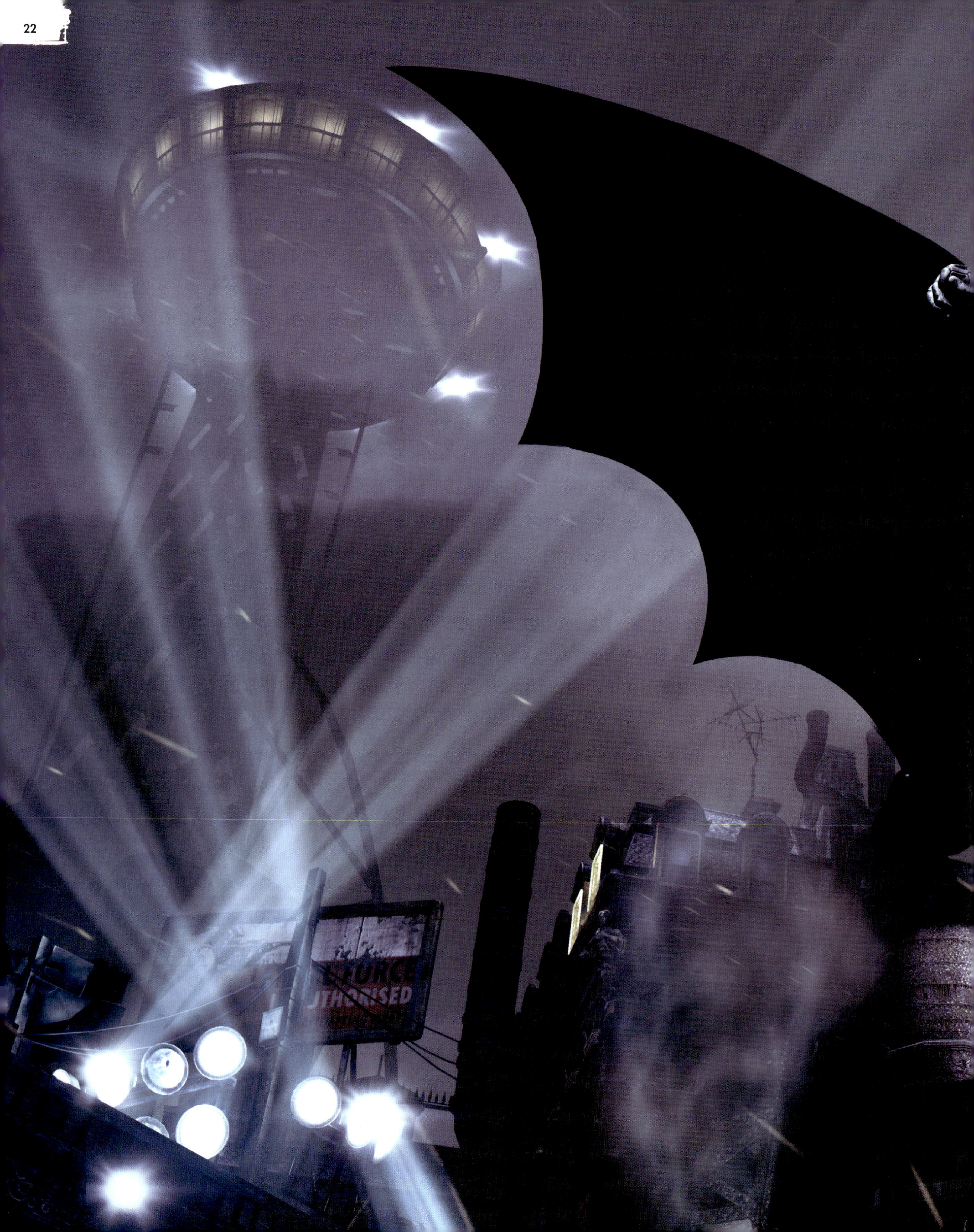
FORCE
UTHORISED

Gotham City Guardian
A true creature of the night, Batman cuts an imposing figure on Gotham City's skyline. He is equal parts salvation and symbol of hope to the innocents of the troubled city, as well as a figure of terror to all criminals.

BRUCE WAYNE

GOTHAM CITY'S PREMIER PLAYBOY AND FAVORITE SON HIDES QUITE A SECRET FROM THE CITIZENS OF HIS BELOVED CITY. IN REALITY, BRUCE WAYNE IS MERELY A MASK THAT BATMAN WEARS TO HIDE IN PLAIN SIGHT.

Few in Gotham City possess as much influence, money, and power as Bruce Wayne. The head of Wayne Enterprises and heir to his family's vast fortune, Bruce has a heart of gold, always contributing to good causes to improve the city he loves. In spite of his philanthropic efforts, Bruce is perceived as a bit aloof, if not empty-headed by friends and associates alike. Only a select few know that Wayne is actually a master strategist and detective, concealing his brilliant intellect in order to deflect suspicion from his nightly activities fighting crime as Batman.

THE MAN BEHIND THE BAT
In order to become Batman, Bruce Wayne secretly trains with the world's greatest martial artists, detectives, and even actors. From the latter, he learns vital skills that help him to mask himself as the Dark Knight, including drastically altering his voice when wearing his cowl.

Only a handful of people closest to Bruce know about his double identity. The chosen few include his trusted allies Nightwing, Robin, Oracle, his loyal butler Alfred, and his business partner, Lucius Fox.

Night of Tragedy
Bruce's parents are gunned down before his eyes on the way home after seeing the film *Mark of Zorro* at Gotham City's Monarch Theatre.

A TRAGIC PAST
After seeing his parents die at the hands of a mugger, Bruce Wayne inherits his family's fortune. Yet that comes as little solace to the heartbroken child who simply wants his mother and father back. Determined to prevent the tragedy that has befallen him from ever happening to anyone else, Bruce puts his pain and his fears to work for him, honing his body and mind to perfection, and embarking on a war on crime as Batman.

"TODAY, I'M STARTING THE CAMPAIGN TO CLOSE ARKHAM CITY."
— Bruce Wayne

▲ **Taking a Knee**
When surrounded by Penguin's men inside Arkham City, Bruce Wayne has no choice but to let a few of the Batman's skills sneak out in order to stay alive.

◄ **Special Delivery**
After being imprisoned by Hugo Strange, Bruce Wayne fights his way to the rooftops where he has a Batsuit delivered to him via an airdrop arranged by his butler, Alfred.

BRUCE WAYNE: PRISONER
While he deliberately projects an aloof image, even Bruce Wayne finds it necessary to get political once in a while. This is the case when he speaks out against Arkham City, a giant prison complex built in the heart of Gotham City. For his efforts, Bruce soon finds himself a prisoner inside the walled-off penitentiary—which is exactly where Batman wants to be.

BATMAN BRUCE WAYNE

DATA FILE
- **REAL NAME** Bruce Wayne
- **OCCUPATION** Head of Wayne Enterprises
- **HEIGHT** 6 ft. 2 in.
- **WEIGHT** 210 lbs.
- **HAIR** Black
- **EYES** Blue

A-List Celebrity
Wayne's face is known to the world, one of the main reasons that Batman stays in the shadows.

Citizen Wayne
An upstanding Gotham City personality, Bruce plays the role of a socialite playboy, never breaking character in his life's grand play.

Playing Politics
Wayne drops his playboy image to campaign against Arkham City.

Man About Town
Befitting his lifestyle, Bruce Wayne's suits are bespoke and expensive.

WAYNE MANOR

THE LONGTIME HOME OF GOTHAM CITY'S FIRST FAMILY, WAYNE MANOR IS A MUSEUM-LIKE TRIBUTE TO THE WAYNE LEGACY, HOUSING AN AMAZING SECRET BENEATH ITS HALLOWED HALLS.

Located outside the city limits of Gotham City proper, Wayne Manor is the impressive home of Bruce Wayne. Maintained by the Wayne family's loyal butler, Alfred Pennyworth, Wayne Manor appears to be just as it was when Thomas and Martha Wayne were still alive, but deep below the mansion is a giant cave system that serves as Batman's secret base of operations, the legendary Batcave.

THE BALLROOM

The Wayne Manor ballroom is a place that Gotham City's high society is very familiar with. It has hosted hundreds of events since its creation. Bruce Wayne holds many fundraisers for charities and good causes here and, although he would rather just cut a check than socialize with the city's elite, his status as a playboy philanthropist helps hide his true career as Gotham City's Dark Knight.

Majestic Home
Wayne Manor serves as a reminder to Bruce Wayne of a glorious past he won't allow himself to forget.

THE GRAND HALLWAY

Bruce Wayne's vast childhood home has numerous impressive features. The Grand Hallway, with its lofty ceiling, marble floor, walls elegantly decorated with ancestral pictures, and imposing fireplace sets the tone for the whole house. As a child, Bruce used to love to play in Wayne Manor's spacious, luxurious rooms. However, after the death of his parents, Bruce set aside childish pursuits and Wayne Manor became just another facet of Bruce's grand disguise.

THE LIBRARY

While Batman uses advanced technology to maintain an elaborate online database and digital file system, Bruce Wayne often visits his family's library during a case for a bit of research or related reading. Housing many valuable, antique volumes, the library is a reminder of how much Bruce, with his constant thirst for knowledge, is like his parents. The library is a very special place for him, and intruders are especially unwelcome.

THE STUDY

One of the most traversed rooms in Wayne Manor since the death of Bruce Wayne's parents is the study, a room that houses not just an impressive fireplace, but also the greatest secret of Wayne's life. Behind the study's grandfather clock is a secret passageway that leads down to the caverns below and to Batman's hideout, the Batcave.

THE WINE CELLAR

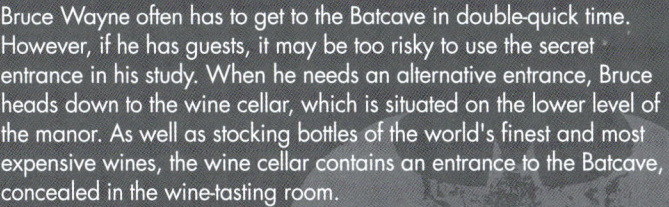

Bruce Wayne often has to get to the Batcave in double-quick time. However, if he has guests, it may be too risky to use the secret entrance in his study. When he needs an alternative entrance, Bruce heads down to the wine cellar, which is situated on the lower level of the manor. As well as stocking bottles of the world's finest and most expensive wines, the wine cellar contains an entrance to the Batcave, concealed in the wine-tasting room.

THE WINE-TASTING ROOM

In the wine-tasting room is an unassuming statue of a man holding a barrel. Like many things in Wayne Manor, however, this statue is not what it seems. The barrel is really a lever and when pulled, a secret entrance to the Batcave is revealed. Bruce can then access his lair via a stairwell and an elevator shaft.

THE BATCAVE

BENEATH STATELY WAYNE MANOR LIES THE HIDDEN BASE OF OPERATIONS FOR BATMAN. A CAVE THAT NOT ONLY ALLOWS THE HERO TO DWELL LIKE HIS NAMESAKE, BUT HOUSES SOME OF THE MOST SOPHISTICATED TECHNOLOGY IN THE WORLD.

Batman is at home in the shadows, so it makes sense that his true home lies in the cold caverns of the Batcave. This subterranean lair is formed within a network of ancient caves that can be accessed from several points inside Wayne Manor. The Batcave houses an array of Batmobiles, Batwings, computer systems, and Batsuits—all of the vital equipment the Dark Knight requires in his crusade against crime.

Batwing
The Batcave is so large, it allows for the takeoff and landing of Batman's impressive Batwing.

Secret Caverns
Bruce literally stumbled on the caves as a child. Only a select few know of their existence.

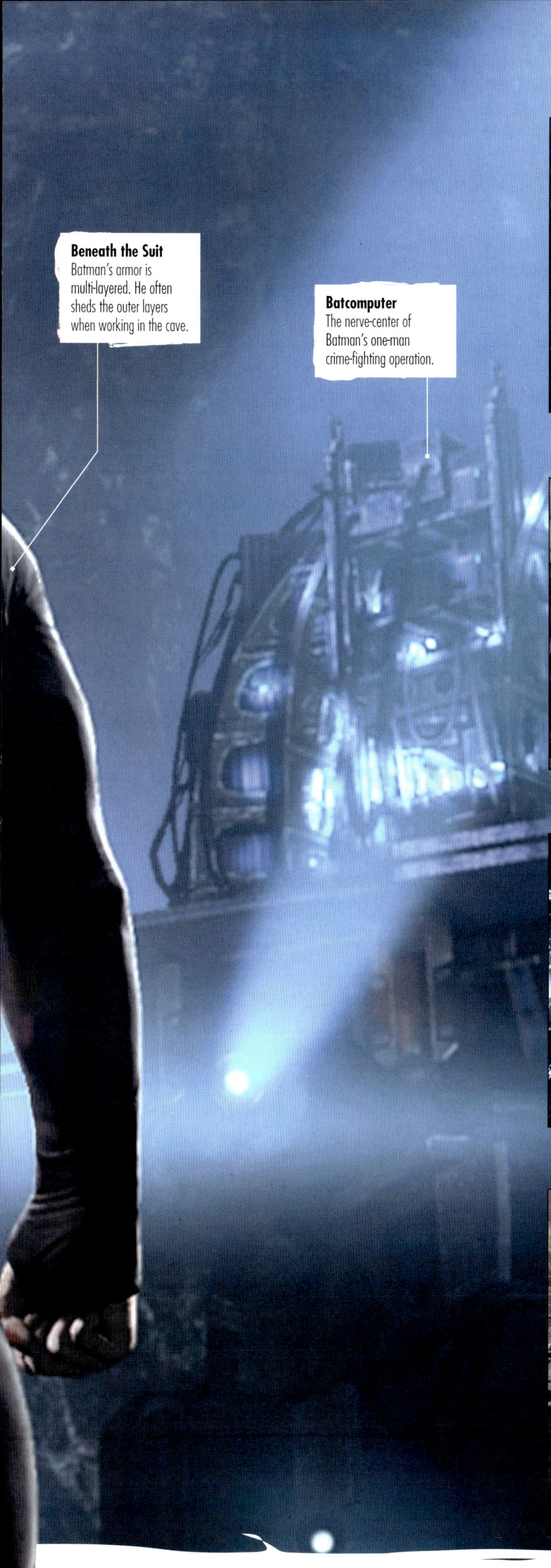
Beneath the Suit
Batman's armor is multi-layered. He often sheds the outer layers when working in the cave.
Batcomputer
The nerve-center of Batman's one-man crime-fighting operation.

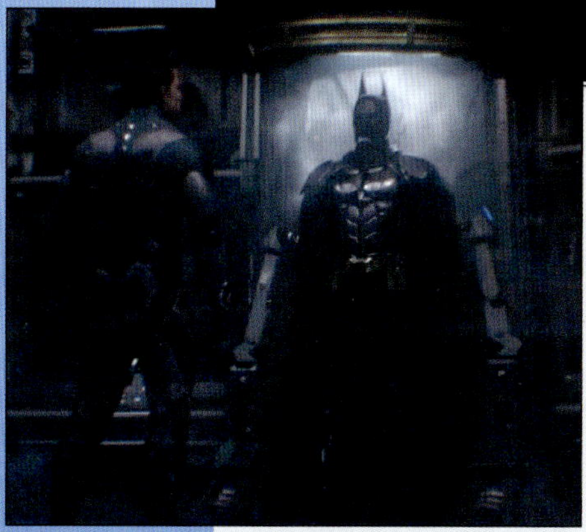

THE BATSUIT CHAMBER

Whenever possible, the Dark Knight updates the technology contained in his famous Batsuit. His armor is constantly being upgraded to allow for greater ease of movement and increased protection. The Batcave houses not just Batman's main suit, but also the many other variations that he has donned over the years, whether for genuine crime-fighting missions or for various experiments and trial runs.

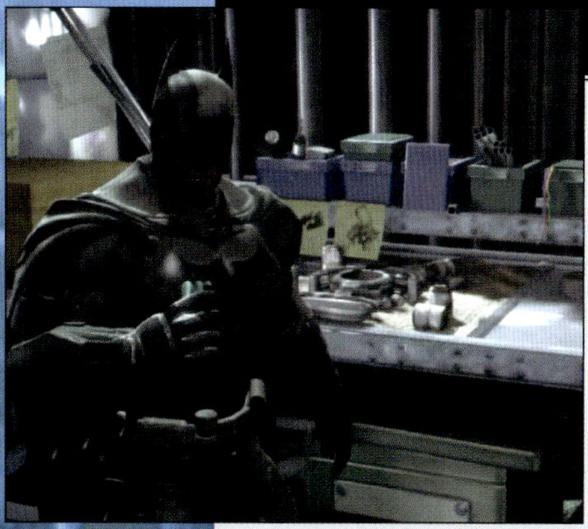

THE WORKSHOP

The Dark Knight's war on crime is a complex one and frequently requires him to develop new, state-of-the-art technologies to aid him on missions and ensure that he lives to fight another day. With Wayne Enterprises' entire technology division at his disposal, Batman often tweaks and designs gadgets for his Utility Belt from the seclusion of the Batcave's workshop.

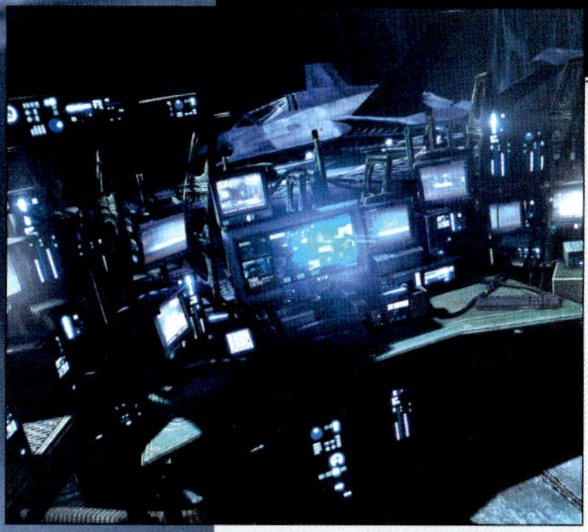

THE BATCOMPUTER

The Batcomputer is Batman's main technological hub and provides him with the vital knowledge he needs to research and track down his criminal opponents. He also uses it to analyze forensic evidence and other crime-scene clues. When Batman is patrolling the mean streets of Gotham City, the Batcomputer is an invaluable tool, enabling the Dark Knight to receive images and data straight to his cowl.

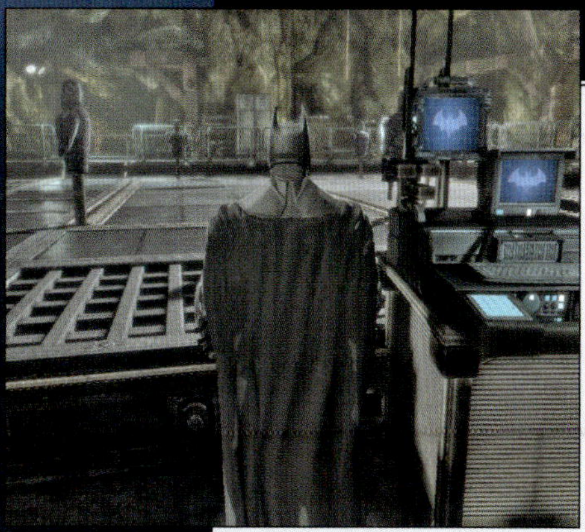

TRAINING CONSOLE

A substantial investment from Bruce Wayne's checkbook, the Batcave's Training Console enables Batman to safely test and improve a wide range of skills. The console creates holographic projections of opponents for Batman to battle, allowing the Dark Knight to test his martial arts and other hand-to-hand fighting techniques in situations that mimic real life to an astounding degree.

Batsuit Chamber
Batman uses his Batsuit Chamber to house a great many variations of his Batman suit, each with a different purpose and function.

THE BATSUITS

BATMAN IS ALWAYS FACING NEW VILLAINS WITH UNIQUE ABILITIES, FORCING HIM TO PREPARE FOR THE UNEXPECTED. THIS MEANS CONSTANTLY UPGRADING AND REDESIGNING THE MOST ESSENTIAL WEAPON IN HIS ARSENAL: THE BATSUIT.

When Batman first decided to become a vigilante and combat Gotham City's criminal element, he realized that he needed to appear much more than a mere man. Only a frightening urban legend could strike fear into the hearts of the superstitious, cowardly lot that prey on the innocent. To that end, Batman developed his Batsuit, a utilitarian, armored costume that not only serves to protect his body and allow for maximum flexibility and movement, but also includes certain dramatic touches, such as a frightening cowl, bat ears, and a flowing cape, that serve to reinforce the Dark Knight's fearsome reputation.

ARKHAM ORIGINS SUIT

One of the earliest suits Batman wears looks more like armor than later incarnations. Batman uses this suit when he first meets the Joker and has to fight numerous assassins on Christmas Eve. He later streamlines the suit so that it is more form-fitting and reduces the vulnerable areas around the costume's joints.

▲ **A Trick Up His Sleeve**
Highly utilitarian, the original Batsuit helps protect against numerous attacks, and is particularly effective when combined with shock gauntlets.

BATMAN THE BATSUITS

ARKHAM ASYLUM SUIT

A finely honed Batsuit that is both sleek and practical, Batman wears this version when he quells the Joker's riots in Arkham Asylum. The suit features large, spiked arm gauntlets and a radio earpiece to contact Oracle and Batman's butler, Alfred Pennyworth. Like his earlier model, this suit features a thick cape that he uses to stun opponents and also to glide through the air.

BATTLE ARMORED TECH SUIT

During his campaign to clean up the streets of the prison known as Arkham City, Batman upgrades to an armored suit to so he can fight with even greater effectiveness. This suit contains layered kinetic dampeners that store the impact energy from combat, and then release it on command when in so-called B.A.T. mode. It is a perfected version of the Shock Gloves Batman uses with his Arkham Origins uniform.

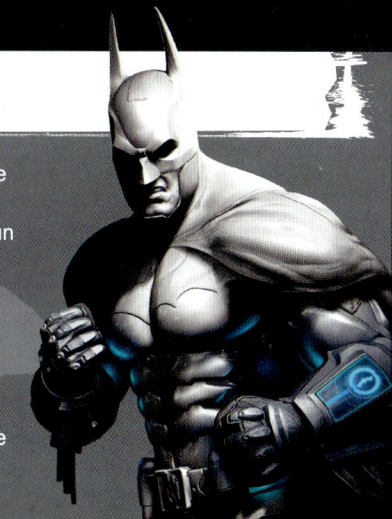

ARKHAM KNIGHT SUIT

When facing the threat of the Arkham Knight, Batman employs two versions of his Batsuit, the latter being his Mark 8 suit. These suits include new arm gauntlet holographic camera displays that allow him not just to talk to his crime-fighting allies, but see them as well. When Batman activates this new technology his eyes glow, making him appear even more intimidating.

ARKHAM ASYLUM ARMORED SUIT

After quelling the Joker's riots on Arkham Island, Batman upgrades his suit to a bulkier, armored version. While similar in appearance to his standard suit, this one gives him the extra protection needed to clean up a few of the loose ends and inmates still lurking in the asylum's shadows. He later takes some of the design and practical elements of this suit and employs them full-time when the Arkham Knight emerges in Gotham City.

EXTREME ENVIRONMENT SUIT

When facing Mr. Freeze, Batman realizes that he needs a way to protect himself from the villain's powerful cryogenic technology. He develops the Extreme Environment suit, also called his XE Suit. With heat-generating gauntlets that can superheat Batarangs, the XE Suit protects Batman from exceptional cold and hot temperatures.

ARKHAM CITY SUIT

Allowing for enhanced ease of movement, this version of the Batsuit is utilized by the Dark Knight when he investigates the situation inside the walls of Arkham City. It has a less bulky Utility Belt than the Arkham Origins or Arkham Asylum suits. The pouch belt houses a variety of gadgets, while giving Batman the freedom to perform necessary aerial moves.

OTHER SUITS

THE BATSUIT CHAMBER IN THE BATCAVE IS HOME TO DOZENS OF DIFFERENT SUITS FOR BATMAN TO UTILIZE IN HIS WAR ON CRIME. SOME SUITS ARE MORE PRACTICAL THAN OTHERS, BUT ALL RETAIN HIS SIGNATURE BAT-MOTIF.

Most at home in one of his standard Batsuits, Batman has been known to change his appearance from time to time. Whether to try out a new type of body armor, or simply to keep criminals on their toes, Batman's wardrobe is ever-shifting, giving the Dark Knight a vital edge.

1ST APPEARANCE

It is said that the Dark Knight donned his original Batsuit on the night of his first foray into crime-fighting. Equipped with an art-deco Utility Belt, small purple gloves, a cape, and a more simplistic bat-symbol, this suit seems perfectly capable of striking fear into the hearts of the superstitious cowardly lot seeking to commit crimes in Gotham City.

ZUR EN ARRH

Years of experience with mind-bending criminals like the Mad Hatter and Scarecrow has made Batman extra cautious and wary when fighting crime. He is constantly aware that when he enters a fight, his mind may be as vulnerable as his body. To that end, he implanted a failsafe in his own head to trigger a "pure Batman" personality if ever the need arose. This ruthless, yet efficient, mindset can result in Batman piecing together a suit out of whatever materials are readily available.

CLASSIC TV SERIES

Resembling something that would perhaps be created for a television program rather than the battlefield, this particular Batsuit is not as practical as other designs. Offering little or no armor, the suit's main benefit is its light weight, allowing Batman the ease of movement to fully display his unarmed combat skills.

1970S BATMAN

While he mostly sticks to shades of dark navy or black these days, Batman has tried out a few brighter suits over the years. One such suit has a capsule belt that keeps the gadgets in his Utility Belt streamlined to his body. While the yellow oval may appear as something akin to a target on his chest, Batman purposely reinforced it to draw gunfire away from vulnerable areas, such as his head.

THE DARK KNIGHT RETURNS

Streamlined and revealing Batman's bulk, this Batsuit isn't far removed from some of his earlier costumes. Yet when worn by Batman, it gives the impression of an older, grizzled crime-fighter. Perhaps this is the costume Batman will wear into retirement in his later years.

YEAR ONE

A suit said to be used early on in Batman's war on crime, this costume is simple, streamlined, and effective. It allows Batman maximum flexibility, albeit with limited protection from gunfire. This suit is ideal for instilling fear in everyone from common criminals out to steal a TV set to Gotham City's many corrupt officials.

GOTHAM BY GASLIGHT

Another drastic departure from his standard suit, this Batsuit looks like it would be more at home in the late 1800s rather than in the current, 21st-century setting of Gotham City. Victorian in style with its elaborate cape, this costume is still highly suitable for stalking the night, on the lookout for anyone who would prey on the innocent.

ANIMATED SERIES

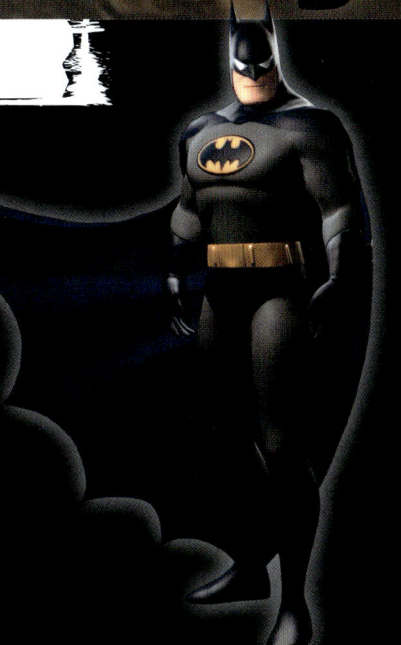

Streamlined and lacking body armor, this costume gives Batman an animated feel with an emphasis on movement. With almost triangular eye slits, and a thin, art-deco Utility Belt, this suit also features a curved ear and the classic yellow oval bat-symbol. It's the perfect look for instilling fear in criminals, from hard-bitten bank robbers to eccentric characters such as Harley Quinn.

KNIGHTFALL

From the outset of his career, Batman has incorporated armor into his suits. However, this particular Batsuit may be a tad overkill. Including a spotlight capable of projecting Batman's symbol upon those he encounters, and utilizing razor-sharp claws on its armored gauntlets, this suit resembles something a vigilante like Azrael would feel comfortable wearing.

LONG HALLOWEEN

Another Batsuit rumored to have been utilized in Batman's early years, this particular uniform shows the evolution of Batman's costume in progress. Employing longer "shorts," and a bluer cape, this suit also has a gold-colored Utility Belt and longer, bat-like ears. A perfect look for taking down any trick-or-treaters trying to take their pranks to the next level.

ONE MILLION

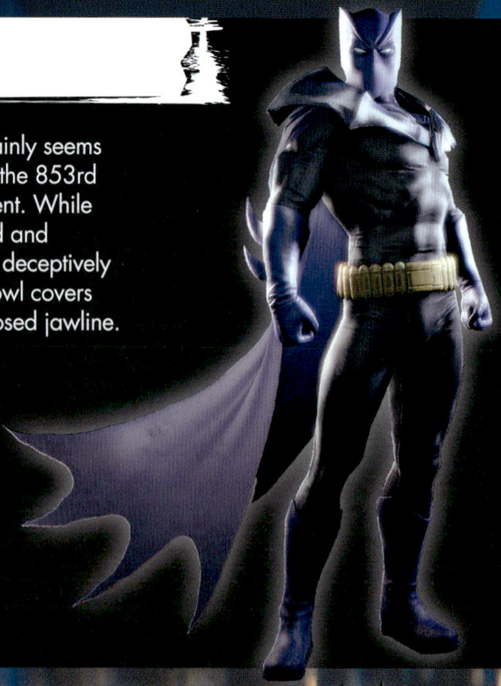

This futuristic suit certainly seems more appropriate for the 853rd century than the present. While it appears streamlined and lightweight, the suit is deceptively armored, while the cowl covers Batman's usually exposed jawline.

DARK KNIGHT OF THE ROUND TABLE

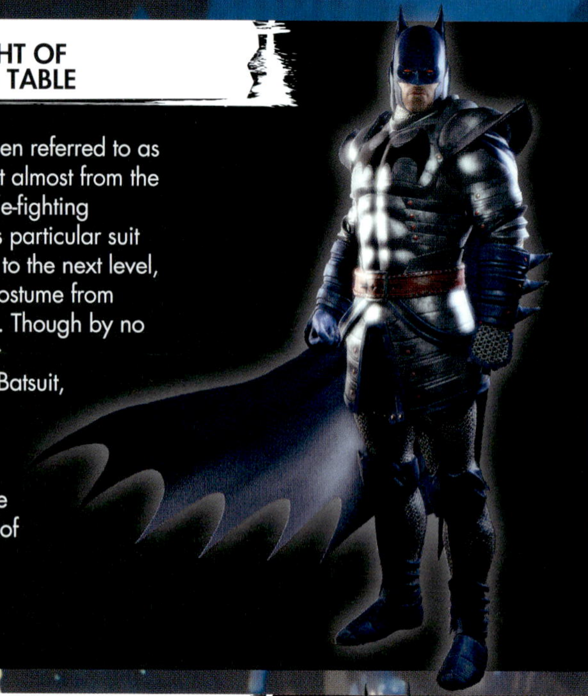

Batman has been referred to as the Dark Knight almost from the start of his crime-fighting campaign. This particular suit takes that idea to the next level, resembling a costume from medieval times. Though by no means as silent as his modern Batsuit, it certainly is armored. It also gives Batman a noble look, reflective of his character.

THRILLKILLER

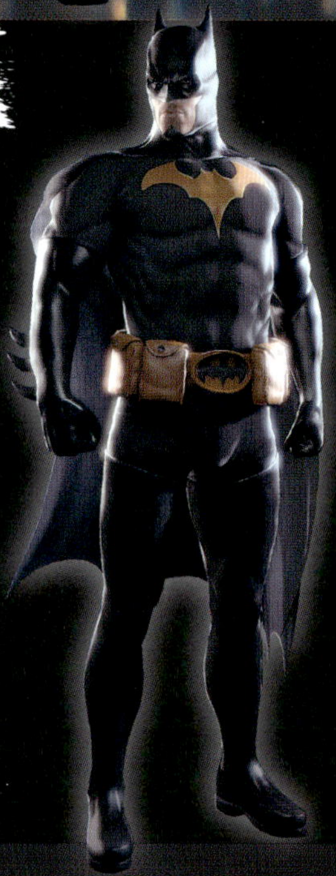

A bit mod in appearance, this Batsuit allows Batman to once again stretch his detective muscles without the heavy bulk of armor. Said to be one of Barbara Gordon's favorite looks for the Dark Knight, this costume employs a yellow insignia and an oval buckle on its Utility Belt.

BATMAN BEYOND

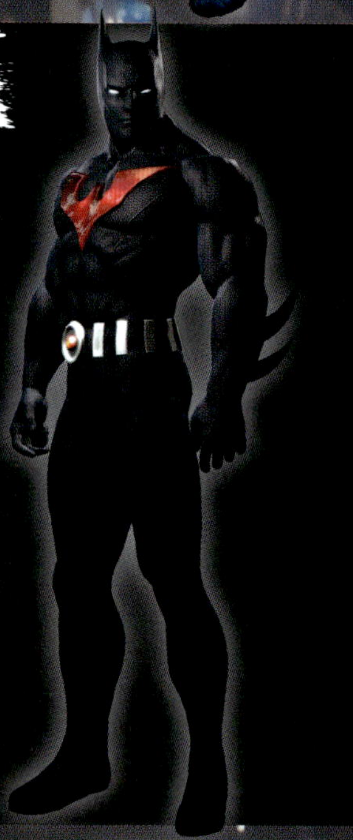

Batman can glide using the heavy-duty material of the cape of his current Batsuit, but this futuristic version gives him gliding capabilities, utilizing red "wings." While this Batsuit might be a bit youthful in style for Bruce Wayne's current tastes, it could, with an eye to the evolution of the Dark Knight, be the perfect fit for someone younger, such as Robin.

BATMAN BEYOND

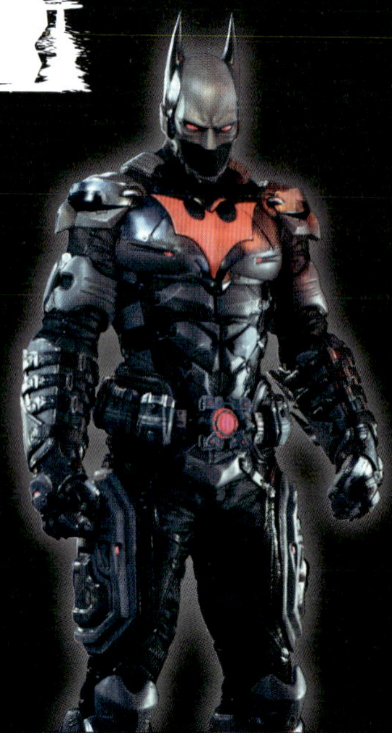

Dedicated to a lifetime of fighting crime, Batman is aware that one day he may need to pass on his mantle. He understands that he needs to have a Batsuit prepared that fits not just his own requirements, but also those of some of his youthful crime-fighting partners. Perhaps modeled in part after the Arkham Knight's militaristic suit, this version of the Batman Beyond look continues the red-and-black motif, but adds a utilitarian feel to the more streamlined, standard Batman Beyond look.

RED SON

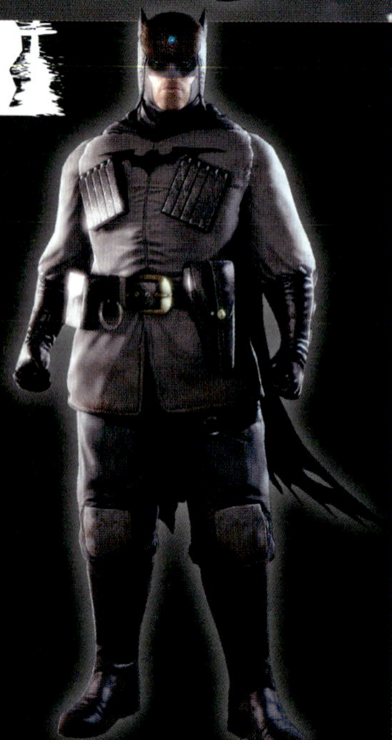

The winters of Gotham City can be cold and harsh. Batman has responded by creating some costumes that offer more insulation from the elements. However, this particular Batsuit would probably be more suited to crime-fighting in Russia than in the Dark Knight's normal environs.

THE ICONIC BLACK AND GRAY

Batman's black and gray look quickly became a standard, right after he first debuted it during the early days of the Joker's career. The colors break up Batman's outline, helping him to avoid the unwanted attentions of the many snipers that have their sights set on him. For missions in which his bulkier, armored suit would be more of a hindrance than a help, Batman switches to a lighter-weight Kevlar material that allows for faster travel and quicker reaction time.

BATMAN INCORPORATED

Appearing like a combination of Batman's more classic looks and his modern suits, this Batsuit is similar to the Earth-One version in that it employs an oval bat-symbol and has a contemporary feel. In addition, the symbol can be illuminated and Batman's logo can be projected on his intended target.

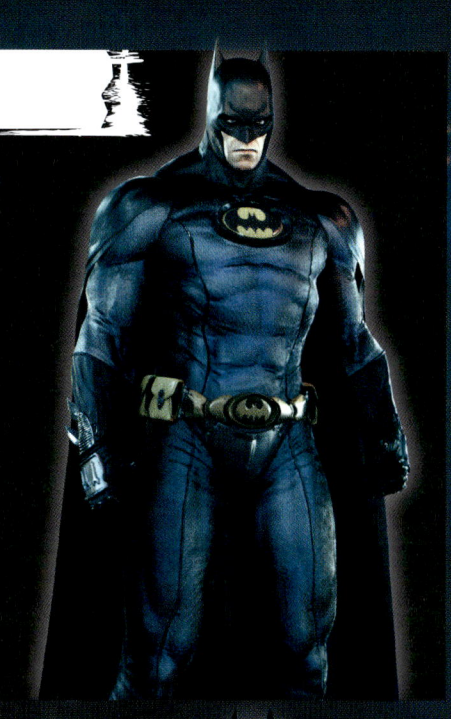

LIBERTY CITY FILES

The Liberty City Files Batsuit employs goggles and a thick, leathery cloak to help protect the Dark Knight's body and mask his movements. A definite departure from his standard wardrobe, this costume almost feels like it would be more suitable for a different era, such as the war-torn world of the 1940s. Unlike other models, this particular suit incorporates a brown belt that matches the strap on the goggles.

SINESTRO CORPS

While a Sinestro Corps Batsuit does indeed reside inside the Batsuit Chamber, when Batman has been seen wearing this particular uniform, he hasn't demonstrated the fantastic powers said to be bestowed upon anyone with a yellow power ring. Perhaps Batman can strike terror enough on his own without the use of otherworldly technology.

ANIME BATMAN

Navigating the many dangers of Gotham City's nights can be tough for Batman, and this particular suit aids him in his patrols by adding extra bulk and padding to his chest, while protecting his shoulders and neck with molded armor. Influenced by foreign media such as anime, this suit features a distinctive-looking Utility Belt and gauntlets that only feature a single spike, as opposed to Batman's traditional three.

BLACKEST NIGHT

The Black Lantern Corps is comprised of reanimated corpses of long-dead crime-fighters, their friends or enemies. However, this particular suit is one of the many options available to the very much alive Dark Knight when riffling through his Batsuit Chamber. However it does not give Batman any of the fantastic powers of a true Black Lantern.

BRIGHTEST DAY

Another Lantern on the emotional power spectrum is the White Lantern. While wearing this uniform and power ring, Batman has never again shown the near-infinite power levels inherent to a White Lantern. An interesting color choice, this Batsuit seems to go against Batman's very nature as Gotham City's Dark Knight.

NOËL

Said to have been employed during a particularly harrowing holiday season in Gotham City, this Batsuit is one of the rare few that connects the cape to the bat-symbol itself. Armored and with a few jagged edges, this suit could quite possibly spook any would-be Scrooge.

NEW 52

A Batsuit appropriate for a new beginning, this suit utilizes a standard pouch Utility Belt with a newly stylized buckle, reinforced, extra-thin body armor sections attached together by seams, and Batman's trademark black bat-symbol. Both a classic and a modern look, this suit signals a bright future for the Dark Knight.

NEW 52 METALLIC

Taking the New 52 suit one step further, the metallic version offers the protection of an extra layer of body armor for the Dark Knight. The result, however, gives the Batsuit a shinier look, one that may draw attention when reflecting streetlights or car headlights. This is sometimes a risk Batman is willing to take, as the sheen of this Batsuit may distract his criminal prey, given the right circumstances.

NEW 52 ARKHAM KNIGHT

While Batman seems to have success with his standard New 52 Batsuit, that doesn't prevent the Dark Knight from upping the ante when given the time to tinker with his costume. In this second version of that suit, the seams of the original give way to segments of thin armor, form-fitted to Batman's exact specifications. Along with a similarly augmented cowl, the overall result is a bulkier, yet practical suit.

DARK KNIGHT

No matter the odds stacked against him, the Dark Knight finds a way to triumph over adversity and rise from the ashes like the proverbial phoenix. This Dark Knight suit is efficient,

with an emphasis on the color black, perhaps inspired by the many ninjas Batman has encountered in his crime-fighting career. Batman has chosen this Batsuit, with its bronze belt and more rounded cowl, to hunt down the likes of the Joker and Bane.

EARTH ONE

A suit that seems to combine all the best elements of Batman's other suits and delivers them in a new and interesting way, this particular uniform once again displays the yellow, oval bat-symbol, but keeps to a dark color scheme. The muted tones are continued in the Utility Belt, which departs from more standard gold or yellow hues.

EARTH 2 DARK KNIGHT

The Earth 2 Dark Knight suit departs from the Dark Knight's usual color palette. Normally preferring black and blue shades that allow him to fade into night's shadows, this red-accented costume is one of the brighter suits currently stored in the Dark Knight's Batsuit Chamber.

INJUSTICE

A costume made of many metal segments, this Batsuit is built for battle, perhaps with the intention of fighting corrupt Super Heroes of immense power. It still employs many of Batman's signature touches, such as his gold Utility Belt and the sharp spikes on his gauntlets.

BEWARE THE BATMAN

Criminals are a cowardly, superstitious lot, and Batman knows how to exploit those qualities with ease. In this all-black "Beware" look, only the hero's Utility Belt breaks the black-on-black color scheme, giving him a more ominous look than ever. Its sleek contours again give Batman an animated feel, albeit one with quite a menacing air about it.

JUSTICE LEAGUE 3000

Another one of Batman's costumes that looks as if it would be right at home in the far future, this Batsuit once again incorporates the color red throughout its design. With a mix of streamlined, thin, Kevlar-like material and armored, reinforced gauntlets, shoulder pads, boots, and cowl, this suit seems as if it would be state-of-the-art even a thousand years from now.

FLASHPOINT

If there are other dimensions and other versions of Earth, perhaps altered by one time paradox or another, Batman's Flashpoint suit looks like it would be ideal. The Flashpoint suit seems to be a costume for a very different Batman with a very different origin. Nevertheless, this look is stored in Batman's Batsuit Chamber. It features red eye slits and armored shoulder plates that can be employed both offensively and defensively.

FIGHTING TECHNIQUES

THE DARK KNIGHT HAS EARNED A FORMIDABLE REPUTATION OVER THE YEARS. NOT ONLY IS HE A FRIGHTENING FIGURE OF THE NIGHT, BATMAN IS ALSO AN EXPERT FIGHTER, ABLE TO IMPROVISE WHEN THE SITUATION CALLS FOR IT.

No matter where Batman tries to concentrate his efforts, he ends up spending the majority of his time stopping petty crimes and taking down members of one gang or another. While his main focus is on major threats like the Joker or the Penguin, stopping street criminals is an essential part of his job, and one he handles with particular style.

▲ **Mixing it Up**
Batman is constantly varying his techniques, using kicks, elbows, knees, and a variety of other strikes so as to not overtax any one part of his body.

Weapons Everywhere
Criminals and Batman alike will employ any handy object as a weapon.

ONE AGAINST MANY
Bruce Wayne's parents were murdered before his eyes by a common street thug. For that reason, Batman takes every mugger or burglar seriously. Unfortunately for the Dark Knight, criminals in Gotham City rarely work alone, forcing Batman to become an expert in fighting multiple opponents at once, using moves like double take-downs.

BATMAN FIGHTING TECHNIQUES

TAKE-DOWN TECHNIQUES

▲ Bad Jokes
Not particularly vigilant, the Joker's thugs are easy prey for a crime-fighter at home in the shadows.

No Holds Barred
Batman went largely unarmed when he first started out, but he learned to use his opponents' weapons against them in a street brawl.

Corner Cover
When taking on armed foes, Batman is forced to rely on stealth. He ducks behind objects or conceals himself in dark corners, attacking enemies when they least expect it.

Block Party
Years of training allow Batman to predict an enemy's attacks. Batman can block and counter most methods of assault, such as blows or knife thrusts.

Down But Not Out
Batman often bounces back and forth between enemies in a brawl, knocking opponents down several times in the course of a single fight.

Running the Gauntlet
Batman's gauntlets are heavily armored for more effective strikes and blocks.

◀ Knockout Punch
While he often uses gadgets or his cape in a fight, sometimes a simple punch is the easiest solution.

PLAYING TO THE ROOM
Batman is such a capable fighter, he can adjust his technique according to his surroundings. When out on the streets, he can dive or pounce on opponents; however, those kinds of opportunities don't come around as often indoors. To increase his chances of success, Batman makes best use of hiding places to surprise attackers, leaping over adversaries in order to take on only one opponent at a time.

THE BATMOBILE

THE ULTIMATE MUSCLE CAR AND ENGINE OF INTIMIDATION, THE BATMOBILE IS THE PERFECT RIDE FOR THE DARK KNIGHT, AS EFFICIENT AS IT IS IMPRESSIVE.

When the Arkham Knight first appears in Gotham City, he comes armed and ready for a fight. Commanding remote-controlled drone tanks, the Knight is prepared for Batman's Batmobile, as if he knows the Dark Knight's technology inside and out. After Batman learns that the Knight's tanks are driverless, he's free to really unleash the weaponized fury of his newest Batmobile, showing the Arkham Knight what this vehicle is truly capable of.

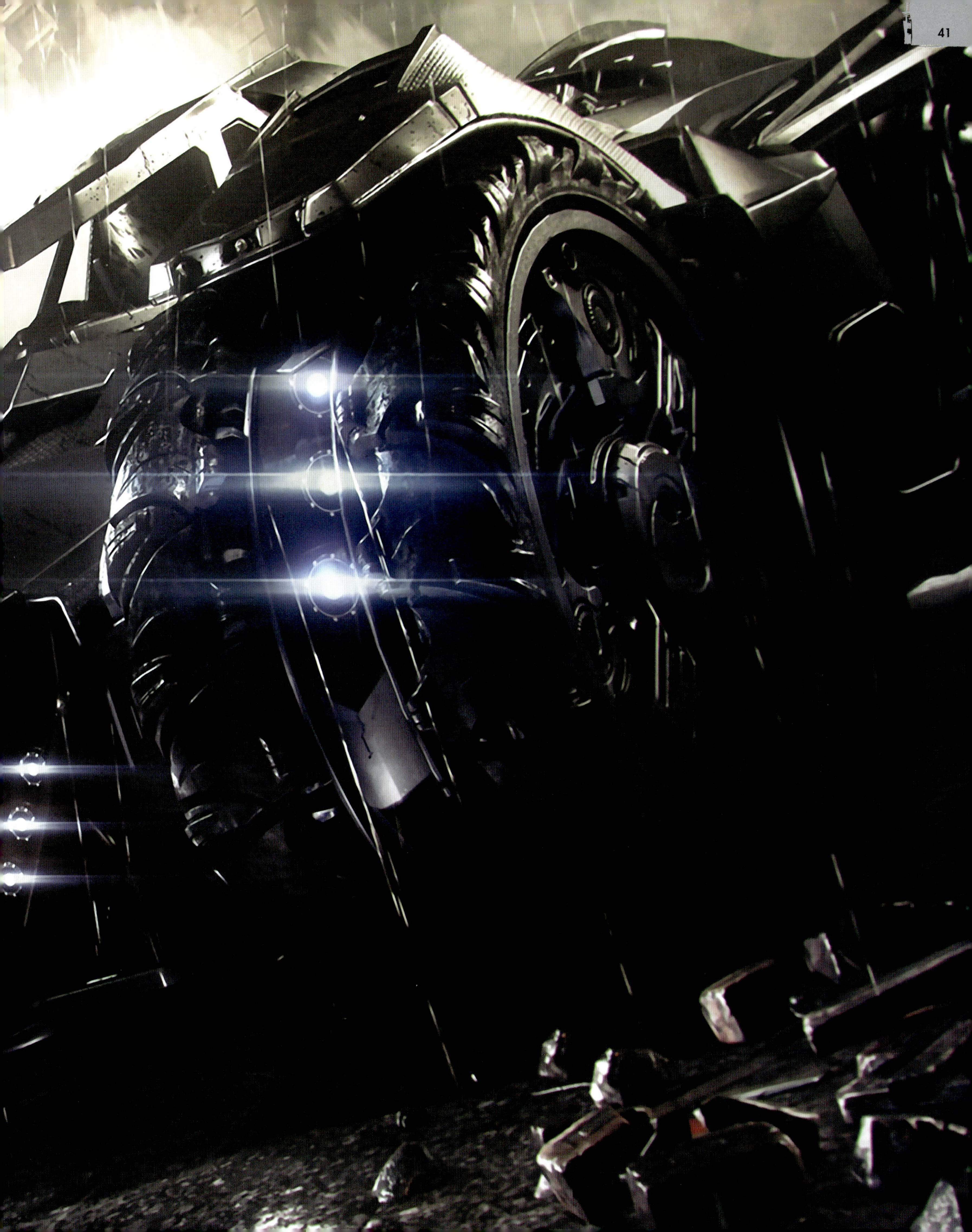

UP CLOSE

BATMAN IS CONSTANTLY IMPROVING HIS OWN ARMOR, SO IT ONLY MAKES SENSE THAT HE CONTINUES TO REWORK THE FAVORITE TOOL IN HIS ARSENAL—THE BATMOBILE.

While it was mostly a souped-up hot rod in the past, the latest version of Batman's Batmobile still contains the aesthetics and abilities of the older model, but with many added features. Now able to propel Batman through the air via an ejector seat, the car makes it possible for Batman to swing into action even faster, adding to his legend as Gotham City's Dark Knight.

▲ **Remote Control Car**
Batman's arm gauntlets do much more than just protect his forearms. They also contain advanced circuitry that allows the Dark Knight to remotely drive his Batmobile in emergencies.

TERRAIN Off-road capabilities

HIDDEN Launches from lake Batcave exit

TRANSFORM Can change to Battle Mode

RAM Can burst through any barricade

ARMOR A high-speed fortress on wheels

Cockpit
Slides open to eject Batman at high speeds, allowing him to glide long distances.

Dynamic Bodywork
Independent body panels slide smoothly over one another as vehicle moves.

Axle-less Wheel
Free-floating mountings allow wheels to move in different directions.

Battle Mode
Bodywork splits during Battle Mode to let wheels steer independently.

BATMAN UP CLOSE 43

BACK

FRONT

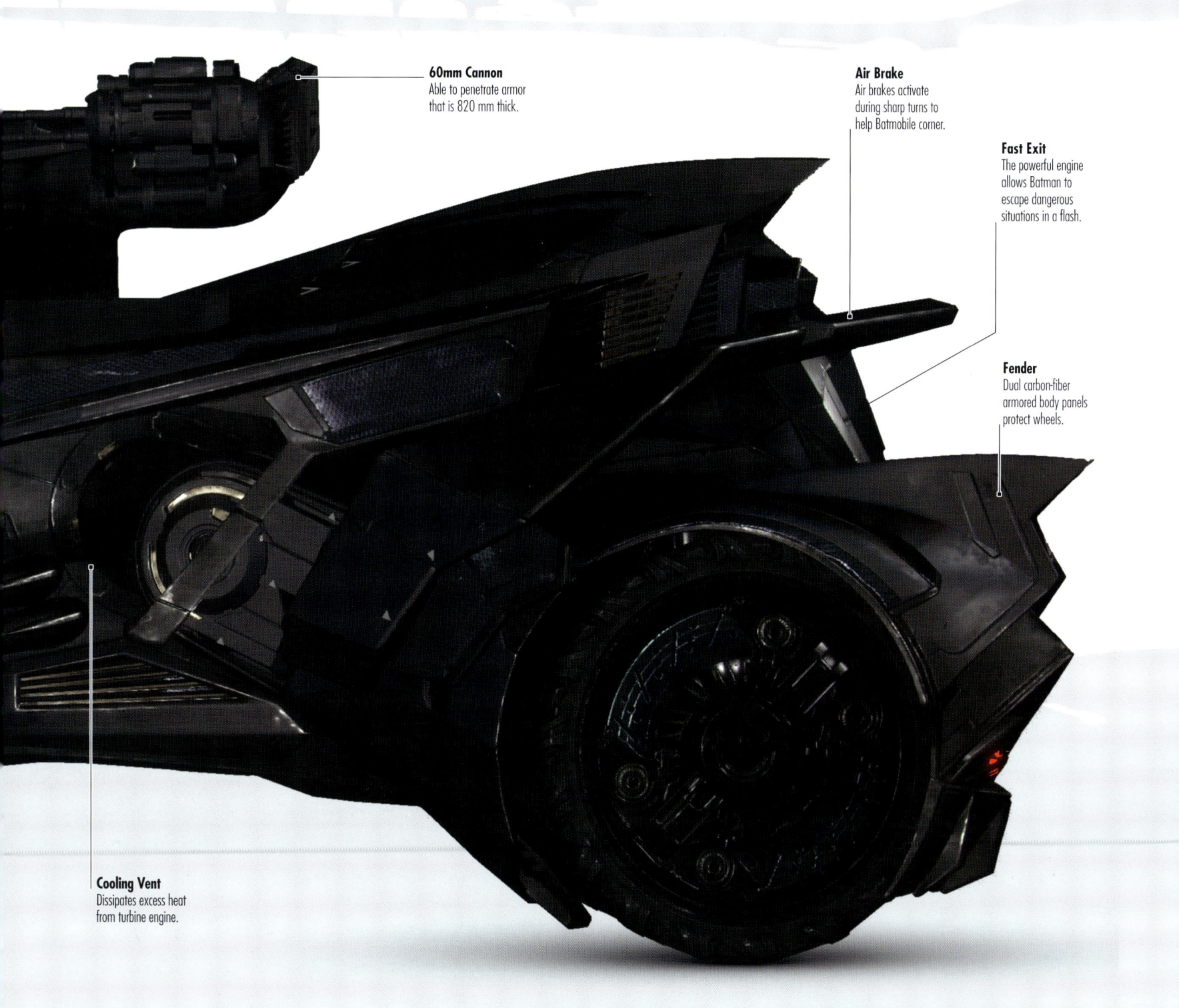

60mm Cannon
Able to penetrate armor that is 820 mm thick.

Air Brake
Air brakes activate during sharp turns to help Batmobile corner.

Fast Exit
The powerful engine allows Batman to escape dangerous situations in a flash.

Fender
Dual carbon-fiber armored body panels protect wheels.

Cooling Vent
Dissipates excess heat from turbine engine.

UNDER THE HOOD

UNLIKE THE PREVIOUS MODEL OF THE BATMOBILE, HIS NEW VEHICLE COMES EQUIPPED WITH THE ABILITY TO SWITCH TO BATTLE MODE. IN EITHER FORM, THE BATMOBILE IS JUST AS FRIGHTENING IN APPEARANCE AS BATMAN HIMSELF, STRIKING FEAR INTO THE HEARTS OF THE CRIMINALS OF GOTHAM CITY.

▲ Car of Shadows
Just like Batman's own suit, the Batmobile is designed to blend in with the night. Jet black and heavily armored, the car has been deliberately designed to look intimidating in order to add to the Dark Knight's fearful image. The car also helps Batman to travel like never before, ejecting him with extra propulsion to enable him to glide at high speeds through the Gotham City night.

UNDER THE HOOD
The Dark Knight has been rigorously refining his signature ride for years, working on the car fairly early on in his career. Having dabbled in many technological fields during his training, Batman is able to improve and update his car himself. However, he often emplys the cutting-edge ideas of Lucius Fox, his long-time friend and employee at Wayne Enterprises.

Engine Block
Turbine engine capable of high sub-sonic speeds.

HUD
Display provides 360° view, with threats prioritized.

Brakes
Electromagnetic brakes can bring vehicle to a rapid stop from extremely high velocity.

Wheel Bearing
Heavy-duty rotating bearing attaches wheel assembly to chassis.

Air Intake
Internal grill is reinforced with a metallic weave bonded with graded diamond particles.

BATMOBILE BATTLE MODE

The Batmobile has been heavily altered to help Batman fight crime on the streets like never before. Able to transform into Battle Mode at the flip of a switch, the car is more of a mobile armory than anything else. Ever since his parents died from gunshot wounds, Batman has been a staunch opponent of traditional guns, but that hasn't stopped him from stocking the Batmobile with heavy firepower designed to remove all obstacles from his path as well as take down enemies in a non-lethal manner.

Wheels of Steel ▶
Heavily armored tires make a rupture nearly impossible for the Dark Knight. Not having to worry about stopping to fix a flat, Batman can afford to use the Batmobile as a battering ram if need be.

RED LIGHT MEANS GO

When the Batmobile switches to Battle Mode, its blue-white headlights turn an ominous red, signaling criminals everywhere that the car is primed and ready to fire at Batman's command. The front of the vehicle opens up, to reveal more of the car's impressive firepower. The extended wheelbase adds to the vehicle's stability, enabling it to strafe.

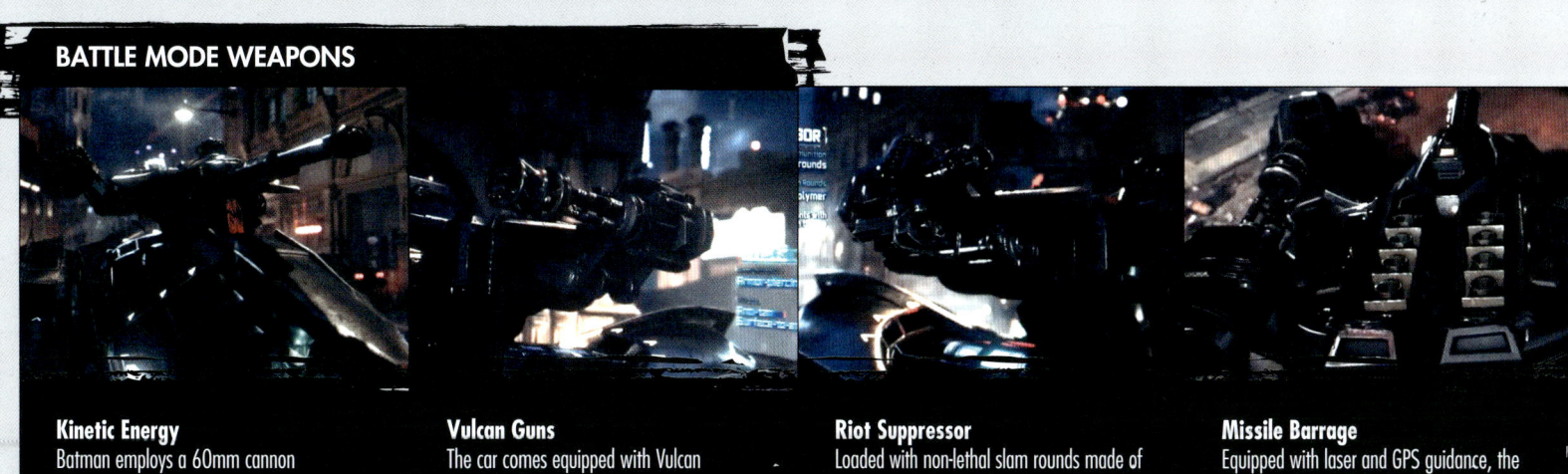

BATTLE MODE WEAPONS

Kinetic Energy
Batman employs a 60mm cannon kinetic-energy penetrator on his new Batmobile. A high-performance device, it can pierce up to 820mm of steel armor.

Vulcan Guns
The car comes equipped with Vulcan Guns that fire armor-piercing incendiary for the strict purpose of anti-tank or surface-to-air combat.

Riot Suppressor
Loaded with non-lethal slam rounds made of medium-velocity flexible polymer, the Riot Suppressor can immobilize combatants with the bare-minimum long-term trauma.

Missile Barrage
Equipped with laser and GPS guidance, the warheads are capable of unleashing a 2kg blast-fragmentation and can simultaneously target up to six hostiles.

BATTLE MODE
The Batmobile has been heavily modified to help Batman fight crime on the streets like never before. Able to transform into Battle Mode at the flip of a switch, the car is more of a mobile arsenal than anything else. Ever since his parents died from gunshot wounds, Batman has been a staunch opponent of traditional guns, but that hasn't stopped him from stocking the Batmobile with firepower designed to take down enemies in a non-lethal manner, as well as remove any obstacles blocking his road.

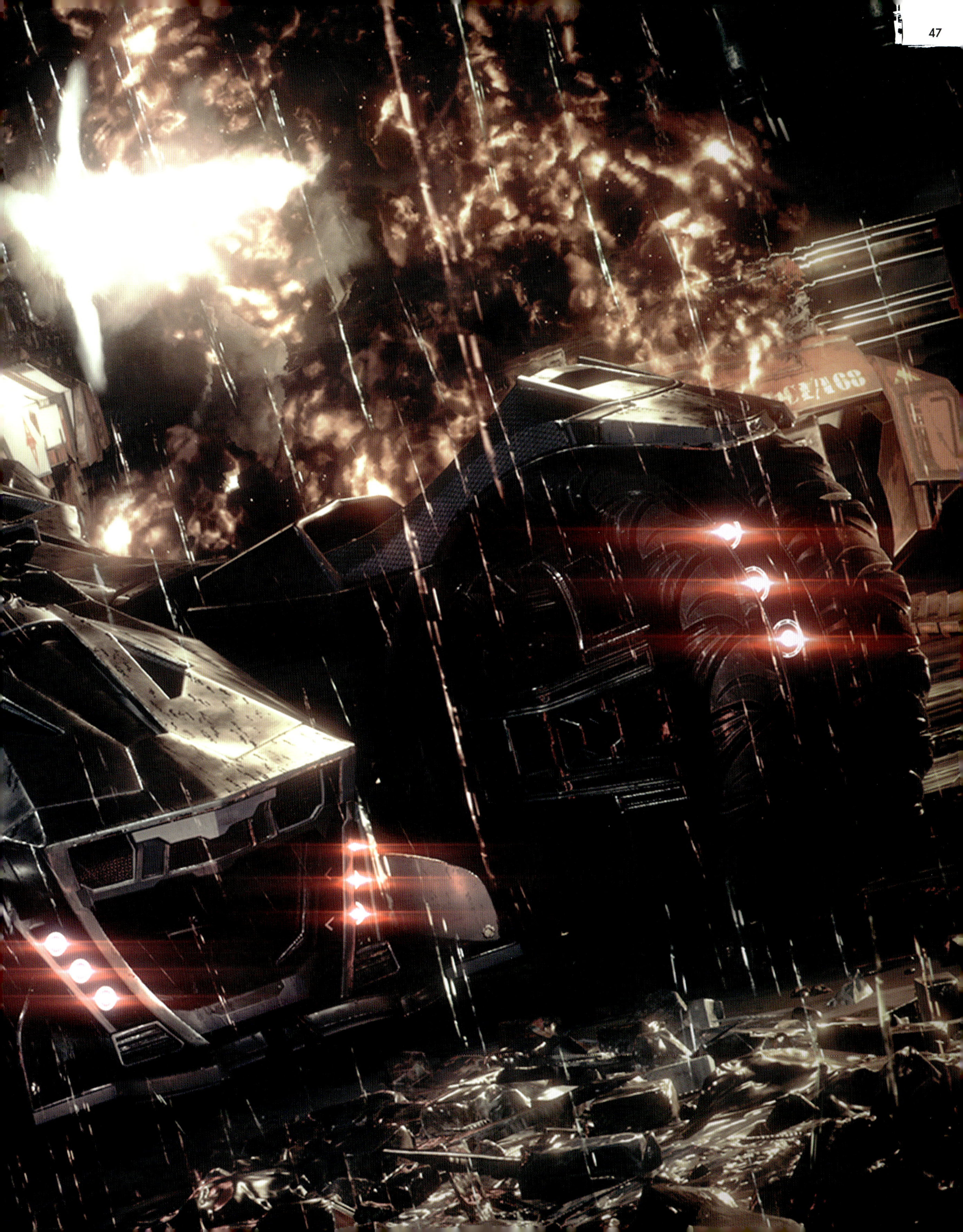

THE BATWING

WHEN BATMAN NEEDS TO GET SOMEWHERE SUPER-FAST HE TAKES TO THE AIR IN HIS TRUSTY BATWING.

Batman began employing his Batwing early on in his career. It's the perfect vehicle for beating Gotham City's crosstown traffic, for fetching vital equipment from the Batcave in a flash, and for getting the Dark Knight to places that he couldn't get to on his own. While he rarely uses the jet for actual combat, the Batwing is second to none when Batman needs to travel in haste.

Fins
The many fins of the original Batwing design help increase stability.

◀ **Drop Points**
The Batwing is designed to get from the Batcave to specific drop points around the city. This allows the Dark Knight to retrieve specific tools, collect his thoughts, and do research on the Batcomputer without significantly interrupting his patrols.

High-tech Craft
The Batwing was developed using Wayne Enterprises technology.

Wings
Streamlined wings aid speedy travel.

BATWING FUNCTIONS

In the Pilot's Seat
The original Batwing lowered a ladder-like platform for Batman. This made entry a snap for the Dark Knight as he could simply step aboard and be raised into the cockpit, ready to take to the air.

Calling a Lifeline
When in need of his Line Launcher while on Arkham Island, Batman typed a command into his arm gauntlet. Soon the Batwing arrived, shattering a wall of glass windows to drop Batman's requested payload.

Special Delivery
When Bruce Wayne was arrested by Hugo Strange and imprisoned in Arkham City, using the Batmobile behind the prison's walls was not an option. Instead, Batman relied on the Batwing to drop his batsuit on a rooftop.

BATMAN THE BATWING   49

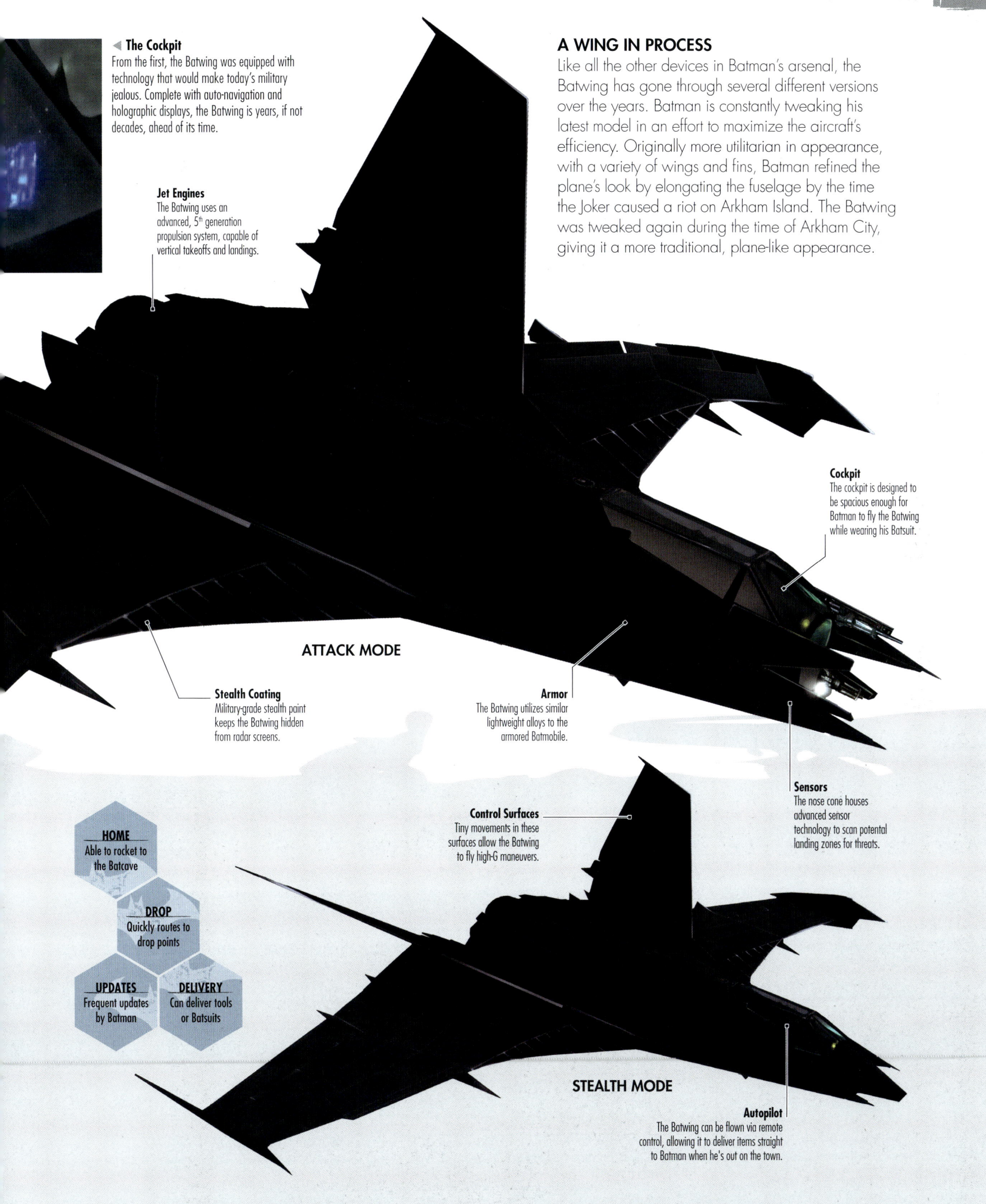

◀ **The Cockpit**
From the first, the Batwing was equipped with technology that would make today's military jealous. Complete with auto-navigation and holographic displays, the Batwing is years, if not decades, ahead of its time.

Jet Engines
The Batwing uses an advanced, 5th generation propulsion system, capable of vertical takeoffs and landings.

A WING IN PROCESS
Like all the other devices in Batman's arsenal, the Batwing has gone through several different versions over the years. Batman is constantly tweaking his latest model in an effort to maximize the aircraft's efficiency. Originally more utilitarian in appearance, with a variety of wings and fins, Batman refined the plane's look by elongating the fuselage by the time the Joker caused a riot on Arkham Island. The Batwing was tweaked again during the time of Arkham City, giving it a more traditional, plane-like appearance.

Cockpit
The cockpit is designed to be spacious enough for Batman to fly the Batwing while wearing his Batsuit.

ATTACK MODE

Stealth Coating
Military-grade stealth paint keeps the Batwing hidden from radar screens.

Armor
The Batwing utilizes similar lightweight alloys to the armored Batmobile.

Sensors
The nose cone houses advanced sensor technology to scan potental landing zones for threats.

HOME
Able to rocket to the Batcave

DROP
Quickly routes to drop points

UPDATES
Frequent updates by Batman

DELIVERY
Can deliver tools or Batsuits

Control Surfaces
Tiny movements in these surfaces allow the Batwing to fly high-G maneuvers.

STEALTH MODE

Autopilot
The Batwing can be flown via remote control, allowing it to deliver items straight to Batman when he's out on the town.

THE BATARANG

PERHAPS THE MOST FAMOUS WEAPON IN BATMAN'S ARSENAL OF CRIME-FIGHTING EQUIPMENT, THE BATARANG HAS BECOME AN ESSENTIAL TOOL FOR THE DARK KNIGHT.

The design seems simple at first: one part boomerang, one part throwing dart, one part calling card. The Batarang is sleek, compact, aerodynamically efficient, and extremely effective. Batman may employ one or more Batarangs to attack criminals from a distance before he engages in close combat. Over time, Batman has created several different variations of Batarang, including Remote-Controlled, Sonic, Sonic Shock, and even Explosive versions.

BATARANG USES

Stunning Work
Batarangs are the perfect tool for stunning the Dark Knight's foes during combat, whether it be Killer Croc or a common thug out to make a name for himself.

Hitting Switches
When Batman needs to hit a button or switch that is out of reach, he makes use of his near-perfect aim and a Batarang to cover the distance for him.

It's Electric
If thrown through an open electric current, the remote-controlled Batarang becomes charged with electricity. It can then power up the device it strikes.

Razor's Edge
The Batarang has razor-sharp edges, perfect for cutting ropes.

▲ By Remote
The remote controlled version of the Batarang is able to speed up and slow down in mid air.

Compact
The Batarang hinges at the center, which allows it to be stored easily in Batman's Utility Belt.

STUN	QUICK-FIRE	BUST	MULTI
Can stun foes from afar	Fast release can aid in combat	Can shatter Joker teeth or balloons	Multi-Batarang throws possible

▲ Heat it Up
When outfitted in his Extreme Environment suit (XE suit), Batman can heat up his Batarangs to a glowing red-hot temperature in order to thaw out frozen objects from a safe distance.

▲ Sonic Shock
Besides the Sonic Batarang, Batman can also employ a Sonic Shock Batarang that not only attracts others to its location, but can take out an opponent as well.

It's a Trap
Batman can use the Sonic Batarang to lure enemies into a trap.

Fake Out
A Sonic Batarang can mimic the high-pitched sound created by the "suicide collars" many Arkham inmates wear.

THE BATMAN BATARANG / SMOKE PELLETS

SMOKE PELLETS

SOME OF THE SMALLEST ITEMS IN BATMAN'S UTILITY BELT MAY BE THE MOST USEFUL, AS IS THE CASE WITH THE DARK KNIGHT'S INVALUABLE SMOKE PELLETS.

Batman develops an affinity for Smoke Pellets during his training days before he adopts the identity of the Dark Knight. They come in handy for making quick escapes or creating enough cover to take down an opponent with ease. In fact, using Smoke Pellets is an almost automatic response from the Dark Knight when faced with an opponent with a shotgun or sniper rifle.

SMOKE PELLET USES

Take the High Ground
Smoke Pellets allow Batman to escape high-risk situations and get to a higher vantage point. If he uses his grapnel gun quickly enough, his attackers can't follow his movements through the thick smoke.

Clouded Judgment
Even when the odds seem stacked against the Dark Knight Detective, by dropping one of his smoke bombs, he can disorient his foes, especially those already nervous about tangling with the legendary Batman.

High Concentration
Bruce Wayne begins to favor the use of Smoke Pellets when training with Master Kirigi in the mountains of North Korea. Without the aid of Detective Vision, Wayne has to use pure concentration to navigate.

Now You See Him...
On impact, the pellet's composite shell breaks open, releasing a cloud of thick smoke. Batman can use the distraction to disarm foes or knock them unconcious.

VARIED Good in combat and predator situations

VISION Detective Vision lets Batman navigate

MULTI Can be used many times in combat

SETTING Useful outdoors or inside

LIMIT Smoke disperses quickly

▲ **Dark Knight Detective**
Thanks to his Detective Vision's thermal imagery, Batman can easily navigate through thick smoke. This automatically kicks in when the Dark Knight hurls a Smoke Pellet.

▲ **Caltrops**
Wayne employs Caltrops when training with Master Kirigi. While they do create a bit of dust in the air when thrown, Caltrops do not create the type of smoke cover Bruce's later Smoke Pellets provide.

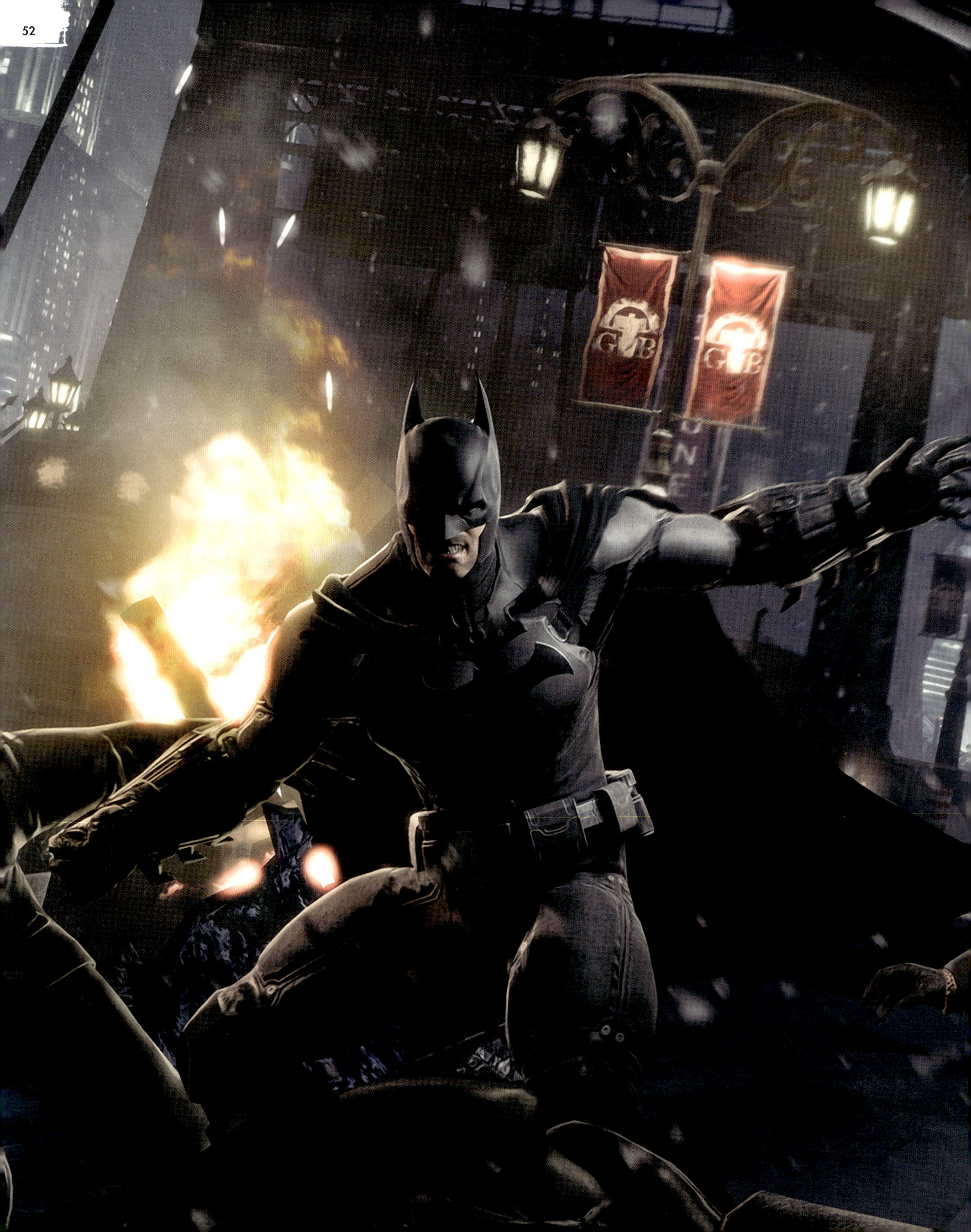
GB
GB

Tools to Fight Crime
The Gotham City night holds many terrors for ordinary citizens, from street thugs out to make a quick buck, to villains like Black Mask and his army of minions. It is because of threats like these that Batman is forced to equip his Utility Belt with such a powerful, high-tech arsenal, and to use razor-sharp Batarangs.

GRENADES

BATMAN'S UTILITY BELT IS ALWAYS STOCKED WITH A VAST ARRAY OF WEAPONS, MANY OF WHICH ACT AS NON-LETHAL GRENADES, ENSURING THE DARK KNIGHT HAS ALL THE FIREPOWER HE NEEDS TO ENGAGE IN ANY FIGHT.

In his early days policing Gotham City, Batman produces miniature Glue Grenades that can be tossed at an opponent from a distance to stop a criminal in his tracks. He also employs Concussion Detonators that can stun enemies with a non-deadly blast. Later, with access to Mr. Freeze's technology, Batman develops the Freeze Blast, a high-tech update to the basic principles of his Glue Grenade.

GRENADE USES

Freeze!
Batman can literally stop an oncoming enemy in his tracks with his Freeze Blast. Unlike the effect of Mr. Freeze's gun, the Freeze Blast wears off fairly quickly.

White-Water Rafting
With either the Glue Grenade or Freeze Blast, Batman can create a makeshift raft. He simply has to throw either gadget into the water and a chemical reaction results in a large, raft-sized platform that he can ride on.

No Police Brutality
With a toss of his Concussion Detonator, the Dark Knight can take out recalcitrant members of the Gotham City Police Department without injuring them. It's an especially helpful tool for Batman in a city that produces both honest and corrupt police officers.

GLUE GRENADE

Simple Design
The Concussion Detonator uses the same basic design as Batman's Glue Grenade.

◀ **Unstable Molecules**
The Glue Grenade proves too unstable, and Batman stops using it after its first trial run.

NUMBERS — Useful for large groups of hostiles

STICK — Glue adheres foes in place for a time

Making an Entrance ▶
The Concussion Detonator is perfect for delivering a little non-lethal shock and certainly gets people's attention.

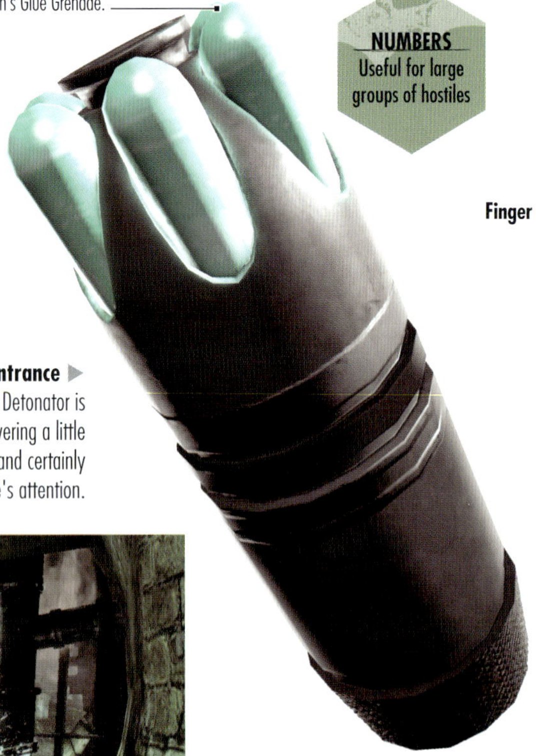

CONCUSSION DETONATOR

◀ **Blowing Off Steam**
When faced with pipes spewing hot steam or noxious gas, Batman can throw either a Glue Grenade or his Freeze Blast at the opening, to seal it off from a safe distance.

FREEZE BLAST

Finger Grip

▲ **Spoils of War**
Mr. Freeze gives Batman the Freeze Blast system in order to help the Dark Knight find Freeze's wife, Nora. Batman later uses it to take down the villain Clayface.

HI-TECH — Advanced variation on Glue Grenade

BATMAN GRENADES/REMOTE CLAW 55

REMOTE CLAW

A CREATURE OF THE SHADOWS, BATMAN IS OFTEN IN NEED OF A WAY TO OBTAIN A HIGHER VANTAGE POINT TO PREY ON THE CRIMINALS OF GOTHAM CITY. HIS REMOTE CLAW AND LINE LAUNCHER LET HIM DO JUST THAT.

First appropriated from the villain Deathstroke, Batman quickly finds plenty of uses for the projectile-firing weapon known as the Remote Claw. By firing at one target and then another, the Remote Claw attaches a line to each and pulls them taut. The Dark Knight later uses this technology to create his own version of the device in the form of his trusty Line Launcher.

REMOTE CLAW USES

Overhead Attack
Batman is constantly looking for ways to take his opponents unaware. Tools like the Line Launcher allow the hero to get the jump on criminals, while keeping himself out of harm's way.

Bringing People Together
The Remote Claw's reel is so powerful it can smash two opponents together if Batman fires the device at both enemies. This stuns them and gives Batman time to act.

Rope Trick
Batman is able to create a tightrope with either the Remote Claw or the Line Launcher. The cords have been specifically designed to hold his weight. The Dark Knight has also been known to use the cord as a zipline, sliding from one end to the other.

Reel It In
The tool's internal reel automatically makes the cord go taut after being fired.

Gas Valve

Anchors Away
The Remote Claw can be fired at no more than two separate anchor points.

Hardened Steel Claw

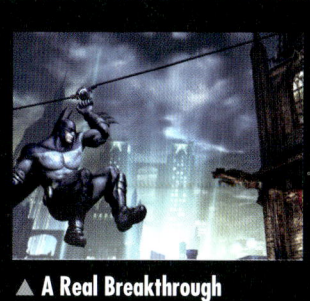

Trigger

▲ **The Hook Up**
Batman uses his grapnel gun to raise himself up to the tightrope created by the Remote Claw. His years of training help him maintain perfect balance as he walks from one end to the other.

▲ **Aiming High**
Batman's sophisticated targeting system is built into his cowl. It feeds him the precise locations at which he must aim the Remote Claw.

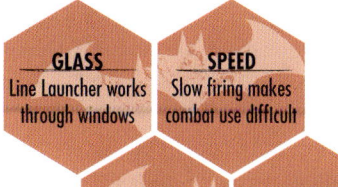

GLASS — Line Launcher works through windows
SPEED — Slow firing makes combat use difficult
USE — Cannot be used vertically
ATTACK — Taut line can launch objects at foes

▲ **A Real Breakthrough**
Using his tightrope as a zipline, Batman can use his momentum to smash through walls that are not structurally sound.

Travel Version
The Line Launcher is much more compact and portable than the Remote Claw.

Hand Held
This newer model offers Batman a comfortable grip.

DISRUPTOR

BATMAN HAS USED TWO DIFFERENT DISRUPTOR TOOLS OVER THE YEARS. WHILE THEY LOOK DIFFERENT, THEIR FUNCTION IS BASICALLY THE SAME: TO SHORT OUT TROUBLESOME ELECTRONICS.

Batman first acquires his Disruptor from the evidence locker at the G.C.P.D. building. The original Disruptor is a bulky device that resembles a rifle or paintball gun. Although he can collapse it quite easily, it is still one of the biggest items in his arsenal. The Disruptor is a tool for causing electronic devices to malfunction, and can also deactivate weapons from a safe distance. Batman later miniaturizes it into a more ergonomic, hand-held version.

DISRUPTOR USES

Severing the Arms
The Disruptor is essential to Batman's campaign against the Penguin's arms dealings. With the simple pull of a trigger, Batman reduces stolen police guns to scrap metal.

Freezing Freeze
Batman's later version of the Disruptor is used mainly for taking out Mr. Freeze's technology. He employs it to good effect during a violent confrontation with the Penguin.

Door Jam
Using the Disruptor to stop a signal jammer is only the first step to opening certain highly guarded doors. Batman's Cryptographic Sequencer is also needed for that particular task.

▲ **Recharged**
During his clash with the Arkham Knight, Batman employed an upgraded version of the Disruptor.

Safety Catch

Charge Housing

▲ **Surprise!**
After being disrupted, a criminal won't even know his gun has been tampered with until he attempts to fire it, allowing Batman to get the drop on him.

◀ **What's Yours Is Mine**
Batman is given a Mine Detonator addition to his hand-held Disruptor from G.C.P.D. Officer Elvis Jones, who decides that the Dark Knight has more use for the device than he does.

Trigger

EMP Pulse Emitter

▲ **Weapon Combo**
The Dark Knight often uses his Disruptor in conjunction with other devices, such as his Cryptographic Sequencer, to unlock doors.

DISRUPT — Can disrupt jammer frequencies
PULSE — Disables security systems
DISABLE — Upgrade to ruin PA systems and mines
UPGRADE — Modified to affect various items
PREP — Used before directly entering combat

BATMAN DISRUPTOR/BATCLAW 57

BATCLAW USES

Clear a Path
Batman can employ the Batclaw to topple crates when he needs to. This is especially useful when boxes are blocking his path and are a good distance away from him.

Capture Claw
When tracking down the Riddler's DataPacks or extortion files, the Batclaw comes in handy to snag out-of-reach hiding places and pull the item back to the waiting Dark Knight.

Stroke of Ingenuity
Deathstroke has a tendency to drop his guard when he is some distance away from Batman. The Dark Knight can take advantage of that thanks to the Batclaw's quick-fire ability.

BATCLAW

WHEN NAVIGATING THE HIDDEN NOOKS AND CRANNIES OF GOTHAM CITY AND ITS BUILDINGS, BATMAN'S BATCLAW IS AN IRREPLACEABLE TOOL TO GET THE DARK KNIGHT WHERE HE NEEDS TO BE.

Batman typically uses his grapnel gun to boost himself to the rooftops of Gotham City, but sometimes the Dark Knight finds it necessary to bring objects to him. On those occasions, he relies on the Batclaw, a sophisticated weapon that shoots a hook from its handle and attaches itself to items like grate covers, crates, or other small objects. Its strong hook firmly attaches to anchor points, but Batman must use his own strength to pull on the Batclaw's line. It also comes in handy in a fight, bringing opponents right where Batman wants them.

- Pnuematic Piston
- Spring-Loaded Claw (Opens on Launch)
- Line Reel

Up the Ante
Only Batman's older model of Batclaw can be upgraded to Ultra.

Triple Strength
Able to shoot three claws at once, the Ultra Batclaw is a much heavier tool.

Ultra Power
When dealing with the riots in Arkham Asylum, Batman upgrades to the Ultra Batclaw, which shoots three hooks at once and can help tear down structurally weak walls.

SNAG Can snag enemies from afar
PUSH Can push foes away if closer than 10 ft.
RETRACT Can be retracted at will
DISARM Able to disarm combatants
UPGRADE Original model can upgrade to Ultra

▲ **Venting Anger**
When a vent grate is too high for Batman to simply pry off, the Batclaw is Batman's go-to tool. After tearing it off the wall with the Batclaw, Batman can use his grapnel gun to lift himself up and gain access the vent.

▲ **Waterway**
When Batman's grapnel line won't reach due to long distances or confined spaces, his Batclaw, with a little improvisation, is the perfect substitute.

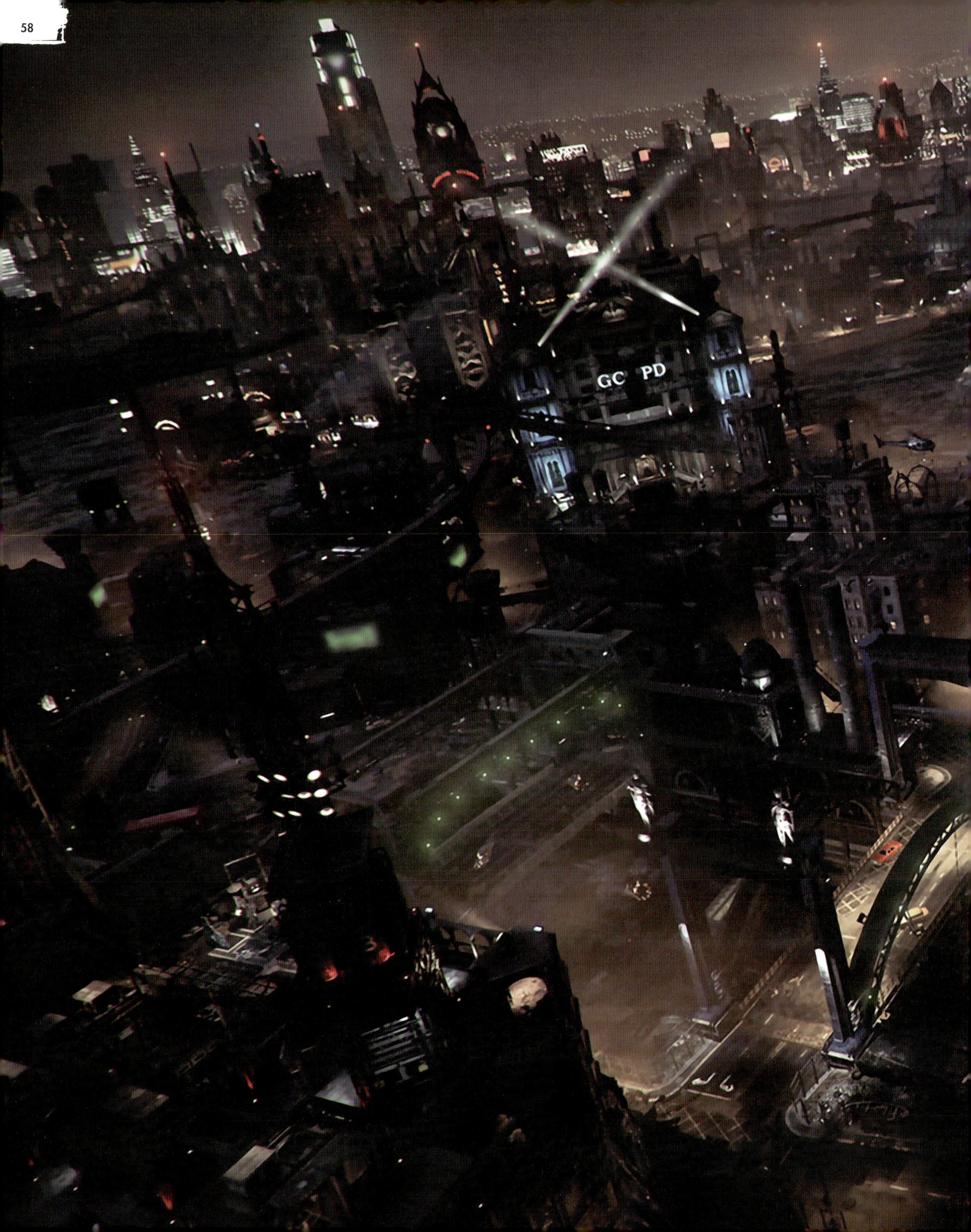
GC PD

Night Flyer
Batman's cape allows him to glide on the wind. It works perfectly in conjunction with his grapnel gun, enabling him to swoop and glide across the Gotham City skyline. By alternating between reeling in the grapnel and gliding on the momentum that creates, Batman can mimic flying. This greatly increases the speed and distance he can travel, enhancing his legend as a creature of the night.

EXPLOSIVE GEL

USED WHEN HUNTING CRIMINALS AS WELL AS WHEN INVESTIGATING INSIDE OLD BUILDINGS, THE EXPLOSIVE GEL IS A POWERFUL ADDITION TO BATMAN'S CRUSADE AGAINST CRIME.

Roadblocks seem to be a regular occurrence for Gotham City's Dark Knight. Whether it be a thin wall of crumbling plaster or a mass of rotting, poorly assembled boards, Batman is often faced with barriers blocking his path. His Explosive Gel quickly gets him through structurally weak walls, and also helps him to make a dramatic entrance to surprise enemies.

Points for Style
The Gel's small, hand-held design allows Batman to "tag" the bat-symbol on each wall that he plans to blow up — Robin sprays his own "R" logo.

▲ **Demolition Man**
The most common use of Batman's Explosive Gel is to demolish walls or floors. After spraying the gel onto the thin barrier he wants to destroy, Batman detonates the gel from a safe distance. When Batman applies gel to a wall, he always sprays a bat-symbol.

Pistol Grip

Explosive Surprise
Batman can use his Explosive Gel rapidly in combat due to the quick-fire trigger.

Nozzle

EXPLOSIVE GEL USES

Wrecking Ball
One way the Dark Knight can take out opponents without putting himself at risk is to detonate a wall that the criminal is standing near, knocking the villain off his feet.

Underfoot
When Batman detonates the floor beneath his feet, he makes a shock entrance in the room below, taking villains by surprise amid the falling rubble.

Increase the Frequency
If needed, Batman can upgrade his Explosive Gel to allow for multiple frequency detonations. This comes in handy when targeting a large group of criminals.

Walled-off Secrets
From the Riddler's trophies to hidden audio files, Gotham City's secrets are often hidden behind weak, easily breached walls.

NO HELP Sound walls cannot be destroyed

STORAGE Often stored in the Batmobile's trunk

TWO-STEP Requires a two-step process

◄ **Off Guard**
When caught in a detonation, Batman's foes tend to drop their weapons, allowing the Dark Knight to deal with them.

BATMAN EXPLOSIVE GEL/SHOCK GLOVES

SHOCK GLOVES

BATMAN IS ALWAYS ADJUSTING AND UPDATING HIS BATSUIT IN ORDER TO BE BETTER EQUIPPED ON PATROLS. ADDING SHOCK GLOVES TO HIS ARSENAL OF WEAPONRY HAS IMMEASURABLY HELPED HIS MISSION.

After the Electrocutioner's death at the Joker's hands, Batman removes the deceased villain's gloves and puts them on. The Shock Gloves become a staple in his quest to defeat the Joker and his assassins, including Bane and his army. Able to transmit electricity to opponents and machinery alike, Batman's Shock Gloves help him to disarm enemies with a single touch, and recharge long-defunct electronics.

SHOCK GLOVES USES

Portable Generator
While exploring various locations, Batman can use his Shock Gloves to charge up old generators and other machinery, allowing him access to otherwise off-limits areas.

Armor Off
One of the greatest benefits of the Shock Gloves is their ability to send current through shields or body armor, helping Batman to take out opponents quickly.

Affairs of the Heart
When Alfred is severely injured by the villain Bane, Batman is able to restart his heart with the help of the Shock Gloves. He even uses the same trick later on Bane himself.

Time Limit
When in combat, it takes Batman a bit of time to charge his Shock Gloves. Also, after significant use, the charge wears off, forcing the Dark Knight to recharge via more combat.

Shock and Awe ▶
The Electrocutioner is not one of Batman's toughest foes, but his technology is impressive. With his Shock Gloves, Batman can even the odds considerably.

Charge Account
Once Batman's battery meter fills up with enough electrical charge, the kid gloves are off, and the Shock Gloves are on.

Recharge
With every strike against an enemy, the Shock Gloves begin to charge.

CHARGE
Electricity generated from combat

The Lights Are On...
The Electrocutioner's ego is his downfall, especially when combined with his extreme reliance on his Shock Gloves.

CRYPTOGRAPHIC SEQUENCER

GOTHAM CITY IS FULL OF WEIRD RIDDLES AND SINISTER PUZZLES. BATMAN'S CRYPTOGRAPHIC SEQUENCER ENABLES HIM TO BRING SOME OF THESE DARK SECRETS INTO THE LIGHT.

Another mainstay of Batman's arsenal, the Cryptographic Sequencer is the perfect device for hacking security codes and gaining access to closed-off rooms and chambers that would be nearly impossible for a civilian to enter. When close to a console, the Sequencer automatically connects Batman to the device. When used in other locations, the Cryptographic Sequencer also allows the Dark Knight to listen in on various radio frequencies.

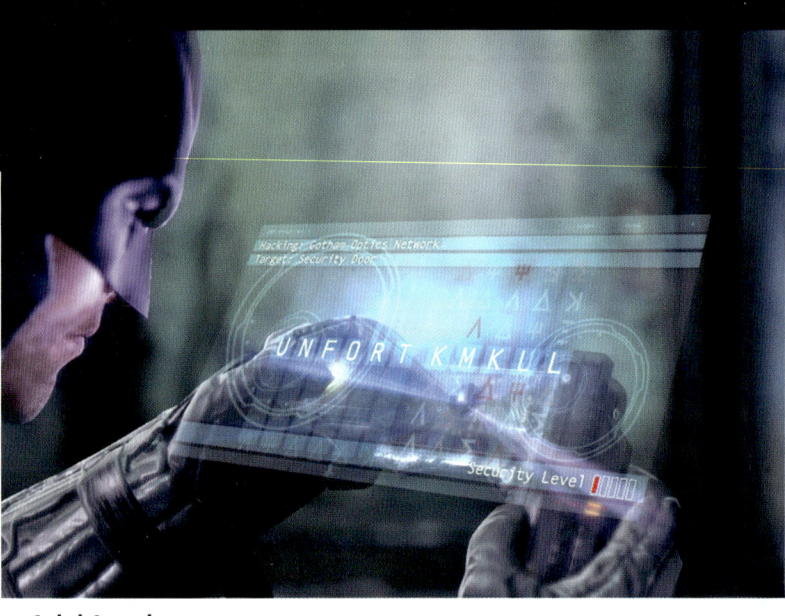

SEQUENCER USES

Bomb Squad
The Cryptographic Sequencer is a multi-purpose tool. It can be used to hack into bombs, making it possible for Batman to diffuse them. However, Batman must then beat a ticking clock.

Radio Days
Batman can use the Cryptographic Sequencer to tap into anything from talk radio to the raving manifestos broadcast by criminals. To listen for any great length of time, Batman must remain stationary.

Gated Community
Batman is constantly facing locked security gates and doors, especially when inside Arkham Asylum or Arkham City. The Cryptographic Sequencer is really his only option if he wishes to continue his mission.

WayneTech
The Cryptographic Sequencer receives WayneTech upgrades to increase its range of effectiveness and to make hacking easier for Batman. These upgrades greatly improve the device's efficiency.

Screenshot
The Cryptographic Sequencer projects a holographic screen for Batman to utilize.

▲ **Coded Conundrums**
Batman uses both thumbs to find the "sweet spot" on the Cryptographic Sequencer, spelling out a word or phrase that unlocks the console.

COMPACT — Folds for easy storage
DETECT — Can listen in on police broadcasts
TUNE IN — Can tune in to radio stations
COMBO — Often used with other tools
ENTRY — Allows entry to highly secure areas

▶ **Riddle Me This**
Batman frequently uses the Sequencer to decipher security codes created by Edward Nashton, also known as Enigma, and later as the Riddler. Riddler's code words and phrases are often dark jokes or insults aimed at Batman.

▲ **Good Vibrations**
Batman can tell how close he is getting to cracking a security code by the intensity of the vibrations from his Sequencer.

Efficient Device
Like most of Batman's gadgets, the Sequencer folds up to take up a minimum of space on his Utility Belt.

REMOTE ELECTRICAL CHARGE

BATMAN DETESTS GUNS, BUT HE HAS NO QUALMS ABOUT USING HIS NON-LETHAL, REMOTE ELECTRICAL CHARGE DEVICE (REC). THOUGH SHAPED LIKE A RIFLE, THE REC SIMPLY GIVES THE DARK KNIGHT A LITTLE EXTRA POWER—QUITE LITERALLY.

After abandoning his Shock Gloves, Batman realizes that he still needs to employ an electrical charge now and again, whether to power-up long inert machinery, or to disable and disarm opponents during hand-to-hand combat. The Remote Electrical Charge weapon is perfect for these purposes, and doesn't weigh the Dark Knight down as much as his Shock Gloves.

ELECTRICAL CHARGE USES

Sticking It to Freeze
By charging machines, Batman can activate the devices, and can also create a magnetic charge. This proves particularly useful when Batman uses magnets to gain the upper hand against Mr. Freeze.

Automatic Door
Locked doors are a common sight for Batman—the criminals of Gotham City don't want him busting into their hideouts. Luckily, the Dark Knight's REC will quickly open electronic doors.

Magnet Manipulation
By charging a dormant magnet with the REC, Batman can attract or repel metal items. He can also swing objects, such as cranes, giving him access to walled-off areas.

Pop Goes the Weasel
When Batman is feeling particularly annoyed by Harley Quinn, he can use his Remote Electrical Charge to pop the heads off the statues she decorates the Steel Mill with.

Shock Attack ▶
Batman's opponents aren't prepared for a blast of electricity, which makes the REC a great weapon to employ in any fight.

Magnetic Personality
With a single shot from his REC's emitter, Batman can charge powerful magnets and cause chain reactions.

Design Sense
Batman often employs a similar utilitarian design for his gadgets, not wanting to fix something that's not broken.

Stock

▲ Getting Tense
Armed enemies nearly always tense up during an electrical attack, and if Batman shoots an armored foe, his enemy is sent flying backward from the impact.

Fore Grip

SPASM Can cause foes to spasm

CHARGE Useful for charging magnets

MISTAKE Causes some foes to attack their allies

COMBO Often used with other weapons

DETECTIVE MODE

THE BUILT-IN DETECTIVE VISION LOCATED IN THE DARK KNIGHT'S COWL PROVES AN INVALUABLE ASSET WHEN LOCATING, OBSERVING, AND TACKLING VILLAINY.

Batman does not have super powers; he relies on advanced technology to help him tackle large groups of criminals or particularly challenging adversaries. Switching to his cowl's Detective Mode gives the Dark Knight a vital edge, activating a combination of night vision and thermal imaging. This allows Batman to navigate with ease in the dark, much like the creatures that inspired his name.

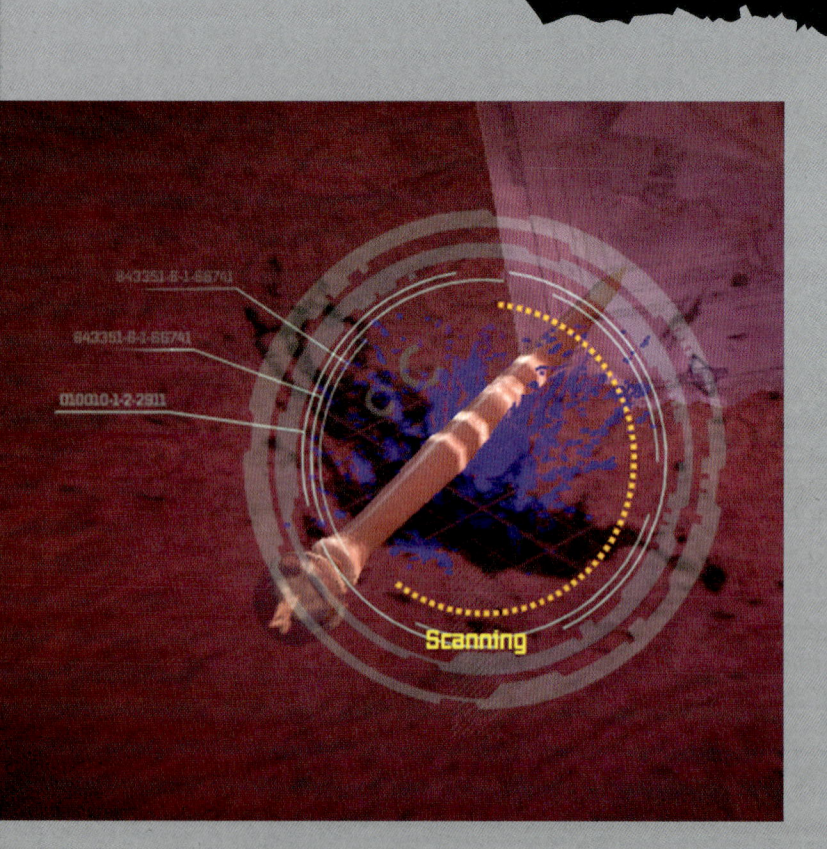

SCENE OF THE CRIME

Detective Mode comes in handy for Batman not just in combat situations. He often employs his cowl's remote link to the Batcomputer in order to analyze crime scenes and gather important clues. Used in tandem with his built-in evidence scanner, Batman can recreate crime scenes, deducing where and how a crime took place.

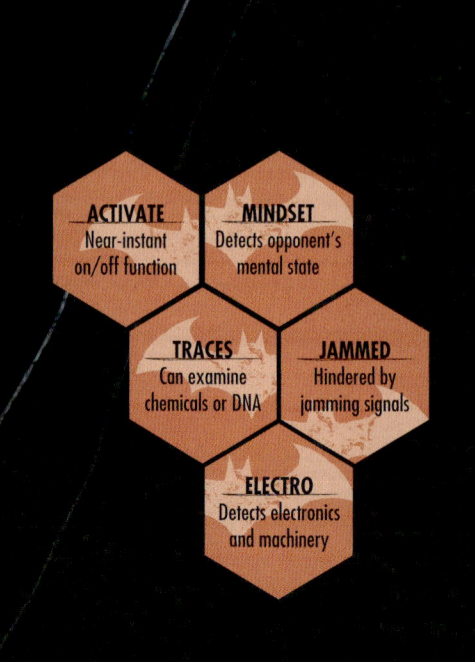

ACTIVATE — Near-instant on/off function

MINDSET — Detects opponent's mental state

TRACES — Can examine chemicals or DNA

JAMMED — Hindered by jamming signals

ELECTRO — Detects electronics and machinery

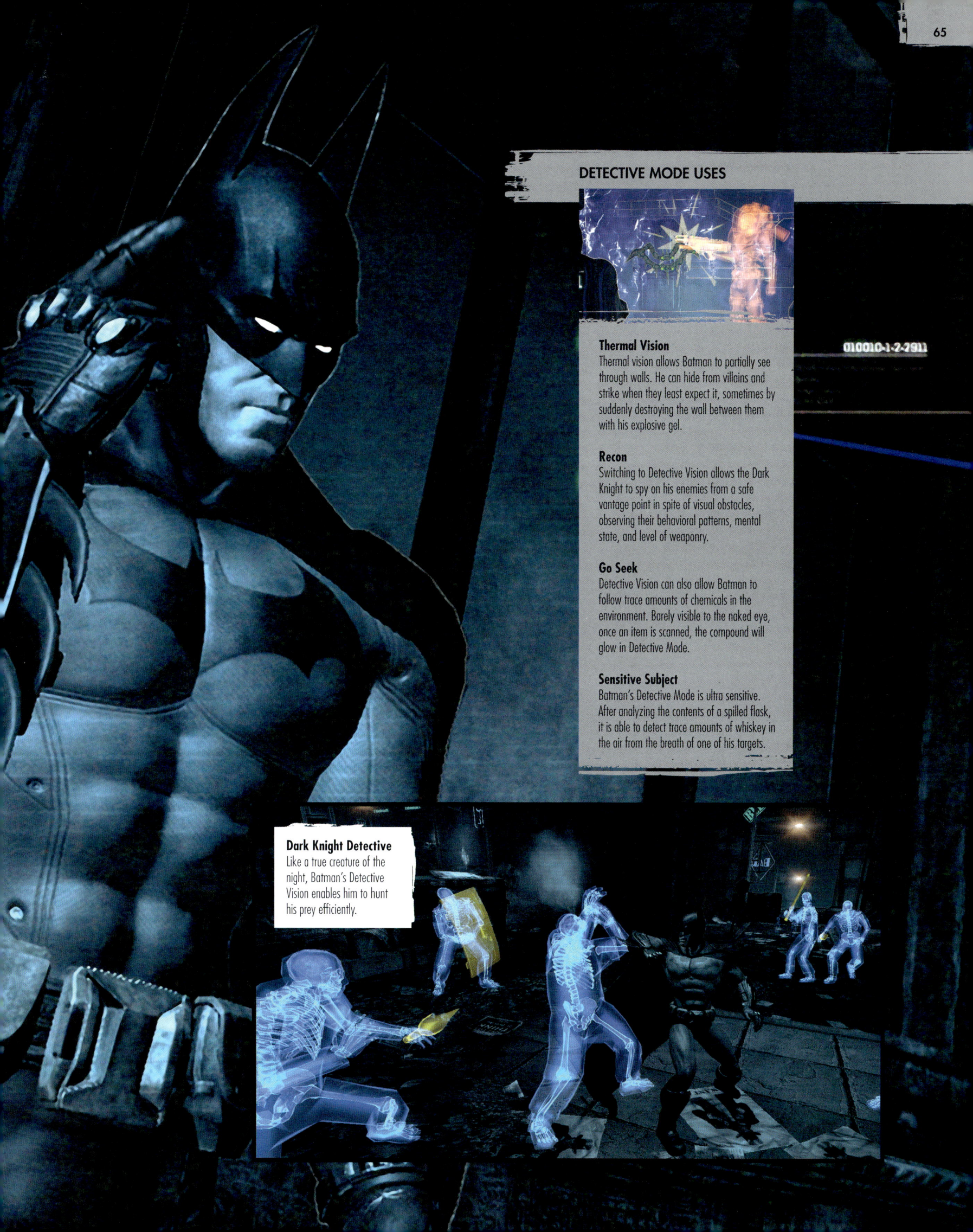

DETECTIVE MODE USES

Thermal Vision
Thermal vision allows Batman to partially see through walls. He can hide from villains and strike when they least expect it, sometimes by suddenly destroying the wall between them with his explosive gel.

Recon
Switching to Detective Vision allows the Dark Knight to spy on his enemies from a safe vantage point in spite of visual obstacles, observing their behavioral patterns, mental state, and level of weaponry.

Go Seek
Detective Vision can also allow Batman to follow trace amounts of chemicals in the environment. Barely visible to the naked eye, once an item is scanned, the compound will glow in Detective Mode.

Sensitive Subject
Batman's Detective Mode is ultra sensitive. After analyzing the contents of a spilled flask, it is able to detect trace amounts of whiskey in the air from the breath of one of his targets.

Dark Knight Detective
Like a true creature of the night, Batman's Detective Vision enables him to hunt his prey efficiently.

Down in Flames
A police helicopter crashes on the streets of Gotham City—another mystery for Batman to solve.

COLD CASES

DURING THE EARLY DAYS OF HIS CAREER, BATMAN FACES A MULTITUDE OF THREATS SOLVING CASES THAT THE G.C.P.D. JUST CANNOT CRACK.

The Christmas Eve that Batman first defeats the Joker sees Gotham City overrun by crime. When not being put through his paces by Black Mask or the Clown Prince of Crime, the Dark Knight has to put his detective skills to the test, investigating everything from a mysterious helicopter crash to an unsolved hit and run. But of all the crimes that take place that night, a shooting in Crime Alley hits the closest to home for the hero.

HELICOPTER CRASH

Alfred informs Batman about an S.O.S. in the Bowery area of Gotham City, and Batman heads to the scene. However, the call is a ruse to corner the Dark Knight with a police helicopter. Before the police can act on their threat of deadly fire, the helicopter is shot out of the air. Batman investigates, eventually discovering that the marksman was none other than the hired hitman Deadshot.

BATMAN COLD CASES

THE DIXON DOCKS SHOOTING

Batman discovers the body of Owen Grant—an investigative reporter who had interviewed Bruce Wayne the previous year—at the Dixon Docks in Gotham City's Amusement Mile. It turns out that Grant has been shot while photographing a ring of counterfeiters led by his killer, Chucky Berks.

THE AMUSEMENT MILE MAULING

Batman learns of a homicide outside the Gotham Casino in the Amusement Mile neighborhood of Gotham City. The victim has been killed by a large fan, which has been thrown at him. The killer in question is Andrew Carter, who has augmented his physique using Bane's technology, losing his mental stability in the process. Batman tracks Carter down and takes down an entire group of Bane's mercenaries at the same time.

THE BURNLEY HIT AND RUN

Outside the Burnley police precinct, Batman discovers the body of S.W.A.T. team member Nate Ramo. Realizing that Ramo has been deliberately hit by a car, the Dark Knight deduces the vehicle's owner, officer John DeMarco. Ramo had evidence against DeMarco, prompting his murder. Batman soon apprehends the crooked cop.

THE COVENTRY FIRE

The Dark Knight overhears an emergency broadcast, which brings him to Coventry, to discover the remains of a fire. A body has been recovered by emergency workers, and Batman uses the victim's dental records to identify him as a small-time arms dealer named Alex Cane. Cane has been shot in the heart and has fallen on an incendiary grenade. After some shrewd deduction, Batman tracks down the killer, apprehending a martial artist named Qing Lu.

THE JEZEBEL PLAZA FALL

An account manager at the Gotham Merchants Bank named Bryan Murphy falls from a building into Jezebel Plaza. Batman discovers Murphy's briefcase in a ventilation shaft, and the fingerprints of con artist Robert Hanes. Batman tracks down Hanes and learns that he and Murphy were partners in a crime gone wrong.

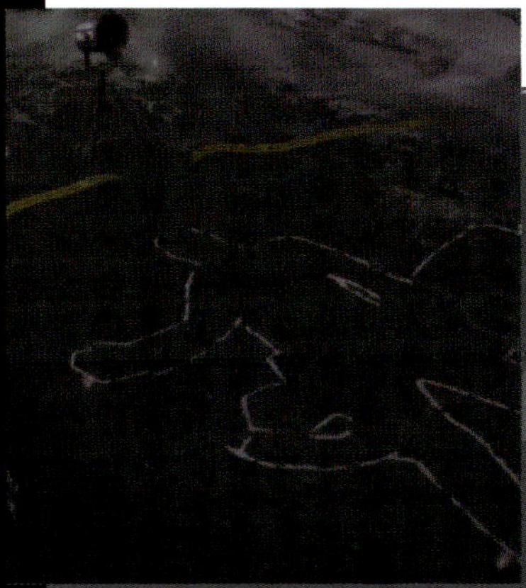

THE CRIME ALLEY SHOOTINGS

Socialites Horace Riley and Clarissa Rodriguez are gunned down in Crime Alley, where Bruce Wayne's parents were killed years earlier. Batman finds it hard not to take the killings personally. A trail of clues leads Batman to track down the gunman, a jealous fellow member of Gotham City's elite named Ian Chase.

GOTHAM CITY

ONLY GOTHAM CITY COULD SPAWN A MAN LIKE THE DARK KNIGHT. A CITY WITH MANY SECRETS AND SHADOWS, THERE IS BEAUTY IN GOTHAM CITY'S FOREBODING ARCHITECTURE AS WELL AS INNOCENTS AMONG ITS MADMEN AND CRIMINALS.

There are plenty of decent men and women living in Gotham City. However, very few of them willingly venture out at night. A place that seems to breed insanity, Gotham City has a way of producing some of the most bizarre and disturbing criminals in the world. The city has seen earthquakes and floods, and faced the near-destruction of its infrastructure and many of its towering skyscrapers, but it survives, a home to the determined, the corrupt, and the insane.

NIGHTLY COMMUTE

Batman has many methods for traversing Gotham City, giving him options when combatting criminal schemes. For fast travel, he sometimes utilizes his Batwing, which can let him off at drop points around the city. Likewise, the Batmobile can be a tremendous asset when Batman needs a high-speed way to journey through the streets. But more often than not, the Dark Knight travels via rooftop, using his cape to glide from building to building.

City of Secrets
Gotham City's rooftops hold many secrets, including trophies left by the Riddler and secret entrances to buildings.

High Life
Batman attaches his grapnel to tall buildings, propelling himself faster through the air than by gliding.

Up On the Roof
The Dark Knight often encounters criminals on rooftops; some possess deadly sniper equipment.

KNIGHT AND DAY

There is a popular theory that Gotham City began its descent into corruption the night that Thomas and Martha Wayne were gunned down in the formerly ritzy neighborhood of Park Row. That fateful night, the city lost two of its brightest stars and beacons of hope and prosperity. A criminal madness began to fester in the city. A madness that Batman has made it his duty to oppose.

BATMAN GOTHAM CITY   69

The Gargoyle That Moves
Gotham City's Gothic design creates the perfect camouflage for Batman.

Ears Like a Bat
Batman is constantly listening in to local broadcasts and police bands, trying to keep his finger firmly on Gotham City's pulse.

OLD GOTHAM
- Gotham Church
- Solomon Wayne Courthouse
- The Final Offer (ship)
- Sionis Steel Mill
- Jezebel Plaza
- Pioneer's Bridge
- The Batcave

NEW GOTHAM
- My Alibi Nightclub
- GothCorp Building and the Gotham Royal Hotel
- Lacey Towers
- Enigma's Headquarters
- Gotham City Police Department
- Blackgate Prison

MAPPING THE CITY

Gotham City is divided into two main halves, and each one is broken down into various neighborhoods. The city is constantly evolving, with buildings built on top of older structures and new neighborhoods constructed to fill the ever expanding population. Despite setbacks, such as the temporary establishment of Arkham City over the majority of Old Gotham, the city somehow continues to thrive and attract new citizens. This is the map Batman used when battling Black Mask early in his crime-fighting career.

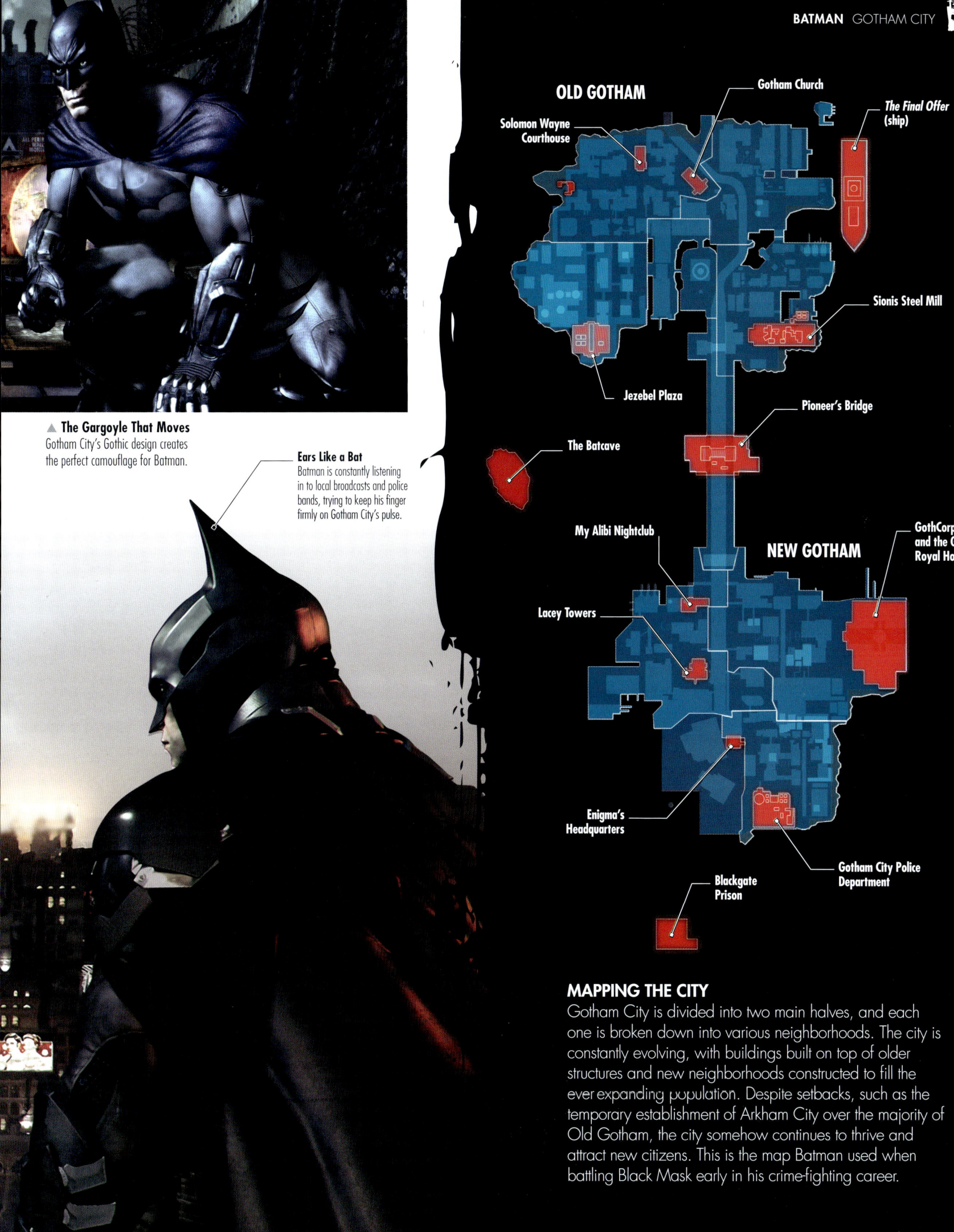

GOTHAM CITY LOCATIONS

A METROPOLIS AS INTEGRAL TO THE CREATION OF THE BATMAN AS THE MUGGER THAT TOOK THE LIVES OF BRUCE WAYNE'S PARENTS, GOTHAM CITY IS EQUAL PARTS BEAUTIFUL AND TERRIFYING.

With its mix of Gothic architecture, art deco, and glass and steel skyscrapers, Gotham City has one of the most remarkable urban landscapes in the world. Gotham City is a perfect fit for a creature of the night like Batman, from its recently modernized areas to the old, walled-off sections that comprise the massive prison of Arkham City. Bizarre gargoyles gaze down balefully on streets and alleys doused nightly with shadows dark enough to conceal the most grotesque secrets.

GOTHAM CITY POLICE DEPARTMENT

In Gotham City, the gangs come in all colors, and according to many of its citizens, blue is one of the most dangerous. When Batman first appeared, the police were just as corrupt as the criminals they brought in on a nightly basis. Luckily, thanks to the efforts of Commissioner Jim Gordon, Gotham City Police Department has cleaned up its act—a bit. Despite the improvement, occasionally there is still a need for Batman to break into a G.C.P.D. branch to deal with cops who have gone bad.

The Bat-Signal
No location in Gotham City is off-limits to the Batman, who seeks out criminals wherever the Bat-Signal shines its light.

GOTHAM ROYAL HOTEL

The Gotham Royal Hotel in the Diamond District is one of the city's grandest hotels—that is until the Joker takes it over. He transforms the building, filling it with freakish items taken from a carnival and defacing the exterior with his crazed messages. At this point, the Joker is a new threat to the Dark Knight, who is shocked by the Joker's depravity, but he soon gets used to the villain's warped antics.

PIONEERS BRIDGE

Pioneers Bridge is the main structure that connects Old Gotham with New Gotham. Batman often swings from the bridge's tall supports, and has tackled trouble on the bridge many times. The worst occasion comes early on in his career when he is forced to confront the arsonist Firefly, who succeeds in destroying a large section of the historic landmark.

BLACKGATE PRISON

Blackgate is a penitentiary located on its own island off the Gotham City mainland. It is here that Batman has his first climactic fight with the Joker. Over time, the Dark Knight deals with several breakouts from the notorious prison, which becomes familiar terrain for the Dark Knight Detective.

GOTHAM CHURCH

Located in Old Gotham's Park Row district, the church has sheltered the worst and best Gotham City has to offer. It is the scene of a confrontation between Batman and Black Mask early on in the hero's crime-fighting campaign. In the days of Arkham City, Gotham Church becomes a sanctuary, housing medical professionals and members of the press, such as Vicki Vale and Jack Ryder.

AMUSEMENT MILE

Amusement Mile was built during Gotham City's industrial boom, but the good times didn't last, and the amusement park became run-down, owing to bankruptcy and flood damage. At one point, it was enclosed inside Arkham City's walls, removing this eyesore from view. The site is often used by villains and, due to its proximity to the sea, is an ideal base for smuggling.

JEZEBEL PLAZA

This decidedly decrepit shopping area captures Gotham City's overall atmosphere. During the time of Arkham City, Jezebel Plaza becomes overrun with criminals. Located in Old Gotham's Bowery, the Plaza is an essential entranceway to the subway for Batman's various missions underground.

SIONIS STEEL MILL

In the heart of Gotham City's industrial district stands the Steel Mill. It was once owned by the Sionis family, whose heir apparent is the criminal Black Mask. During the construction of Arkham City, the Joker uses the mill as his hideout. After his death, Harley Quinn occupies the building as a twisted memorial to her "puddin'."

MONARCH THEATRE

Bruce Wayne's life would have been very different had his parents not taken him to see *Mark of Zorro* at the Monarch Theatre. After Thomas and Martha Wayne were murdered outside the movie house, the neighborhood of Park Row fell into ruin. Batman later returns to the theatre to combat the Joker in the villain's final battle.

ACE CHEMICALS

There are two Ace Chemical sites in Gotham City. One is in Park Row. The other is a manufacturing plant separated from the nearby neighborhood by a small bridge. Long connected to Batman's past as the site that saw the creation of the Joker—when, as the Red Hood, he fell into a vat of chemicals—the plant is also the scene of some of Batman's battles with the Arkham Knight.

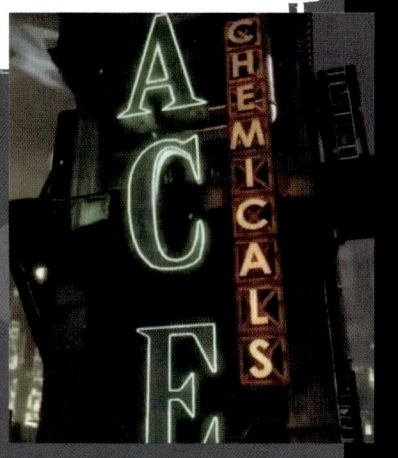

MY ALIBI NIGHTCLUB

A popular dance club located in the Coventry neighborhood of New Gotham, My Alibi is known to be the haunt of various criminal cartels. It is in this shady establishment that the Dark Knight must face Bane's right-hand man, Bird. It is also where Batman goes in search of the components of a cryodrill that he needs to stop Mr. Freeze.

BAUDELAIRE

When Poison Ivy chooses a hideout, she does so with flair. Her flower shop lair is named after Charles Baudelaire, the famous poet who wrote the poem, *Les Fleurs du Mal*, which translates as "Flowers of Evil." Poison Ivy customizes the Park Row shop to her liking and has mind-controlled guards to keep intruders at bay.

LACEY TOWERS

The criminal Black Mask is known as a high roller in Gotham City before the Joker makes his grand entrance onto the criminal scene. Black Mask then takes up residence in the Coventry neighborhood's posh Lacey Towers, until his girlfriend is murdered by the Joker during his successful takeover of Black Mask's entire illegal operation.

THE JOKER'S FUNHOUSE

The Joker earned his nickname as the Clown Prince of Crime in part due to his over-the-top sense of style. In fact, the villain has been known to convert eccentric hideouts in his own image in as little as a handful of days. He converts a funfair into the perfect location to brew his deadly toxin, attracting the criminal Bane in the process. It is up to the combined efforts of both Batman and Robin to shut down the rival gang leaders' operations.

GOTHCORP. BUILDING

Batman always believed that Ferris Boyle was one of the few members of Gotham City's high society that he could respect. However, when investigating the origins of Mr. Freeze in Boyle's GothCorp Building in the Diamond District, Batman discovers Boyle is as corrupt as the monstrous villain he helped create.

SOLOMON WAYNE COURTHOUSE

Named after one of Bruce Wayne's ancestors and located in Park Row, the Solomon Wayne Courthouse has housed many faces from Batman's Rogues Gallery. The courthouse has also been the site of many epic battles; Batman confronts the villain Anarky there during his early years wearing the cape and cowl, and fights Two-Face at the courthouse during the days of Arkham City. The Dark Knight even encounters the jailed Calendar Man in the building's lower level.

ICEBERG LOUNGE

Accessible through the Museum, the Iceberg Lounge is Penguin's home away from prison. Complete with a giant iceberg, this den of iniquity is the perfect hangout for Gotham City's underworld and is a highly lucrative asset to the Penguin's already impressive bankroll. In order for Batman to reach the Lounge, he has to traverse an icy indoor pool housing a very hungry orca whale.

INSTITUTE FOR NATURAL HISTORY

The Institute for Natural History was designed to be a cultural hub for denizens of Gotham City with a thirst for knowledge and discovery but when Arkham City is built, the Park Row museum is taken over by the Penguin who transforms it into an elaborate hideout, connected to his Iceberg Lounge. The museum's displays are turned into macabre trophy cases containing the villain's victims—including deceased members of rival gangs.

WONDER TOWER

Wonder Tower is an impressive edifice located above the underground metropolis of Wonder City, near the center of Old Gotham. It is the launching point for Hugo Strange and Rā's al Ghūl's crazed plot to destroy Gotham City, and is the place where not just Strange, but also the "immortal" Rā's al Ghūl, finally meet their deaths.

WONDER CITY

Hidden away below the streets of Old Gotham is Wonder City, an abandoned attempt at creating a future metropolis utopia. Housing a Lazarus Pit at its core, Wonder City now stands as a buried failure, with lifeless sentinel robots littering its halls. This fantastic underground world is the perfect hideout for Rā's al Ghūl during the time of Arkham City.

ORACLE'S CLOCK TOWER

Situated in the Cauldron district of Bleake Island, the Clock Tower is an impressive building. It appears to be an ordinary apartment complex but few know the secrets it contains. On the other side of the large clock face is the home base of Oracle, Batman's go-to source for information regarding the criminal fraternity of Gotham City, as well as anything else that is going on in the city that only an information guru can dig up.

WAYNE ENTERPRISES

Wayne Tower is the skyscraper headquarters of Wayne Enterprises and proudly boasts the logo of Gotham City's favorite son. Overseen by Bruce Wayne and his loyal employee Lucius Fox, Wayne Enterprises is responsible for many charity programs and has an impressive research facility that (mostly unknowingly) has contributed to Batman's arsenal over the years.

WAYNE MANOR

Despite his love for Gotham City, Bruce Wayne didn't actually grow up inside the city limits. His home, Wayne Manor, is located north of Old Gotham, connected via a bridge. However, since the manor houses the Batcave, Batman has easy access to the city, via the incredibly speedy Batwing and Batmobile.

PINKNEY ORPHANAGE

Bruce Wayne naturally feels sympathetic to orphans, having lost his parents to a senseless act of violence at a young age. That makes his time at the Pinkney Orphanage all the more disturbing, when he is forced to save Catwoman from the Riddler's latest scheme and the villain's technologically advanced robot suit.

FALCONE SHIPPING YARD

An elusive crime family that has been around since the beginning of Batman's career, the Falcones are feared throughout Gotham City. The Falcone family conduct their "business affairs" in the relative security of their own shipping yard. However, Batman certainly doesn't respect this mob family's "turf."

LADY OF GOTHAM STATUE

The Gotham City skyline boasts an impressive array of giant skyscrapers and iconic landmarks. One of these landmarks is the famous Statue of Justice, also known as the "Lady of Gotham" by the city's residents. The statue becomes the location of a criminal campaign led by the villain Deacon Blackfire.

BATMAN GOTHAM CITY LOCATIONS 75

STAGG INDUSTRIES

Not all of Gotham City's many monsters operate in the shadows or are regular inmates of Arkham Asylum or Blackgate Prison. Some criminals function openly in broad daylight, posing as legitimate businessmen. One such is Simon Stagg, whose corrupt company is named Stagg Industries. Stagg is secretly in cahoots with Scarecrow.

PANESSA STUDIOS

The elaborate movie studios known as the Panessa Studios, contain many old props and sets. At the studios, the Dark Knight is forced to confront several people who have been infected with the Joker's toxic blood, and are slowly adopting the Clown Prince of Crime's infectious personality.

PRETTY DOLLS PARLOR

At the Pretty Dolls Parlor, Batman encounters the twisted scientist Professor Pyg. While the villain himself doesn't represent the most dangerous physical threat to the Dark Knight Detective, Professor Pyg's army of Dollotrons certainly helps to tip the scale in his favor.

THE HIDEOUT

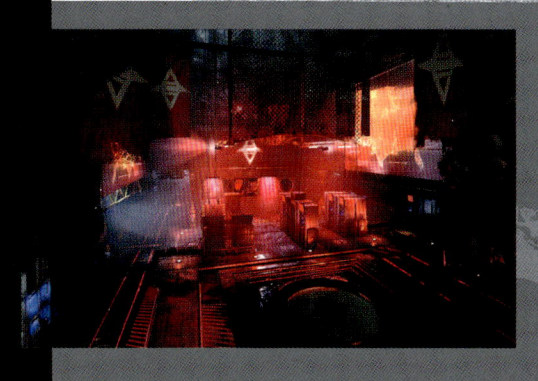

Stockpiled with weapons and decorated with flags bearing his logo, the Arkham Knight's bunker is the perfect location for the vigilante to restock his arsenal or merely collect his rather conflicted thoughts.

MIAGANI BOTANICAL GARDENS

The Miagani Botanical Gardens is in the Bristol district of Miagani Island. Designed so that citizens can enjoy the beauty of nature, the gardens cover several acres, with statues, greenhouses, and conservatories containing rare plants. The gardens are targeted by Gotham City's plant-loving villain Poison Ivy but, surprisingly, when Batman meets Poison Ivy there they are not enemies. Instead, they are uneasy allies, worried about Gotham City—and its plant life.

PAULI'S DINER

Pauli's Diner started off as an ordinary diner and favorite eatery of Gotham City locals, but the doomed restaurant becomes a home to horrors and atrocities that shock the entire city. Used as a testing site for Scarecrow's latest fear toxin, the diner erupts into chaos, and the city soon follows suit when Scarecrow threatens to release his gas throughout Gotham City.

City of Secrets
Gotham City boasts many impressive views, even if a closer look reveals the corruption and chaos hiding in the shadows.

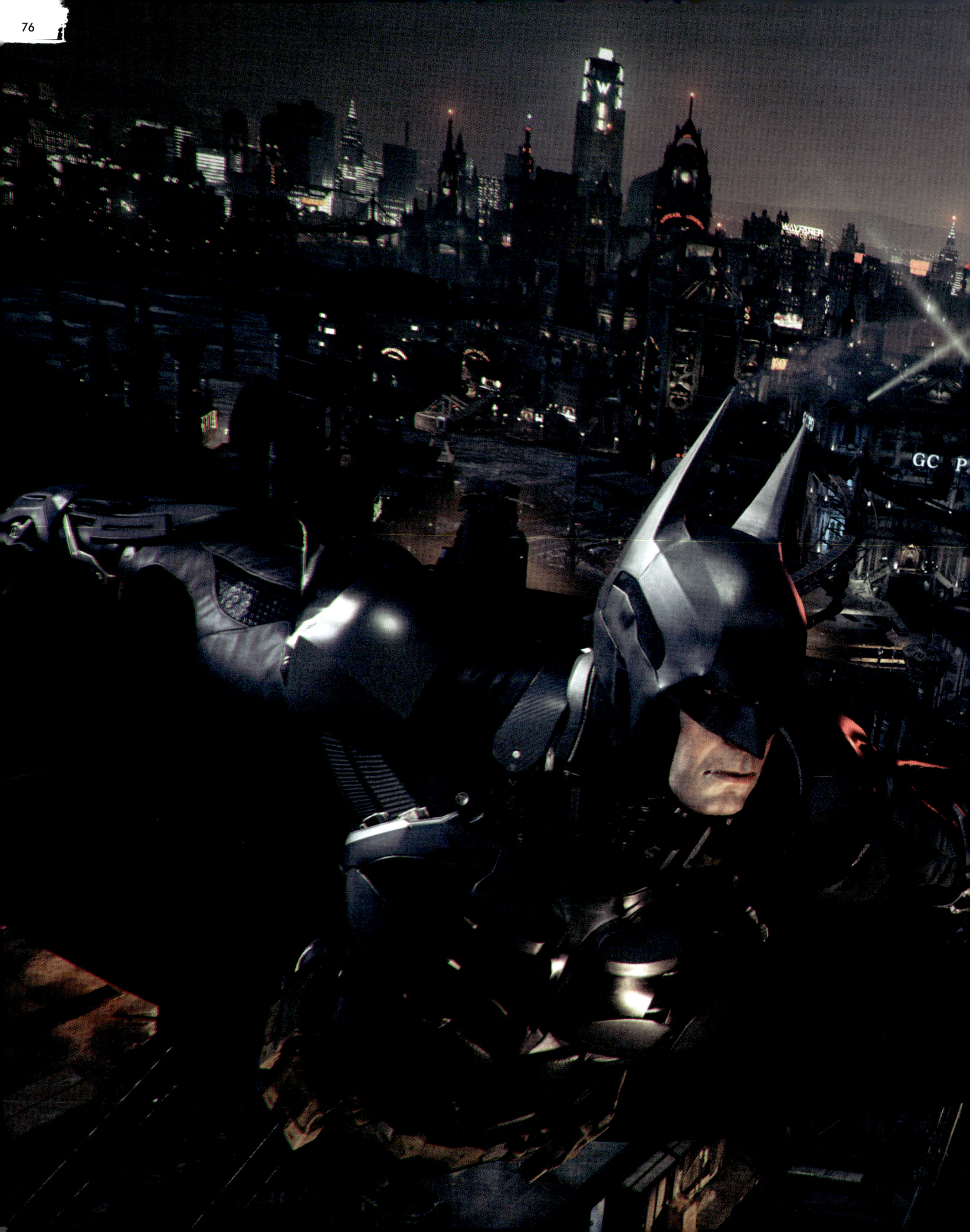
GC P

The Heart of the City
Bruce Wayne's family has invested in the well-being of Gotham City for generations. Solomon Wayne, Bruce's ancestor, was a very influential figure. He helped the architect Cyrus Pinkney use the city as a canvas for his dark imagination. By the time Bruce was born, the Waynes had become synonymous with Gotham City. As the last of the Wayne line, Bruce feels a deep need to help Gotham City in any way he can, both as a billionaire citizen, and as Batman.

CITY SOCIETY

THE SEETHING METROPOLIS OF GOTHAM CITY IS HOME TO ALL WALKS OF LIFE, FROM THE NOBLE AND RESOURCEFUL TO THE DEVIOUS AND CORRUPT.

As both Bruce Wayne and Batman, the Dark Knight has a unique insight into the movers and shakers of Gotham City society. Bruce spends his days rubbing shoulders with the rich and famous, observing how his "peers" present themselves to the public, and how they behave behind closed doors in the company of their friends. Bruce then spends his nights throwing punches at the criminals of Gotham City as Batman, discovering along the way that many of his well-to-do associates in the business world have close ties to the not-so-well-to-do in the underworld.

VICKI VALE

OCCUPATION Investigative journalist
HEIGHT 5 ft. 7 in. · **WEIGHT** 121 lbs.
EYES Blue · **HAIR** Blonde

Fascinated by Batman and his heroic actions, Vicki Vale captures the first images of the Dark Knight on film and manages to record his historic first fight with the villain Bane. Brave, resourceful, and often in the most dangerous places, Vicki later files reports from inside the walls of Arkham City itself. Undeterred by her experiences in Arkham City, Vicki continues to report some of the most groundbreaking news in Gotham City.

JACK RYDER

OCCUPATION Investigative reporter
HEIGHT 6 ft. · **WEIGHT** 194 lbs.
EYES Blue · **HAIR** Black

A reporter known for hiding in the shadows until he nabs his exposé, Jack Ryder also hosts a controversial TV talk show in which he attempts to get at the truth in typically aggressive style. Imprisoned in Arkham City for saying the wrong things to the wrong people, Ryder sets up camp at Gotham Church with other members of the media, including reporter Vicki Vale. He is later captured by Deacon Blackfire, forcing Batman to come to his rescue.

MAYOR QUINCY SHARP

OCCUPATION Mayor
HEIGHT 5 ft. 8 in. · **WEIGHT** 190 lbs.
EYES Blue · **HAIR** Gray

The former Warden of Arkham Asylum, Quincy Sharp makes the move into politics with the help of Hugo Strange. However, unknown to even Sharp himself, he is Strange's puppet, controlled through hypnosis and the power of suggestion by the mastermind into erecting and ruling over the massive Arkham City prison.

LUCIUS FOX

OCCUPATION Wayne Enterprises employee
HEIGHT 5 ft. 10 in. • **WEIGHT** 170 lbs
EYES Brown • **HAIR** Black (white temples)

Bruce Wayne's confidant and business associate, Fox knows Wayne's double identity. Fox supplies Batman with gear and information to aid his crime crusade. When Hush kidnaps Fox, Batman repays his loyalty by rescuing him.

City of Contradictions
Gotham City attracts all types of people, from the philanthropic to the apathetic, from the sympathetic to the psychopathic.

SIMON STAGG

OCCUPATION C.E.O. of Stagg Industries
HEIGHT Unknown • **WEIGHT** Unknown
EYES Blue • **HAIR** White

The unscrupulous head of Stagg Industries, Simon Stagg becomes a criminal threat in league with Scarecrow. Stagg's greed causes him to develop the Cloudburst weapon for the villain, the perfect method for dispersing fear gas.

WARDEN JOSEPH

OCCUPATION Blackgate Prison Warden
HEIGHT 5 ft. 11 in. • **WEIGHT** 195 lbs.
EYES Dark brown • **HAIR** Black

An expert administrator, Warden Joseph first meets Batman when the Dark Knight saves his life during a prison riot. Despite being surrounded by corruption, Joseph manages to keep himself and his record clean.

CYRUS PINKNEY

OCCUPATION Architect
HEIGHT 5 ft. 10 in. • **WEIGHT** 165 lbs.
EYES Brown • **HAIR** Brown

Gotham City owes its uniquely dark and grotesque visual style to architect Cyrus Pinkney, who worked closely with Bruce Wayne's ancestor Judge Solomon Wayne. Pinkney died on the eve of his 40th birthday, back in the mid-1800s.

THOMAS AND MARTHA WAYNE

OCCUPATION Surgeon/Philanthropist •
HEIGHT 6 ft. 1 in./5 ft. 8 in. • **WEIGHT** 180 lbs./135 lbs. • **EYES** Blue/Brown
HAIR Black/Brown

Born into wealth, Thomas Wayne and Martha Wayne tried to help the citizens of Gotham City and did a great deal for charity. When they are gunned down on Park Row by a mugger, Gotham City becomes a much darker place.

FERRIS BOYLE

OCCUPATION C.E.O. of GothCorp
HEIGHT 6 ft. 4 in. • **WEIGHT** 220 lbs
EYES Blue • **HAIR** Black (gray temples)

Ferris Boyle is viewed as a humanitarian by most people, and Bruce Wayne even considers him a like-minded soul in his quest to help Gotham City. However, it later transpires that Boyle is a weapons manufacturer and willing to do whatever it takes to make a profit.

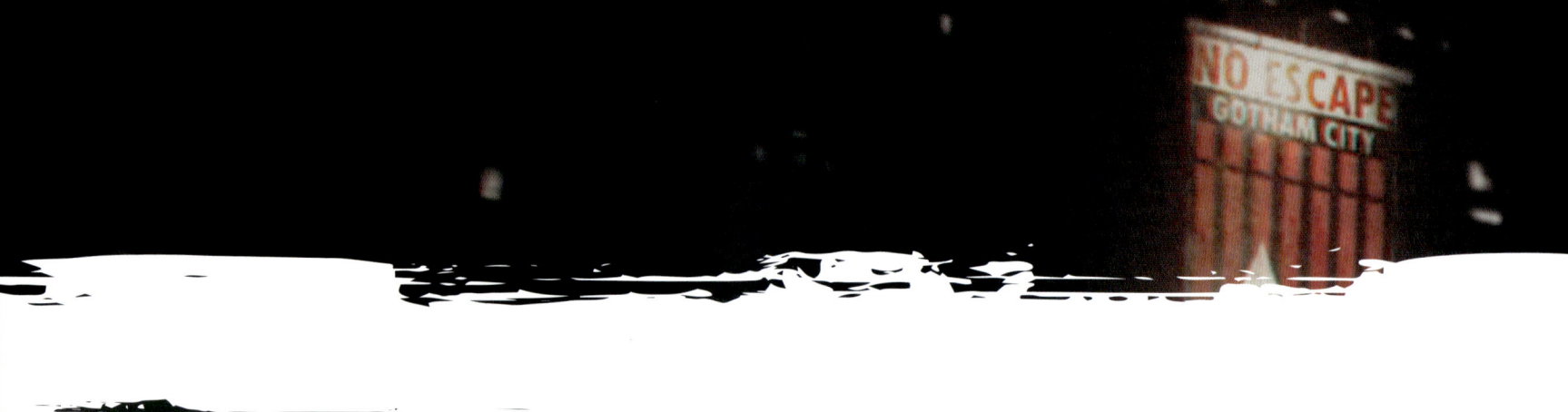

ALLIES

NEARLY EVERYONE IN GOTHAM CITY HAS A SAD STORY TO TELL. FOR MOST, THE CITY BREAKS THEM AND BRINGS THEM DOWN TO ITS SORRY LEVEL. BUT THERE ARE A RARE FEW WHO DRAW STRENGTH FROM THEIR WOUNDS AND, ALONGSIDE BATMAN, BECOME SOMETHING BETTER.

One of Batman's allies watched his parents fall to their deaths during a trapeze act. Another watched her father constantly struggle against a disturbingly corrupt police force. Another found heroes when he had nothing else to keep him going, and one realized that the law he'd spent his entire life trying to uphold just wasn't enough to make a real difference. They are the men and women who have refused to let Batman take on Gotham City's monsters all by himself. They are his allies, and in the Dark Knight's quiet, reflective moments, the people he considers friends.

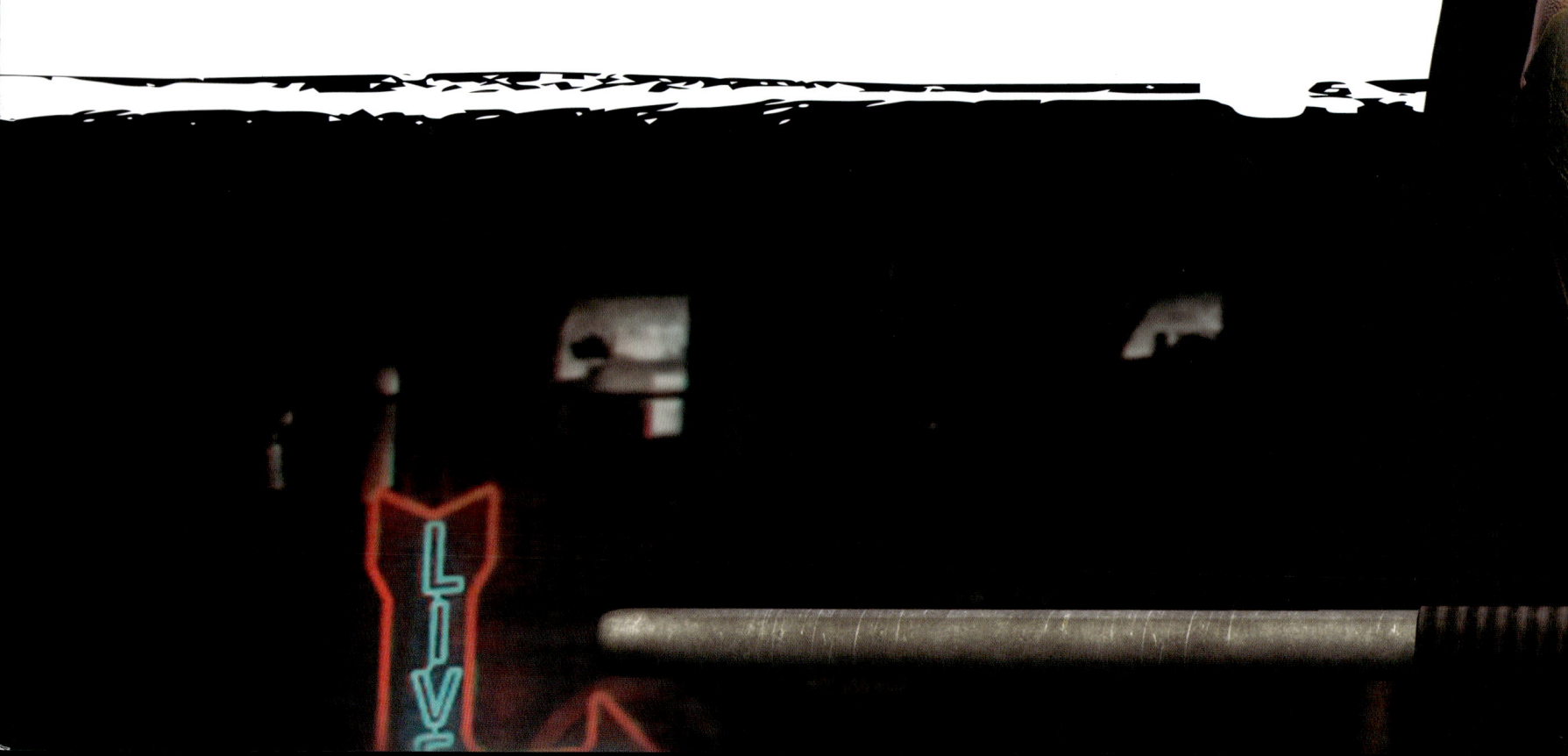

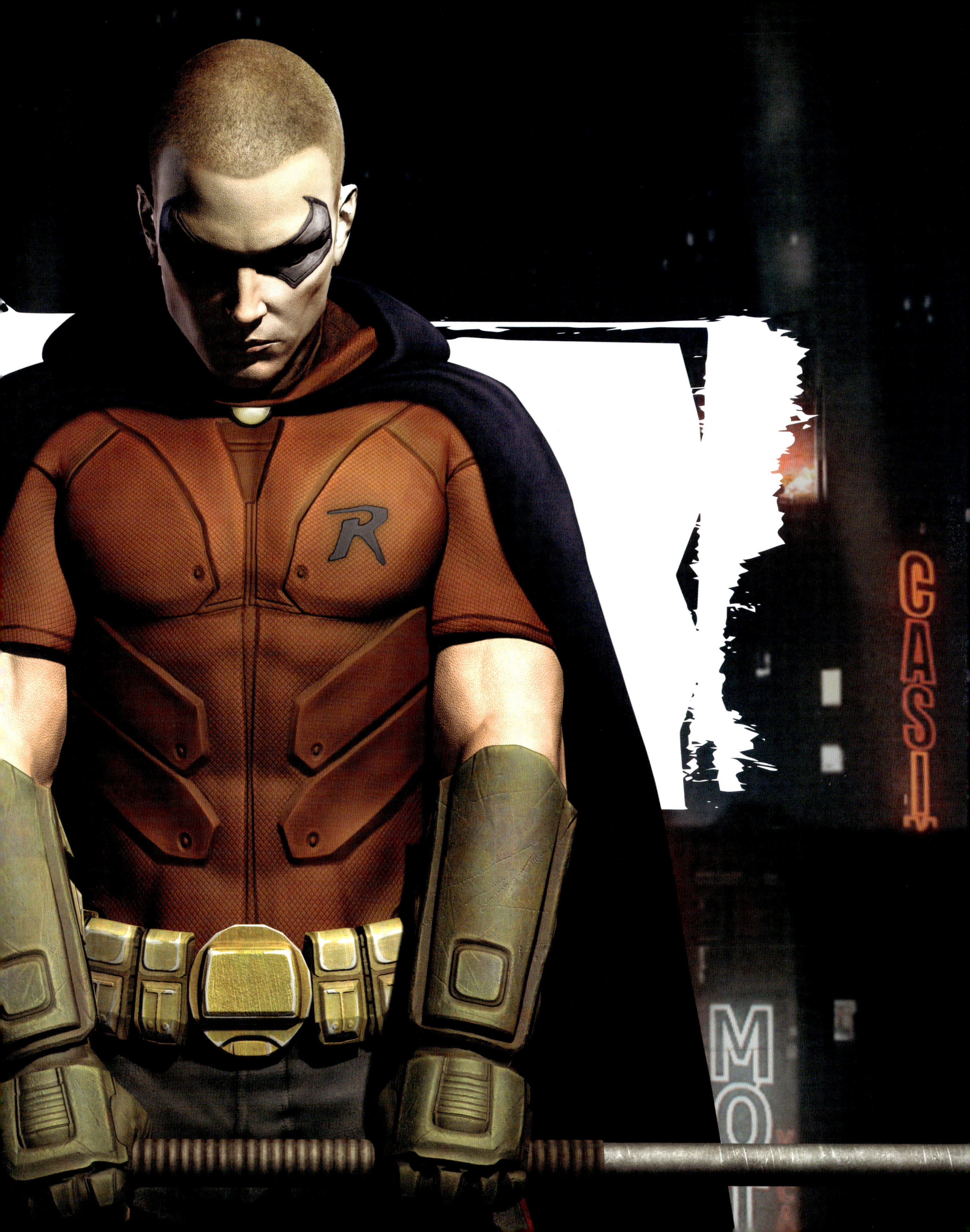
CASI
MO

ROBIN

HE'S BEEN CALLED A SIDEKICK AND THE BOY WONDER, BUT DESPITE THESE LOWLY LABELS, ROBIN IS TRULY A FORCE TO BE RECKONED WITH. A TRAINED MARTIAL ARTIST AND AN EXCELLENT DETECTIVE, ROBIN IS NEARLY AS ADEPT AS BATMAN AT FIGHTING CRIME.

Tim Drake is not the first hero to assume the mantle of Robin. Two others came before him: Dick Grayson, the hero now known as Nightwing, and Jason Todd, who later adopted the name and guise of the vigilante called the Red Hood. However, Tim is loyal to the Dark Knight to a fault, and has even married one of Batman's closest allies, Barbara Gordon, the heroine known as Oracle.

A PARTICULAR SET OF SKILLS
Robin's abilities complement the Dark Knight's. As Robin, he moves a bit quicker on his feet than his mentor, and prefers a different set of weapons. During the time of Arkham City, he relies heavily on shurikens rather than batarangs, and even uses shurikens of the remote control variety. Robin also employs a bullet shield and snap flash grenades in battle.

JOKING AROUND
The relationship between the various Robins and the Joker is a long and storied one. While Dick Grayson faces the Clown Prince of Crime a time or two when Batman first starts his career, Jason Todd is later captured and tortured by the Joker—a life-changing and traumatic event.

▲ **The Original**
Dick Grayson's Robin costume is quite different from Tim Drake's. Like Batman's suit at the time, Grayson's Robin costume is segmented and bulkier.

"IF YOU NEED ME, YOU KNOW WHERE I AM."
—Robin

LONE KNIGHT
When the Arkham Knight rears his head in Gotham City and Scarecrow threatens the metropolis with his fear gas, Robin attempts to help Batman on his mission. Worried about his partner's welfare, Robin realizes that the Dark Knight has the Joker's poison still running through his veins. Robin does his very best to help, suggesting Batman take a break from fighting crime, but Batman prefers to face the dangers head on.

◄ **Voice of Reason**
When Batman is obviously a danger, thanks to the Joker's machinations, Robin attempts to save him from himself.

ALLIES ROBIN 83

DATA FILE

- **REAL NAME** Tim Drake
- **OCCUPATION** Crime-fighter
- **HEIGHT** 5 ft. 10in.
- **WEIGHT** 170 lbs.
- **HAIR** Black
- **EYES** Blue

Detective Mode
Like Batman's, Robin's mask can switch to Detective Vision.

R Symbol
When Drake took over as Robin, he updated Grayson's R symbol.

Gauntlets
Robin wears protective gauntlets, similar to those worn by his mentor.

The Cape
Robin can use his cape to stun opponents.

Bo Staff
Robin's weapon of choice can retract when necessary.

Robin Beyond
Much more in touch with his human side, Robin seems destined for a happier future than the Dark Knight.

NIGHTWING

THE ORIGINAL BOY WONDER AND BATMAN'S FIRST PARTNER IN HIS WAR ON CRIME, DICK GRAYSON HAS GROWN UP AND TAKEN FLIGHT AS A HERO IN HIS OWN RIGHT KNOWN AS NIGHTWING.

As one of the few living people on the planet who can boast that they have been trained by Batman, Nightwing is an expert martial artist and hand-to-hand combatant. Nearly rivaling his mentor when it comes to fighting techniques, Nightwing excels in areas that require acrobatic skills and agility. This has led him to develop his own arsenal, including escrima sticks that carry an electric current and wrist darts.

LIGHT KNIGHT

Part of a famous circus act named the Flying Graysons, young Dick witnessed the death of his mother and father when a local mob boss had them killed in order to extort money from the circus. He was raised by the sympathetic Bruce Wayne and his butler Alfred Pennyworth, so Dick didn't have the same lonely upbringing as Batman, giving him a brighter outlook on life. Dick originally partners Batman as Robin, but they begin to differ in their ideas on how to combat criminals, so Dick assumes the new identity of Nightwing and decides to work alone.

Evening Up the Odds
Nightwing's athleticism and martial arts skills mean that he can take on more than one opponent and win with ease.

TRAIL OF BLÜD

Nightwing battles Black Mask during the time of Arkham City and brings the crime boss to justice after a vicious fight in a subway. However his prime concern is his adopted hometown of Blüdhaven, a shipping town not far from Gotham City. When the Penguin's arms deals begin to affect Blüdhaven, Nightwing heads to Gotham City to partner Batman once again.

MEETING OF MINDS

Although out to prove he's his own man, Nightwing is not too proud to go to Batman for help. During the time of the Arkham Knight, Nightwing shares intel with his mentor about the Penguin's arms deals. The crime boss is smuggling weapons out of Blüdhaven using North Refrigeration trucks. Nightwing gives Batman a Disruptor to help the crime-fighter take down the Penguin's operation.

◀ **Night and Knight**
Nightwing's arrival in Gotham City coincides with the emergence of the mysterious criminal called the Arkham Knight.

ALLIES NIGHTWING   85

DATA FILE

- **REAL NAME** Richard "Dick" Grayson
- **OCCUPATION** Crime-Fighter
- **HEIGHT** 6 ft.
- **WEIGHT** 175 lbs.
- **EYES** Blue
- **HAIR** Black

Night Vision
The lenses in Nightwing's mask allow him to access Detective Mode.

The Suit
Nightwing's blue symbol is the only splash of color on his otherwise black suit.

Winging It
Around the time Jason Todd becomes the second Robin, Dick branches off on his own and assumes the identity of Nightwing.

Escrima Stick
Nightwing can throw his escrima stick with great accuracy over long distances.

Armor
Nightwing's suit is made of a lightweight, yet sturdy armor.

ALFRED

THE SUBSTITUTE FATHER FIGURE IN BRUCE WAYNE'S LIFE, LOYAL BUTLER ALFRED PENNYWORTH NOT ONLY KNOWS ABOUT BRUCE'S DOUBLE LIFE, HE ALSO SERVES AS HIS RIGHT-HAND MAN IN THE BATCAVE.

When a young Bruce Wayne saw his parents gunned down before his eyes in a dark Gotham City alley, the task of caring for the devastated boy fell on the shoulders of the family butler, Alfred Pennyworth. When Wayne returned from intensive training abroad to begin his campaign as the Dark Knight, Alfred began to assist his employer, continuing to take care of him as best he could.

LOYAL TO A FAULT
Alfred is constantly working for Batman from behind the scenes. He orchestrates weapons drops via the Batwing to give the Dark Knight a tactical edge during his crime-fighting missions, and is constantly working on the Batcomputer to supply Batman with additional information and tips to help defeat whatever foe Batman is up against. While he'd rather see his employer give up his vigilante lifestyle for a corporate office, Alfred tries to keep "Master Bruce" alive any way that he can.

History Repeating?
Batman can't stand the thought of losing another father, and experiences a flashback to the death of his parents as he is saving Alfred.

JACK OF ALL TRADES
Alfred has a military background and has also worked in the theater. He has been able to pass on these diverse but extremely useful skill sets to Batman. In addition, his battlefield medical experience has saved Batman's life a time or two. But when Alfred is gravely injured following an unexpected attack on the Batcave by the criminal known as Bane, it is Batman who has to save Alfred's life, fighting despair and heartache to do so.

> "IT'S HIGH TIME YOU REALIZE THAT YOU ARE A MAN NOT AN ISLAND."
> — Alfred

Learning Curve
It took some time before Alfred realized how effective Bruce Wayne was in his war on crime, despite helping him every step of the way.

THE ORIGINAL ALLY
When Batman begins taking his crusade against crime seriously, Alfred has his doubts. While the Dark Knight fails to see his own weaknesses, Alfred can see that Batman is still Bruce Wayne—a human being with faults who is not invincible or infallible. Alfred expresses his concern several times, but it takes his near death to convince Batman to accept his loyal butler's help in his mission against Gotham City's underworld.

ALLIES ALFRED 87

Telltale sign
Alfred's hair has gone from black to gray, perhaps in part due to raising the challenging Bruce Wayne.

DATA FILE

- **REAL NAME** Alfred Pennyworth
- **OCCUPATION** Butler
- **HEIGHT** 6 ft.
- **WEIGHT** 160 lbs.
- **HAIR** Gray (formerly Black)
- **EYES** Blue

Here to Help
When the Arkham Knight attacks Gotham City, Alfred helps Batman combat this new threat. The butler obtains information on the Knight's drones, telling Batman that they are driverless and thus remote-controlled.

Suited and Booted
Alfred is always immpeccably dressed in a suit and bow tie — whatever the occasion.

Helping Hand
When Batman seems to be in an impossible situation during a mission, Alfred often has sage advice or a solution up his sleeve.

Like Father…
As the former butler to Bruce's parents, Thomas and Martha Wayne, Alfred is fully aware of the stubborn streak that runs in the Waynes' bloodline.

JAMES GORDON

FORMING A FRIENDSHIP ON THE FIELD OF BATTLE, COMMISSIONER GORDON HAS GONE FROM BATMAN'S UNEASY ALLY TO ONE OF THE FEW PEOPLE THAT THE DARK KNIGHT CALLS A FRIEND.

While it took some convincing from Alfred Pennyworth, Batman realized that he needed an ally inside Gotham City's police force. Many officers of the G.C.P.D. were known to be corrupt and on the payroll of various criminals, but Captain Jim Gordon was as full of integrity as he was true grit, and he soon became an essential helpmate in Batman's nightly war on crime.

PROVING HIS WORTH

Jim Gordon meets Batman when the Dark Knight is starting his crime-fighting career. Although sharing Batman's outlook, Gordon is hesitant to trust the man in the Batsuit, just as Batman is wary of trusting a cop in the overwhelmingly corrupt G.C.P.D. But when Batman stops Firefly's reign of terror on Pioneer Bridge, Captain Gordon finally sees Batman for what he is—a true hero who cares more for Gotham City's well-being than for his own. Later, after Gordon helps Batman end a riot in Blackgate Prison, the highly respected police captain ends up in the media spotlight. It is only a matter of time before he rises through the ranks and is promoted to Commissioner of Police, making him an even more useful ally to the Dark Knight.

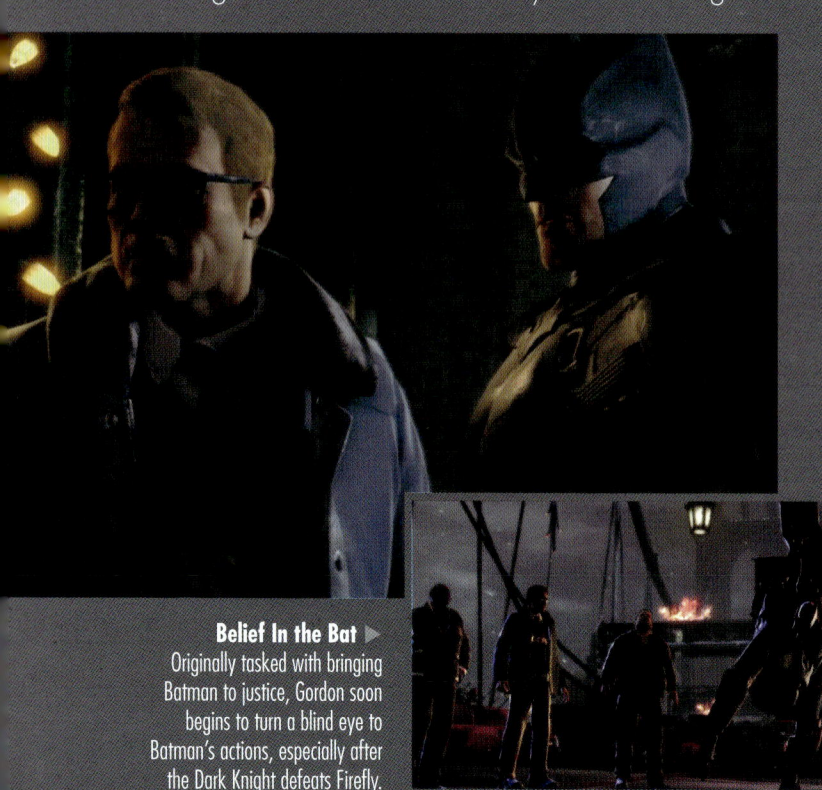

GET GORDON

Commissioner Gordon becomes an unwilling hostage when the Joker takes over Arkham Asylum. With the entire island under the Joker's control, Gordon is caught unaware when Officer Frank Boles turns out to be on the Clown Prince of Crime's payroll and attacks the Commissioner. Luckily, Batman is able to locate Gordon and rescue him after tracking Gordon's tobacco brand of choice, Wild Country.

▲ **Pranking the Police**
When the Joker is delivered to Arkham Asylum, it is just business as usual for Gordon. But then the madman escapes.

"YEAH, IT'S BEEN A HELLUVA NIGHT."
Commissioner Gordon

FRIEND OR FOE?

By the time the Arkham Knight emerges in Gotham City, Batman and Commissioner Gordon have become close allies, with Gordon prepared do almost anything to help the Dark Knight. However, through manipulation and fear, Scarecrow manages to drive a rift between the two old friends. Gordon's daughter, Barbara, becomes involved in the situation, changing the way that the Commissioner views the clandestine activities of his longtime crime-fighting partner.

Belief In the Bat ▶
Originally tasked with bringing Batman to justice, Gordon soon begins to turn a blind eye to Batman's actions, especially after the Dark Knight defeats Firefly.

A Rainy Day
Their long battle against Gotham City's criminal underbelly has taken its toll on both Gordon and Batman.

ALLIES JAMES GORDON

Ace Detective
Gordon is a skilled detective, making him respect Batman's abilities all the more.

Room to Work
As Gotham City's Police Commissioner, Gordon can ensure that the police force allows Batman to act in his city without interruption.

DATA FILE

- **REAL NAME** James W. Gordon
- **OCCUPATION** Police Commissioner
- **HEIGHT** 6 ft.
- **WEIGHT** 180 lbs.
- **EYES** Blue
- **HAIR** White (formerly Brown)

Badge of Honor
Gordon has worked his way up the G.C.P.D.'s ranks, and may have even loftier ambitions.

Good Cop
Gordon is proud of his job, despite the fact that he's often surrounded by corrupt officers.

GOTHAM CITY P.D.

ONCE THE MOST CORRUPT POLICE DEPARTMENT IN THE NATION, THE G.C.P.D. HAS WEEDED OUT THE CRIMINALS IN ITS RANKS IN RECENT YEARS, BUT MANY OFFICERS STILL OPPOSE BATMAN.

When Batman first starts out, there are only a few members of the police willing to take a stand against corruption, while the majority of the force forgets the "protect and serve" part of the job. The G.C.P.D. improves a great deal when Commissioner Gordon takes control of the department, although some corrupt members remain. As an unlicensed vigilante, Batman often finds himself at odds with the police. So much so that he is forced to break into police headquarters on occasion.

LIEUTENANT BRANDEN

REAL NAME Howard Branden ▪ **OCCUPATION** G.C.P.D. S.W.A.T. Lieutenant ▪ **HEIGHT** 6 ft. 3 in. **WEIGHT** 230 lbs. ▪ **EYES** Blue ▪ **HAIR** Brown

Branden is one of the dirtiest cops ever to taint the ranks of the Gotham City Police Department. He works directly with the equally corrupt Commissioner Loeb when Batman first begins to appear in Gotham City. On the take of nearly every criminal syndicate, Branden often uses fear and intimidation to extort money to supplement his already undeserved income.

ALLIES GOTHAM CITY P.D. 91

COMMISSIONER LOEB

REAL NAME Gillian B. Loeb
OCCUPATION Commissioner of Police
HEIGHT 5 ft. 7 in. ▪ **WEIGHT** 210 lbs.
EYES Brown ▪ **HAIR** Gray

When Batman first begins his crime-fighting career, the G.C.P.D. is run by Gillian Loeb, the polar opposite in moral character of his later replacement, James Gordon. Loeb uses his authority to become the equivalent of a gang leader—only the members of his gang are paid in tax dollars and wear police badges. Because of his willingness to work with various mob gangs, Loeb actually manages to achieve peace between Gotham City's criminal families.

DETECTIVE BULLOCK

REAL NAME Harvey Bullock
OCCUPATION Police Detective ▪ **HEIGHT** 6 ft. 1 in.
WEIGHT 295 lbs. ▪ **EYES** Brown ▪ **HAIR** Brown

Harvey Bullock isn't one of the first police officers to jump on the Batman bandwagon. In fact, he is pretty dubious about Batman from the start. Formerly corrupt, Bullock sees a hero in James Gordon and becomes fiercely loyal to him. With that loyalty, Bullock soon begins to see how useful the Dark Knight is in cleaning up Gotham City, and over the years he becomes a reluctant ally of the hero.

Friendly Fire?
The Gotham City Police Department has been both friend and foe to the Dark Knight. During his first few years, Batman constantly has to deal with corrupt or obstructive officers. Under Commissioner Gordon, however, the G.C.P.D. is much more supportive of Batman's mission.

ORACLE

BARBARA GORDON IS NOT ONLY COMMISSIONER GORDON'S DAUGHTER, SHE'S ALSO ORACLE—THE COMPUTER EXPERT WHO HAS SUPPLIED BATMAN WITH INVALUABLE INFORMATION OVER THE YEARS.

Barbara Gordon is a Batman fan from the first. While her father doubts that a masked vigilante armed with high-tech gadgets can have noble intentions and the city's wellbeing at heart, Barbara, while just a teenager, immediately seems to recognize the good within the Dark Knight, helping him with information. She later becomes his trusted ally and a hero in her own right as Batgirl. After being shot by the Joker and confined to a wheelchair, Barbara graduates to the role of Oracle, computer hacker extraordinaire.

HERO WORSHIP

Batman first encounters the young Barbara Gordon when he breaks into police headquarters to gain access to the National Criminal Database. Instead of being scared by the Dark Knight's intimidating presence, Barbara immediately begins to help the vigilante. Batman seems to be a hero of hers, and she covers for him when the police barge in by insisting that Batman has never been there.

▲ **Plundering the Penguin**
Barbara Gordon supplies Batman with the locations of six missing weapons caches that have been stolen by the Penguin.

CRIME-BUSTING TEAM-UP
After assisting Batman at police headquarters, Barbara Gordon soon makes contact with the Dark Knight again to ask him a favor. Evidence crates containing dangerous weapons have been stolen from the police precinct, and Barbara doesn't want them to fall into the wrong hands. With Barbara's assistance, Batman locates the weapons and deactivates them with his Disruptor. This is just the start of Barbara's highly successful partnership with the Dark Knight.

Clock Tower HQ
Surrounded by high-tech equipment, Oracle operates out of the famous Gotham City Clock Tower.

ASKING THE ORACLE
By the time the Joker takes over Arkham Island, Barbara has long since assumed the role of internet information broker Oracle. Keeping her identity secret from the public, Oracle's double life as the now wheelchair-bound Barbara Gordon is only known by Batman, Robin, and a select few. An expert computer hacker and a legend on the internet, Oracle is able to supply Batman with information others would be unable to obtain, helping the Dark Knight on innumerable occasions.

> "JUST WHEN YOU THINK IT CAN'T GET ANY WORSE..."
> *Oracle*

ALLIES ORACLE

DATA FILE

- **REAL NAME** Barbara Gordon
- **OCCUPATION** Information Broker
- **HEIGHT** 5 ft. 11 in.
- **WEIGHT** 126 lbs.
- **EYES** Blue
- **HAIR** Red

Calm Under Pressure
A brilliant tactician, Oracle is able to remain calm even in the direst emergencies.

In Constant Contact
Oracle is able to relay messages to Batman at almost any time.

A Beautiful Mind
Oracle possesses an eidetic memory that gives her the uncanny ability to remember nearly everything she reads and sees.

Loyal Ally
Even after Barbara Gordon is paralyzed from the waist down and confined to a wheelchair, she remains dedicated to helping Batman.

Eve of Destruction
During the fateful Christmas Eve when Batman is forced to fight off eight assassins who are out for his blood, Gotham City has an eerie calm about it. Christmas bells ring from old Gothic clocks, and a light snow covers the city's usually grimy exterior. A mix of dark and light, Gotham City certainly proves a dramatic background for Batman's heroic efforts.

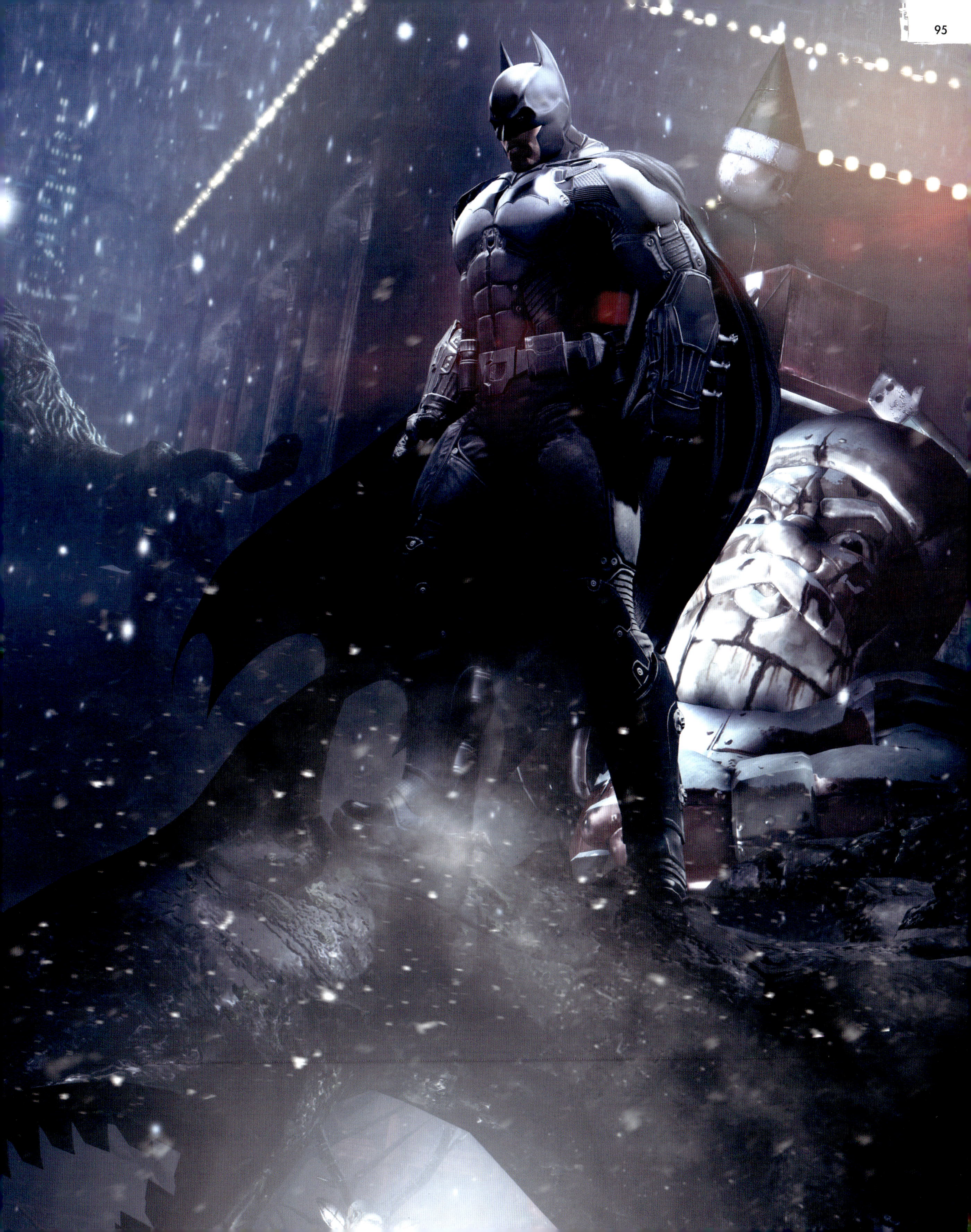

AZRAEL

A MYSTERIOUS PRESENCE IN GOTHAM CITY, AZRAEL IS A HERALD OF THE TERRIBLE TRIAL THAT IS TO COME FOR THE DARK KNIGHT.

A costumed mystery man, Azrael is seemingly as at home on the nighttime rooftops of Gotham City as the Dark Knight himself. With no real idea of this enigmatic man's identity, agenda, or even what side of the law he stands on, Batman hasn't quite decided how to deal with this so-called avenging angel.

THE WATCHER IN THE WINGS
When they first meet on a rooftop near the Courthouse in Park Row, Azrael admits that he has been watching Batman to test whether or not the Dake Knight is "ready." Azrael then extends a flaming dagger from his costume's forearm and uses it to scrawl a mysterious symbol on the roof that seems to have no meaning whatsoever. The man then disappears in a puff of smoke and sparks, leaving Batman with only one option left: to analyze the symbol and try to track Azrael down.

Another Dark Knight?
When Batman attacks Azrael with a batarang, the mysterious figure effortlessly catches it.

◀ **Reading the Signs**
The strange markings left by Azrael lead Batman to the church in Park Row and a meeting with the costumed figure who has been trailing him.

THE SYMBOLS
Despite Batman's training, Azrael still has a tendency to surprise the wary Dark Knight. He appears on the top of Amusement Mile's defunct Ferris wheel, as well as several other rooftops in Gotham City, watching Batman from the shadows and leaving bizarre symbols in his wake. After four such encounters, Batman assembles the symbols, and overlays the result on a map of Arkham City. The combined symbols lead the Dark Knight to Gotham City's famous church in Park Row.

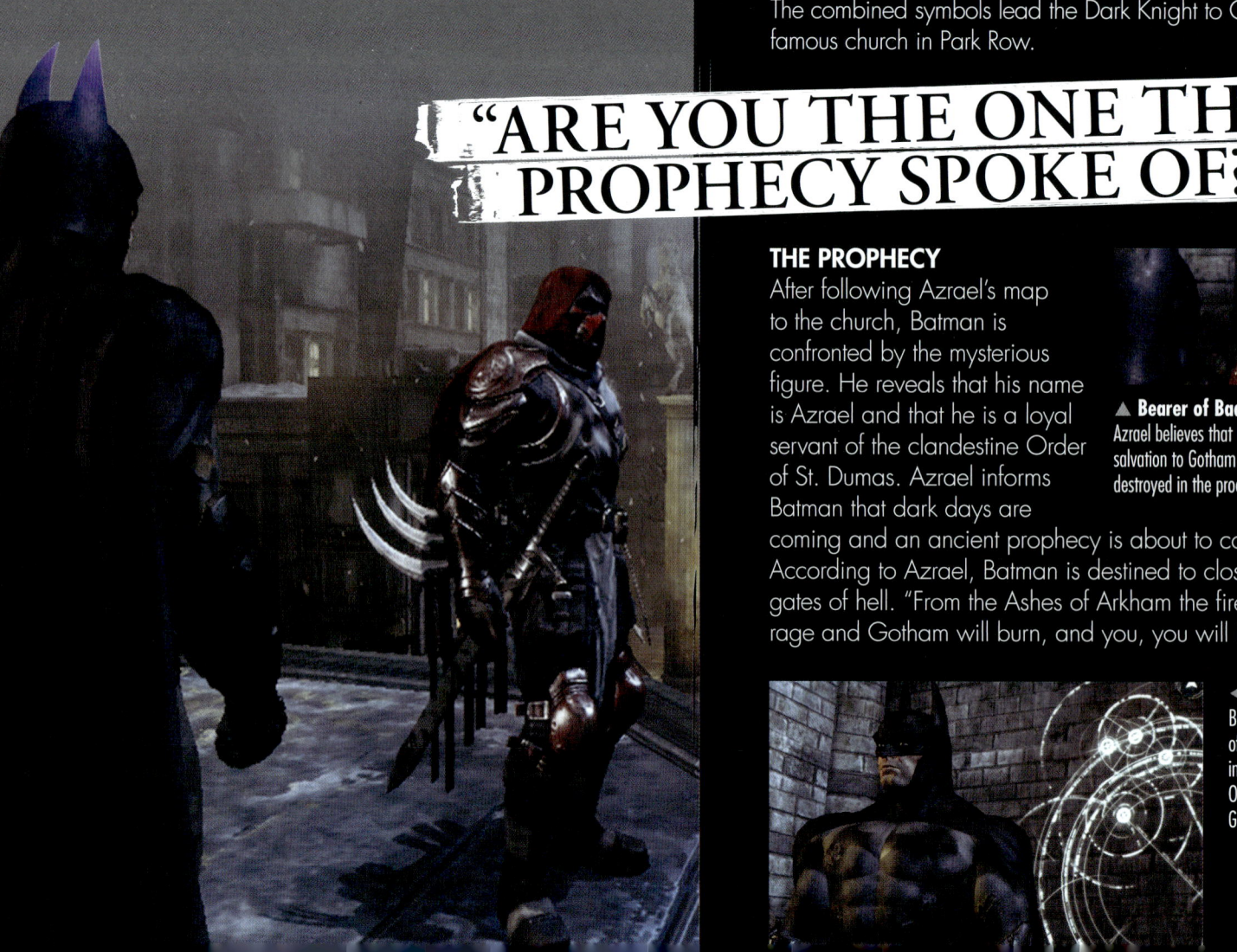

"ARE YOU THE ONE THE PROPHECY SPOKE OF?"
Azrael

THE PROPHECY
After following Azrael's map to the church, Batman is confronted by the mysterious figure. He reveals that his name is Azrael and that he is a loyal servant of the clandestine Order of St. Dumas. Azrael informs Batman that dark days are coming and an ancient prophecy is about to come true. According to Azrael, Batman is destined to close the gates of hell. "From the Ashes of Arkham the fires will rage and Gotham will burn, and you, you will burn, too."

▲ **Bearer of Bad Tidings**
Azrael believes that Batman will bring salvation to Gotham City but will be destroyed in the process.

◀ **Fiction Versus Fact**
Batman doesn't think much of Azrael's prophecy. He is more interested in learning about the Order of St. Dumas, yet another Gotham City secret society.

ALLIES AZRAEL 97

DATA FILE

- **REAL NAME** Michael Lane
- **OCCUPATION** Disciple of the Order of St. Dumas
- **HEIGHT** 6 ft. 2 in.
- **WEIGHT** 210 lbs.
- **EYES** Brown
- **HAIR** Black

Hooded Figure
Azrael has taken great pains to mask his identity.

Friend or Foe?
One of the few people alive who can teach Batman a thing or two about stealth, Azrael's allegiances have yet to be proven.

Masked Man
Only Azrael's eyes are visible behind the mask.

Protective Armor
The armor worn by Azrael has both medieval and religious associations.

Razor Sharp
Lethal blades protrude from the gauntlets.

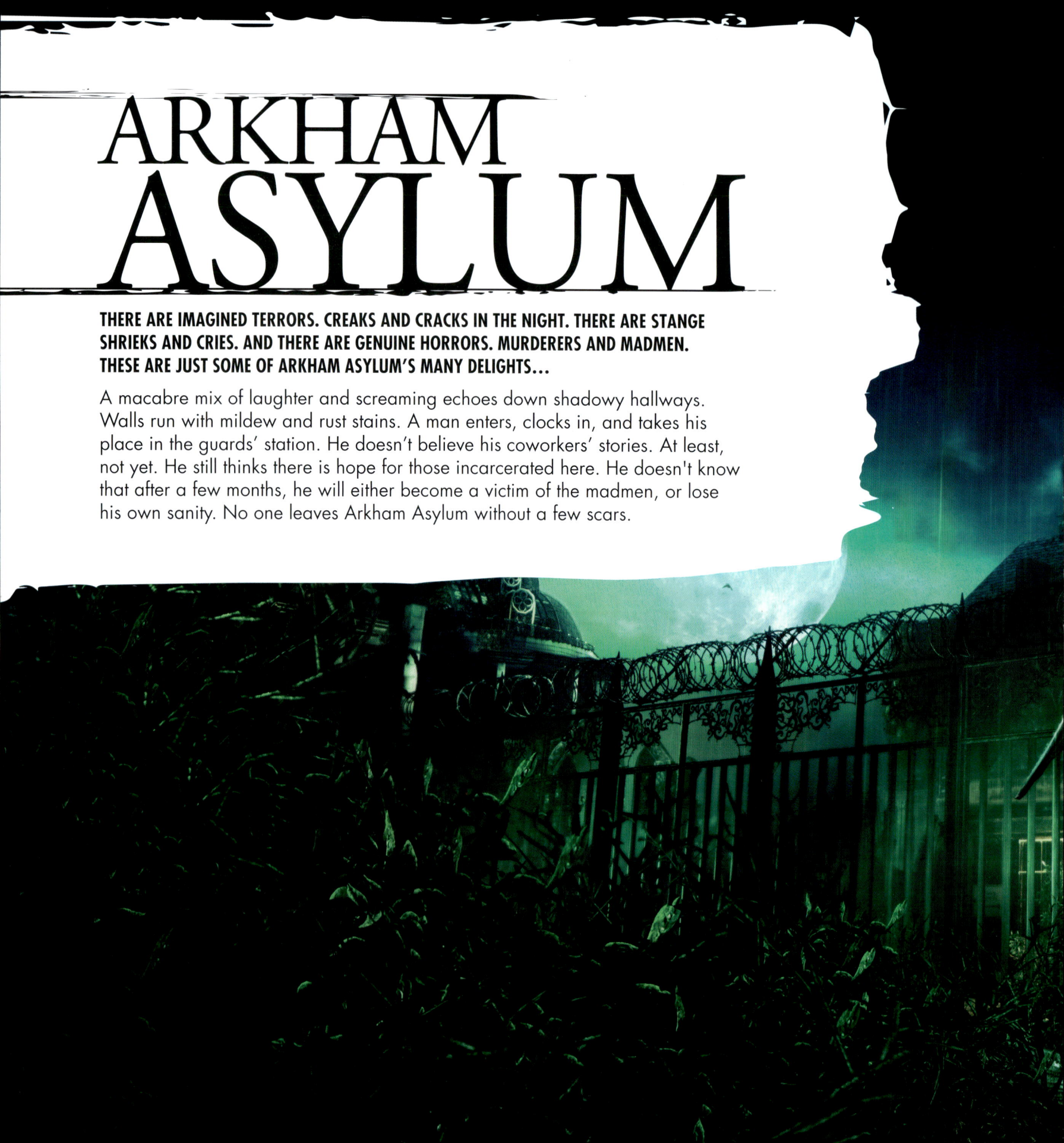

ARKHAM ASYLUM

THERE ARE IMAGINED TERRORS. CREAKS AND CRACKS IN THE NIGHT. THERE ARE STANGE SHRIEKS AND CRIES. AND THERE ARE GENUINE HORRORS. MURDERERS AND MADMEN. THESE ARE JUST SOME OF ARKHAM ASYLUM'S MANY DELIGHTS…

A macabre mix of laughter and screaming echoes down shadowy hallways. Walls run with mildew and rust stains. A man enters, clocks in, and takes his place in the guards' station. He doesn't believe his coworkers' stories. At least, not yet. He still thinks there is hope for those incarcerated here. He doesn't know that after a few months, he will either become a victim of the madmen, or lose his own sanity. No one leaves Arkham Asylum without a few scars.

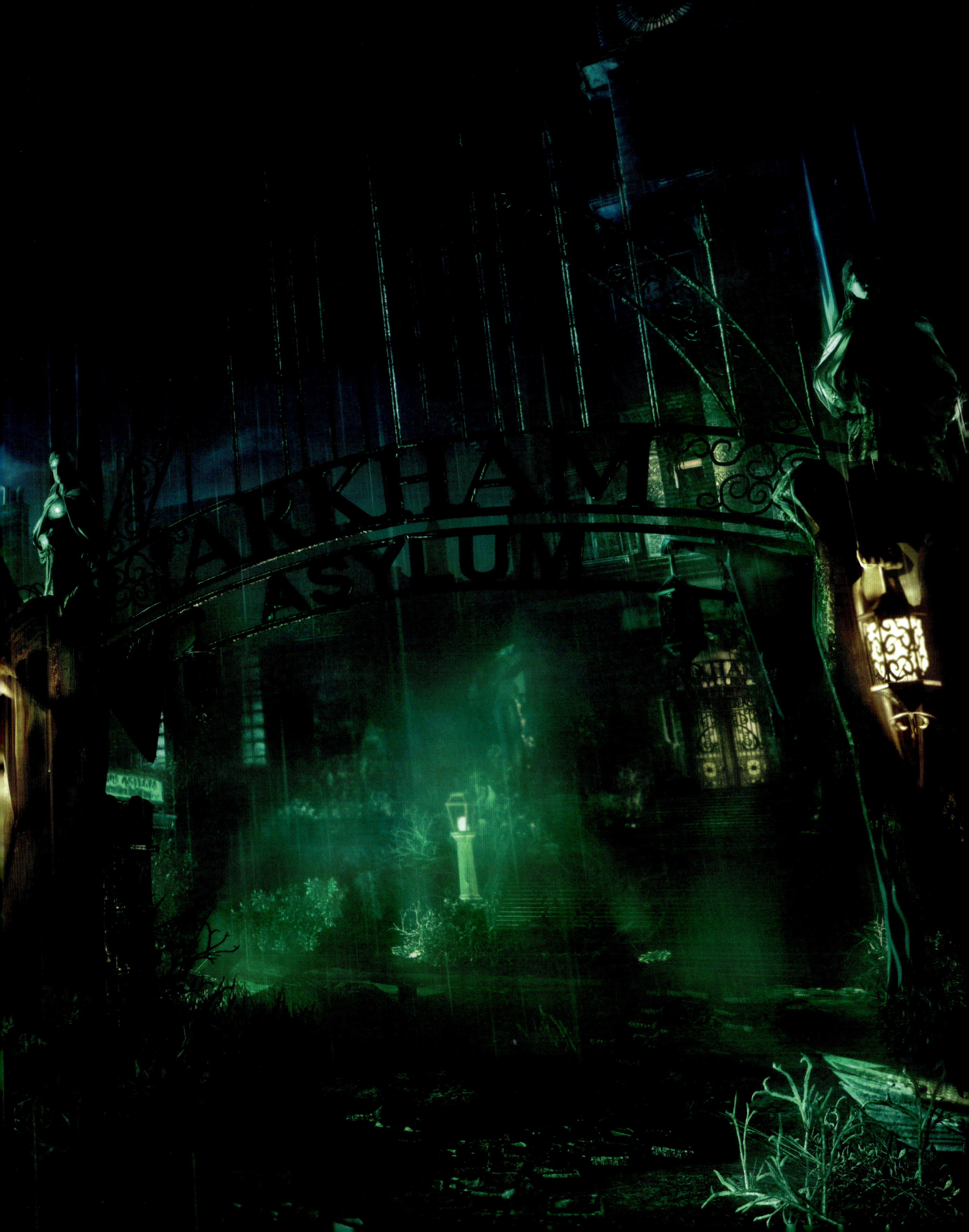
ARKHAM
ASYLUM

HOUSE OF NIGHTMARE

HAUNTED BY A PAST THAT IT SEEMS UNABLE TO ESCAPE, HOME TO THE MOST TWISTED AND EVIL CRIMINAL MINDS, ARKHAM ASYLUM CASTS A LONG, DARK SHADOW OVER GOTHAM CITY.

The Arkham family—a true Gotham City institution—consisted of a long line of respected doctors, lawyers, and politicians, all attempting to make the city a better and safer place to live. Amadeus Arkham's contribution to his family's legacy was to convert their island home into the Elizabeth Arkham Asylum for the Criminally Insane. Amadeus never imagined that this fateful decision would forever taint his family name.

OPENING THE ASYLUM

Amadeus Arkham named his asylum after his mother, Elizabeth, who suffered her own mental breakdown. He dedicated his life to curing people like her, but found himself in over his head when forced to treat Martin "Mad Dog" Hawkins—the man who had murdered Amadeus's own wife and daughter! Although the case was hugely challenging, Amadeus thought that he was making progress and, in his eccentric fashion, began recording his notes on the subject…

WRITTEN IN STONE

Arkham Asylum hides many dark secrets, some of which emanate from Amadeus Arkham himself. The founder of this august institution chronicled his notes about murderer "Mad Dog" Hawkins on pieces of stone hidden around the property. Each of these tablets is later found by Batman. The Dark Knight discovers that these engravings are credited to the "Spirit of Arkham," a mysterious entity that appears to be advancing Amadeus's work.

Home From Home
Batman has made many trips to Arkham Asylum over the years. He even has his own Batcave beneath the property.

A Place of Nightmares
Gloomy and wrapped in mystery, Arkham Asylum is not the most pleasant of healing environments.

THE ARKHAM CURSE

Amadeus Arkham believed that he had cured "Mad Dog" Hawkins but, just as Hawkins was about to sign his release papers, he used the pen to stab and kill Amadeus's secretary. This was the beginning of the end for Amadeus, who soon lost his sanity, becoming an inmate in the very institution he had created.

Grave Warning
Amadeus Arkham died while still an inmate at the Asylum. His untended grave lies in the grounds.

◀ If You Can't Beat 'Em…
After his descent into madness, Amadeus Arkham became a patient in his own asylum. During his stay, Arkham covered the floor and walls of his cell with his crazed writings.

Arkham Mansion
The former Arkham family home is still the main Arkham building.

◀ A Haunted House?
After his death, Amadeus Arkham seemingly haunts the asylum, leaving cryptic messages. It later transpires that the notes are written by the warden, Quincy Sharp, acting as the "Spirit of Arkham." Arkham Asylum's macabre legacy inspired Sharp to embrace his own disturbed impulses.

No Stone Unturned
Batman has explored all the nooks and crannies of Arkham, even its rooftops.

INTENSIVE TREATMENT

Often filled with some of the worst criminals in Gotham City, the Intensive Treatment ward of Arkham Asylum is just one of the many buildings on Arkham Island. It is also the home away from home for the Clown Prince of Crime known as the Joker. But no matter how "intense" his treatment, the Joker seems to be immune to any help that Arkham Asylum has to offer.

ARKHAM ASYLUM LOCATIONS

PENITENTIARY

Located in Arkham West, the notorious Penitentiary houses the dangerous criminals of Arkham. It includes an Extreme Incarceration ward that is filled with the worst inhabitants of Arkham Island. Infamous villains like Mr. Freeze and Clayface call that wing home because their amazing abilities and powers make them grave escape risks and threats to staff and inmates.

DARK, DISTURBING, AND FOREBODING—ARKHAM ASYLUM IS NO TRADITIONAL HOUSE OF HEALING, BUT IT'S AN APPROPRIATE ONE FOR GOTHAM CITY.

The Elizabeth Arkham Asylum for the Criminally Insane was built on the estate of the Arkham family, on a private island off Gotham City. It was Amadeus Arkham who chose to convert his ancestral home into an asylum, and the vast grounds still house many secrets of generations past. Arkham Asylum is extensive and offers many amenities, such as the stunning Botanical Gardens, as well as impressive views of the Gotham City skyline.

Medical Malpractice
Arkham's medical facility is on Arkham West and is the main hospital for patients needing emergency treatment.

MEDICAL FACILITY

Arkham Island has its own medical facility to treat its disturbed inhabitants, however inmates' actual physical condition does not seem to be of paramount concern for some of the doctors.
The medical facility is home to the laboratories of Dr. Penelope Young, as well as other doctors, such as Dr. Kellerman and Dr. Chen. It also has a sanatorium, an experimental chamber, and an x-ray room.

BOTANICAL GARDENS

The beautiful Botanical Gardens were originally intended to be a tranquil place where inmates could sit and reflect on one of the many benches, one of which is dedicated to Thomas and Martha Wayne. It was hoped that the gardens would help bring peace to Arkham's troubled souls, but like the rest of the island the gardens have an ominous atmosphere. Before long they are at the heart of criminal activity when Poison Ivy builds a Titan production facility there.

House of Horrors
Many of Arkham's facilities have fallen into disrepair, helping to add to the institution's haunting atmosphere.

ARKHAM MANSION

Taking up the majority of Arkham East, Arkham Mansion is a huge building, which contains the private office of Warden Sharp and his associates. Dr. Penelope Young also has an office here, and the massive building contains an extensive library and a rather disorganized records room. Just like Batman's own Wayne Manor, Arkham Mansion contains its own dark secrets, such as the walled-off room in which Quincy Sharp plots the creation of Arkham City.

ARKHAM ASYLUM ARKHAM ASYLUM LOCATIONS 105

ARKHAM GROUNDS

A major priority at Arkham Asylum is security, something anyone familiar with the institution's history would find very ironic. Despite the asylum's guard towers and expensive equipment, breakouts are common on the island, allowing the most depraved criminals to return to Gotham City to terrorize the innocent over and over again.

THE SEWERS

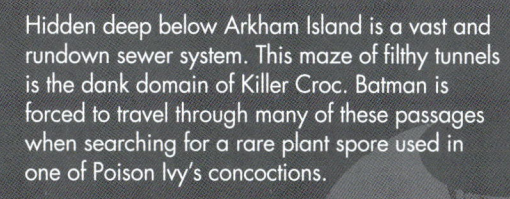

Hidden deep below Arkham Island is a vast and rundown sewer system. This maze of filthy tunnels is the dank domain of Killer Croc. Batman is forced to travel through many of these passages when searching for a rare plant spore used in one of Poison Ivy's concoctions.

ARKHAM ISLAND BATCAVE

Batman discovers the vast network of caverns under the surface of Arkham Island after saving the life of a suicidal inmate during one of his trips to Arkham. Batman decides to save time and energy by creating a satellite Batcave right under Arkham Island itself. A perfect place to store heavy artillery and to keep an eye on his old foes, the Arkham Batcave becomes an important place of refuge for Batman when the Joker takes over the asylum.

ARKHAM STAFF

WORKING WITH THE WORST CRIMINALS IN GOTHAM CITY LEAVES ITS MARK ON EVEN THE MOST RESILIENT AND INTELLIGENT MINDS. ARKHAM STAFF RISK THEIR SANITY EVERY DAY THEY GO TO WORK.

Fully aware of the Arkham "curse," employees at Arkham Island come into their jobs expecting horror, and their worst fears are soon confirmed. Whether agreeing to participate in the madness and therefore perpetuating it, or deciding to stand strong against the corruption inside Arkham's terrifying halls, the people who have worked on Arkham Island are certainly a breed of their own.

AMADEUS ARKHAM

OCCUPATION Psychiatrist • **HEIGHT** 5 ft. 11 in. • **WEIGHT** 175 lbs. • **HAIR** Brown • **EYES** Blue

Amadeus Arkham had his first brush with mental illness after his father died of a mysterious disease. His mother, Elizabeth, survived, but in a state that Amadeus referred to as a "dream." After naming Arkham Asylum after his mother, Amadeus tragically saw his own wife and daughter murdered by Martin "Mad Dog" Hawkins. Amadeus eventually went insane and became an inmate at his own institution after attempting to treat his family's killer.

DR. PENELOPE YOUNG

OCCUPATION Head of Research • **HEIGHT** 5 ft. 6 in. • **WEIGHT** 121 lbs. • **HAIR** Brown • **EYES** Blue

Dr. Young starts her career with the best of intentions, but becomes tempted by a force as malevolent as the devil himself, the Joker. The Joker secretly hires Dr. Young to develop his Titan drug. She eventually attempts to back out of the deal, but the Joker is not known for his tolerance, and Dr. Young becomes another of his many victims.

Doctoring the Evidence
Dr. Penelope Young proves quite the capable actor, able to hide in plain sight as an Arkham staffer despite her crimes.

Spot the Difference
At Arkham, an ID tag may be the only distinguishing feature between a member of staff and a patient.

AARON CASH

OCCUPATION Former Arkham Guard, current Police Officer ▪ **HEIGHT** 6 ft. ▪ **WEIGHT** 185 lbs. ▪ **HAIR** Black ▪ **EYES** Brown

Aaron Cash is one of the few good apples to work at Arkham. He is a security guard at the asylum before transferring to the Gotham City Police Department to work with Commissioner Gordon. Despite his upstanding moral character, the asylum takes its toll on Cash—his hand gets bitten off by the villain Killer Croc.

FRANK BOLES

OCCUPATION Arkham Asylum Guard ▪ **HEIGHT** 6 ft. ▪ **WEIGHT** 185 lbs. ▪ **HAIR** Black ▪ **EYES** Brown

A guard at Arkham for eight years, Frank struggles from the start with drinking on the job. When the Joker stages a riot on Arkham Island, it is revealed that Boles is secretly working for the Clown Prince of Crime when he helps kidnap Commissioner Gordon. He is later "repaid" for his loyal service to the Joker by being murdered by the smiling villain.

WARDEN QUINCY SHARP

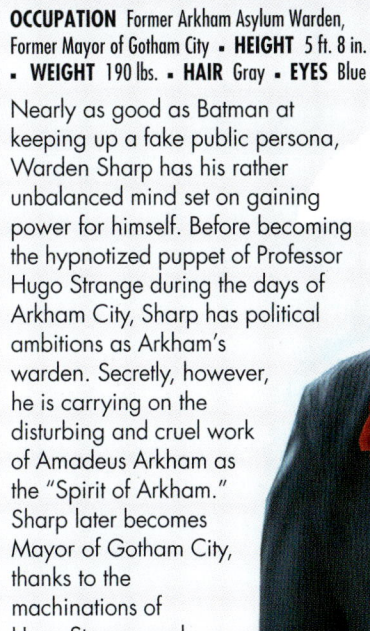

OCCUPATION Former Arkham Asylum Warden, Former Mayor of Gotham City ▪ **HEIGHT** 5 ft. 8 in. ▪ **WEIGHT** 190 lbs. ▪ **HAIR** Gray ▪ **EYES** Blue

Nearly as good as Batman at keeping up a fake public persona, Warden Sharp has his rather unbalanced mind set on gaining power for himself. Before becoming the hypnotized puppet of Professor Hugo Strange during the days of Arkham City, Sharp has political ambitions as Arkham's warden. Secretly, however, he is carrying on the disturbing and cruel work of Amadeus Arkham as the "Spirit of Arkham." Sharp later becomes Mayor of Gotham City, thanks to the machinations of Hugo Strange and Rā's al Ghūl.

Darkness Inside
Sharp's dark side, the "Spirit of Arkham," harbors feelings of intense hatred and violence toward Arkham's inmates.

Tightening Security
Sharp kept a close watch over Arkham Asylum and made sure its security worked like a well-oiled machine—until the Joker got free.

ENEMIES

BATMAN ROUTINELY ENCOUNTERS SICK, TWISTED CRIMINALS. HE IS SURE THAT HE CAN STOP THEM DOING HARM, AND PERHAPS EVEN HELP THEM. BATMAN REFUSES TO BELIEVE IN THE EXISTENCE OF PURE EVIL—BUT THAT DOESN'T STOP GOTHAM CITY FROM TRYING TO CHANGE HIS MIND.

The shadows in Gotham City aren't like those in any other town. They're darker, more impenetrable, and what they hide should never be brought to light. There's a conflicted, homicidal man with two faces, one handsome and one hideous. There's a brutalized and brutal human crocodile who dwells in the sewers. There's a woman with pale green skin and a kiss of death, and a man dressed in straw and burlap, just waiting to create another nightmare. Worst of all, is a pale, green-haired man who can't stop grinning—terrifying atrocities are hilarious to him, and destroying Batman is the greatest joke of all.

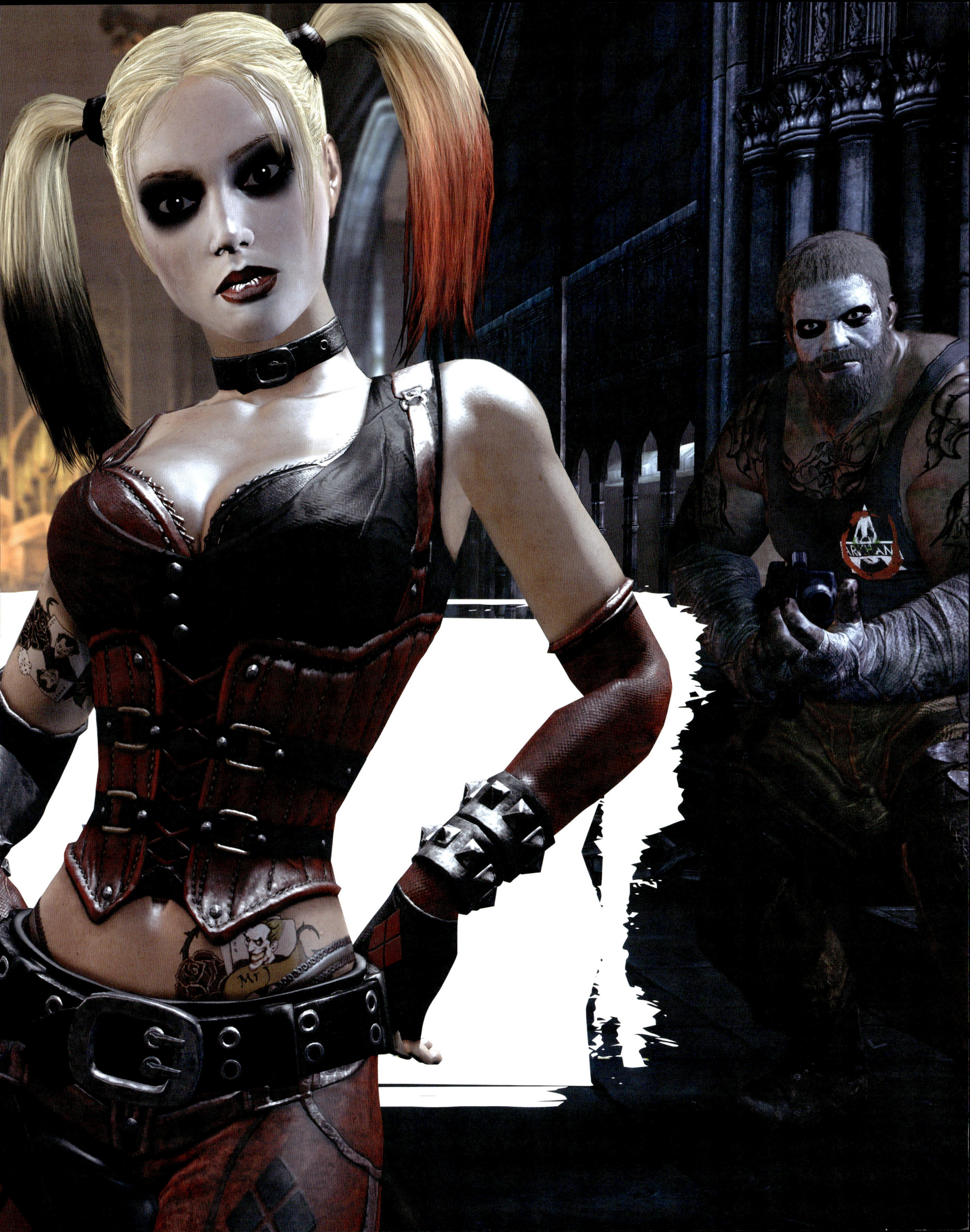

THE JOKER

BATMAN'S GREATEST AND MOST TWISTED FOE IS THE JOKER. HE IS KNOWN AS GOTHAM CITY'S CLOWN PRINCE OF CRIME, AND CONTINUES HIS REIGN OF TERROR EVEN AFTER HIS SUPPOSED DEATH.

With his dead white skin, green hair, and sickeningly exaggerated grin, the Joker is no clown. Obsessed with Batman and the motivations behind the Dark Knight's war on crime, the Joker seems only truly happy when making Batman's life as bizarre and disturbing as possible. The Joker revels in his insanity, caused by a series of tragic events in his past. Criminal acts, including murder, mean nothing to this totally amoral criminal. To him, they are all just part of the "fun."

THE RED HOOD

The Joker's origins remain clouded by his own exaggerations and skewed outlook, but it is believed that the criminal was once a failed stand-up comedian, forced to become a masked thief called the Red Hood. After Batman confronts the villain during a heist at Ace Chemicals, the Red Hood plunges into a vat of toxic chemicals. Moments later, emerging white-faced with green hair and grimacing ruby red lips, the Joker is born.

The Joker's Funhouse
The Clown Prince of Crime wastes no time in making Batman run his twisted gauntlet in Arkham Asylum.

UNDER NEW MANAGEMENT

One of the Joker's most notable crimes is when he takes over Arkham Asylum, and all of Arkham Island. It is all part of the Joker's calculated plan to create an army of behemoths using the drug Titan, as well as to poison the city's water supply at the same time. Luckily, Batman is locked in the Asylum during the subsequent breakouts, and the Dark Knight is able to curb the Joker's campaign at the eleventh hour.

"WELCOME TO THE MADHOUSE, BATMAN!"
The Joker

Clash of the Titans?
The Joker also injects Batman with the Titan strain, but the Dark Knight manages to give himself an antidote, preferring to battle the Joker on his own terms.

JOKER POWER

Relying on his wits and devious nature to prove a challenge for the Dark Knight, the Joker has never been Batman's physical equal. However, near the end of his takeover of Arkham Island, the Joker injects himself with the Titan strain, an enhanced form of the super-steroid known as Venom. Suddenly, for the first time in his life, the Joker is more than a match for Batman—he is a brawny monster able to pick the Dark Knight up in his claw-like hand with ease.

ENEMIES THE JOKER

No Laughing Matter
With pale skin and bright green locks permanently dyed from a toxic bath, the Joker's appearance is as unique as it is terrifying.

For Comic Effect
The Joker loves the color purple, and normally dresses accordingly.

Deadly Joke
The Joker has been known to decorate his lapel with an acid-squirting flower.

Under the Hood
Already teetering on the verge of insanity, the Joker embraced his crazy side after his accidental chemical bath.

DATA FILE
- **REAL NAME** Unknown
- **OCCUPATION** Criminal
- **HEIGHT** 6 ft.
- **WEIGHT** 160 lbs.
- **EYES** Green
- **HAIR** Green

Titan Trauma
After his Titan injection, the Joker becomes deathly ill.

Expect the Unexpected
Whatever the Joker has in his pockets, it's safe to assume it's both disturbing and lethal.

Examining the Joke
The Joker's visage is a frightening one and has been ever since he first started out on the pathway to legendary criminal. While his sense of style has evolved over the years, the Joker's signature grin has remained a tried and true part of his character, instilling fear as quickly as Batman's own intimidating appearance.

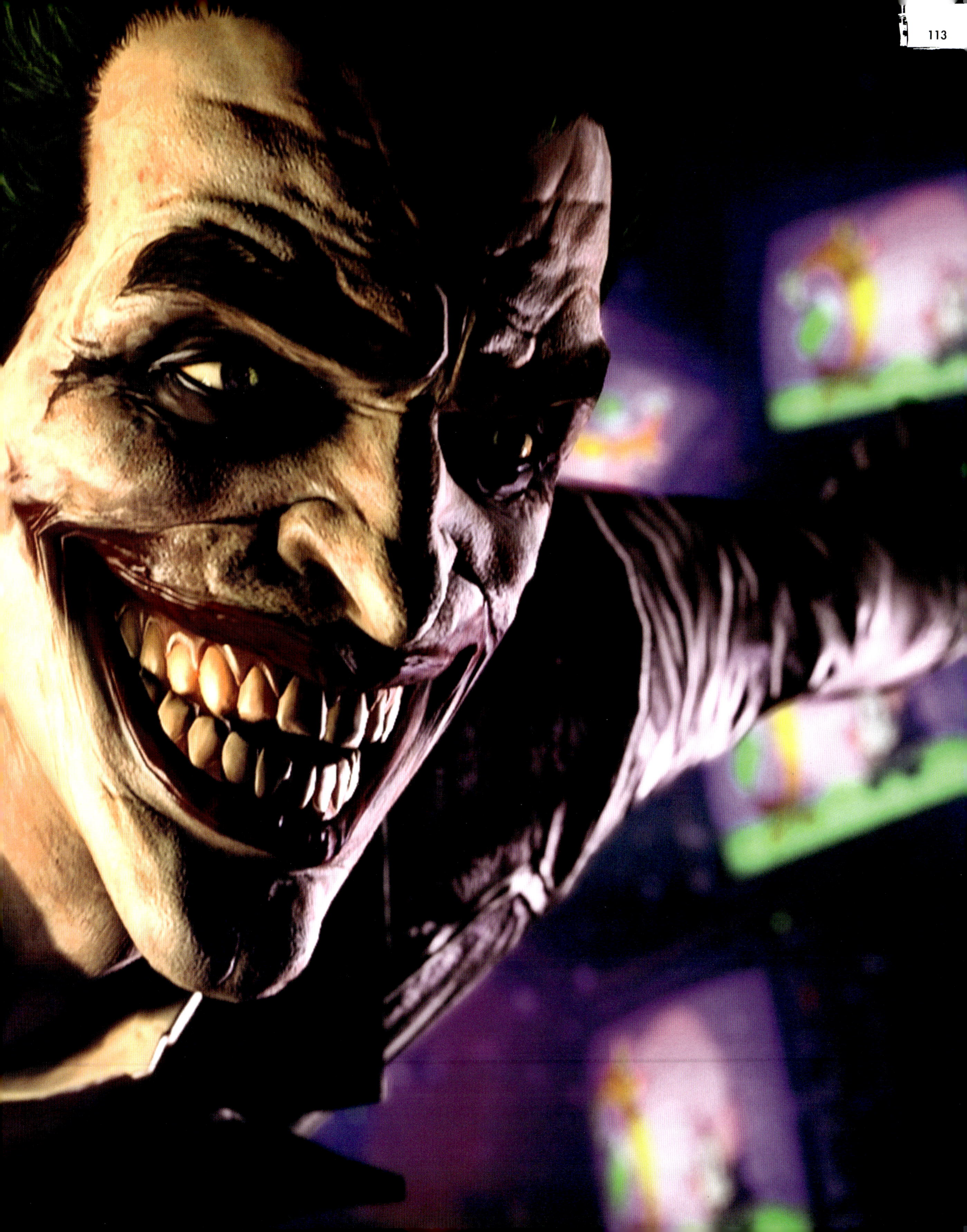

HARLEY QUINN

THE JOKER'S RIGHT-HAND WOMAN AND THE PROVERBIAL LOVESICK PUPPY, HARLEY QUINN GIVES UP HER CAREER AND REPUTATION TO BE AT HER "PUDDIN'S" SIDE.

Harleen Quinzel is the doctor at Blackgate Prison tasked with evaluating the Joker when he is first apprehended by the Batman. She quickly falls in love with her patient, finding in him an excuse to cut loose and embrace her darker tendencies. While not much of a physical threat to Batman, despite her gymnastic aptitude, Harley's mind is nearly as insidious as her boyfriend's, and that is a true danger to Gotham City.

WORK CLOTHES
Harley Quinn has never been one to keep the same uniform for an extended period of time. She often switches her costume from caper to caper. For example, she adopts a nurse's uniform when she helps the Joker take over Arkham Asylum and swaps to a more street-appropriate look when she and her "puddin'" set up shop in Arkham City. When the Arkham Knight begins appearing in Gotham City, Harley dons a new outfit, complete with a black skirt.

▲ **Sharp Dresser**
Harley Quinn's costume for the takeover of Arkham Asylum includes the badge of then Warden, Quincy Sharp.

> "TODAY'S THE JOKER'S BIG HOMECOMING AND YOU'RE THE GUEST OF HONOR."
> — Harley Quinn

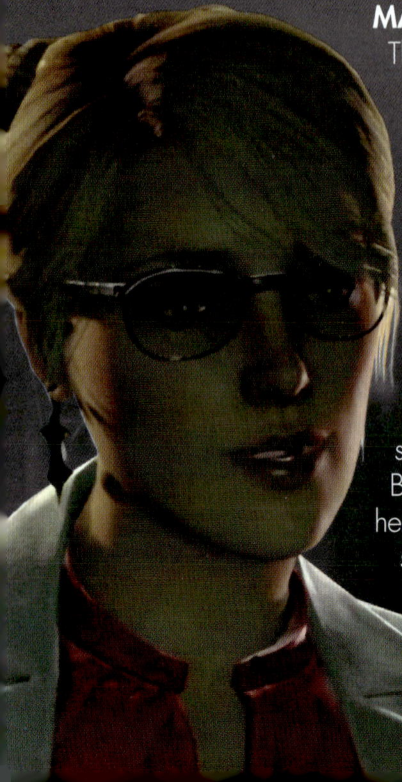

MAD LOVE
The Joker is a master manipulator, and when confronted with an impressionable personality like that of Dr. Harleen Quinzel, he's quite able to mold and shape it as he pleases. When Harleen first meets "Mr. J," he has just been captured by Batman. It is Harleen's job to give the Joker a psychiatric evaluation and as she listens to him speak, she mistakes his fascination with Batman for an infatuation with herself. The doctor is very quickly smitten, and it is likely that she has a hand in the Joker's subsequent escape.

▲ **Harley Quinn's Revenge**
After the Joker's death, the mourning Harley builds a bizarre shrine dedicated to her lost love. She and her gang capture Batman and place him at its center.

THE MOURNING AFTER
The Joker is a huge influence on Harleen Quinzel. He helps her make the change to Harley Quinn, suggesting the nickname during their first meeting in Blackgate Prison. The Joker is such a massive part of her life that when he apparently dies due to poisoning from the Titan drug, Harley dramatically changes her appearance once again. Her mourning attire is much darker than her previous looks, as is her mind. She even refuses to leave the Steel Mill despite Arkham City's shutdown.

ENEMIES HARLEY QUINN

Cute But Lethal
Harley changes the color of her signature pigtails to match her outfit.

DATA FILE

- **REAL NAME** Dr. Harleen F. Quinzel
- **OCCUPATION** Criminal
- **HEIGHT** 5 ft. 7 in.
- **WEIGHT** 140 lbs.
- **EYES** Blue
- **HAIR** Blonde

Tattoos
What these red-and-black roses symbolize is perhaps known only to Harley.

Agile Attacker
Harley is not particularly strong, but she is an Olympic-level gymnast.

Love Sick
Harleen is instantly sympathetic toward the "misunderstood" clown when she meets the Joker, and soon falls madly in love with him. The Joker is a negative influence on her and she becomes almost as depraved as he is.

Mr. J
Harley keeps the Joker close to her heart by tattooing him on her body.

Deadly Girl
Harley is always armed, and will not hesitate to kill in the name of love.

Diamonds Are Forever
Harley's clothes often feature a strong playing card theme.

Clowning Around
After a half-hearted attempt to take the Mayor of Gotham City hostage, the Joker is strangely willing to be captured by Batman.

ENEMIES ARKHAM TAKEOVER 117

The Ringmaster
The Joker is exactly where he wants to be when Batman brings him back to Arkham Asylum. He becomes the ringmaster of his own dark circus.

ARKHAM TAKEOVER

IN PERHAPS HIS MOST AMBITIOUS SCHEME YET, THE JOKER TAKES OVER ARKHAM ASYLUM, TRAPPING BATMAN INSIDE HIS MAKESHIFT HOUSE OF HORRORS.

When a fire at Blackgate Prison causes hundreds of inmates to be transferred to Arkham Asylum, including many members of the Joker's gang, Batman has his hands full maintaining order. To make matters worse, the Joker then invades City Hall. Batman easily captures the Clown Prince of Crime and takes him to Arkham, but soon realizes that something is seriously wrong. And indeed it is. All the players are in now place, and the Joker's trap is about to be sprung...

▲ The Titan Joker
Batman battles the Joker on the roof of Arkham Asylum as news helicopters buzz overhead.

THE METHOD IN HIS MADNESS

The Joker has been developing a new brand of super steroid called Titan with the help of one of Arkham Asylum's own doctors, Dr. Penelope Young. He plans to release it into Gotham City's water supply and cause a massive outbreak of violent mayhem among the population. To achieve this aim, he arranges for his crew, who are mostly imprisoned in Blackgate, to be shipped to Arkham, and for Harley Quinn to help him take over Arkham Island itself. Trapped inside the asylum, Batman first has to figure out the Joker's plot, and then defeat his many henchmen and allies.

After defeating many of his old enemies while fighting his way through the asylum, Batman discovers Joker's masterplan and puts a stop to it. But when a burst of fireworks summons him to a showdown with the Joker, the Dark Knight doesn't realize what he's letting himself in for.

While crew from the *Jack Ryder Show* film the dramatic confrontation on the asylum roof, the Joker quickly injects himself with the Titan formula. Holding Commissioner Gordon captive, the villain—now a hulking brute—battles the Dark Knight, using every bit of his newfound strength. Fortunately Batman comes to the fight armed with his Ultra Batclaw, and soon bests the Joker, restoring order to Arkham Asylum.

THE PENGUIN

DESPITE HIS DIMINUTIVE SIZE, THE PENGUIN IS ONE OF THE BIGGEST PRESENCES IN GOTHAM CITY, SERVING AS THE HEAD OF AN ENORMOUS CRIME EMPIRE.

To say the Penguin has a chip on his shoulder is an understatement. Originally born into a wealthy family, Oswald Cobblepot was sent to live overseas by his family. When the Cobblepots lost their fortune, Oswald began to develop his cutthroat attitude, turning to a life of crime amidst the gangs of London. He returned to Gotham City, complete with his nickname the Penguin, and quickly became the town's premier arms dealer.

"I'M WHAT YOU MIGHT CALL, A COLLECTOR."
The Penguin

BIRDMAN OF GOTHAM
One of Batman's first dealings with the Penguin is when he confronts him aboard a cargo ship. The bird-like criminal is running a casino on the ship, as well as his arms-dealing business. At war with the Falcone crime family, the Penguin is determined to rise to the top of Gotham City's criminal underworld; he does so by dealing in stolen weapons from the G.C.P.D.'s evidence locker. With the help of Barbara Gordon, Batman manages to put a stop to that particular crime, but not the Penguin's criminal empire.

▲ Gaining Arms
Despite Penguin's grisly appearance and cruel nature, beautiful women like Candy and Tracey Buxton are happy to work for the powerful crime lord.

AN EYE FOR TROUBLE
When he first encounters Batman, the Penguin doesn't have the "monocle" that later becomes his trademark. During a bar brawl, Cobblepot is struck in the face with a broken beer bottle, a piece of which becomes lodged in his eye. Doctors determine that removing the glass would be fatal so it remains there—a macabre eyepiece that gives Cobblepot his unique appearance. Cobblepot gets revenge on his assailant by putting out his eyes, leaving the blinded man at the mercy of the freeway traffic during rush hour.

Home Invasion
Despite Penguin's many impressive security precautions, Batman manages to make his way into the criminal's inner sanctum and takes down the bird-themed villain.

EMPEROR PENGUIN
After the construction of Arkham City, the Penguin bases his crimonal operations inside Gotham City's Natural History Museum. There he shows off many of his dead opponents as trophies in the museum's display cabinets. Adjacent to the museum is the Penguin's Iceberg Lounge, which is protected by a large indoor body of water containing a giant shark. The Penguin sets himself up like a modern-day Roman emperor, creating a gladiatorial ring within his lair where criminals fight each other for the chance to be in his gang.

ENEMIES THE PENGUIN

DATA FILE

- **REAL NAME** Oswald Chesterfield Cobblepot
- **OCCUPATION** Black Market Racketeer
- **HEIGHT** 4 ft. 10 in.
- **WEIGHT** 175 lbs.
- **EYES** Blue
- **HAIR** Black

Makeshift Monocle
The Penguin's "monocle" is actually the bottom of a broken beer bottle.

Showing Off
A fondness for fat cigars is just one ostentatious sign of wealth displayed by the Penguin.

A Rainy Day
The Penguin's signature umbrellas have been known to host deadly weapons.

Only the Best
With plenty of illegal assets, the Penguin can afford expensive clothes.

Bird of Prey
Though he pretends to be a distinguished gentleman, employing an English accent and dressing in fancy clothes, the Penguin can't disguise the fact that he's just a criminal thug at heart.

THE RIDDLER

ONE OF THE CRAFTIEST MEMBERS OF BATMAN'S ROGUES GALLERY, THE RIDDLER IS CONSTANTLY CHALLENGING THE CAPED CRUSADER TO A DUEL OF WITS, THOUGH HE RARELY WINS.

Edward Nashton wasn't great at games, until he started cheating. He has a natural love for puzzles and riddles, and he takes great satisfaction in triumphing over others in a mental arena. This desire to win makes him more interested in competing against Batman than actually completing his crimes.

A TRUE ENIGMA

When Batman first meets the Riddler, the criminal goes by the name Enigma. He is secretly gathering extensive information on many influential people he considers corrupting presences in Gotham City, and embarks on an elaborate extortion plot. His plans bring him into conflict with Batman, who plays along with Enigma's games, besting him at every puzzle thrown his way. The Dark Knight finally discovers that Enigma is actually Edward Nashton, a disgruntled former member of the Gotham City Police Department's cyber crimes unit.

RIDDLE ME THIS

When the Joker takes over Arkham Island, Batman has plenty of problems to deal with. Added to that number are the challenges set by the Riddler, Enigma's later alias of choice. The Riddler hides many of his so-called Riddler Trophies around the Asylum grounds, and hacks into Batman's cowl in order to plague him with riddles relating to the Asylum and its inmates.

◀ **Universal Solvent**
Batman solves the Riddler's clues by locating the solutions in various hiding places in Arkham Asylum and scanning them into his cowl.

"I ALWAYS KNEW I WAS BETTER THAN YOU."
— The Riddler

Checkmate ▶
Batman manages to free the Riddler's final hostages, and tricks the Riddler into believing that he, too, has an explosive charge on him that requires his constant movement.

Dramatic Death Traps
The Riddler goes to great lengths to create his complex conundrums, and does so with flair — even using curtains that he opens for an extra dramatic reveal.

GETTING RIDDLED

The Riddler ups the ante after Arkham City is constructed. Not content to merely blackmail Gotham's elite or try to confound Batman, he raises his stakes and kidnaps a medical team. This leads Batman on a not-so-merry chase to locate the villain's many hideouts and free the new prisoners. Eventually, Batman catches up to the villain, only to find that the Riddler's remaining hostages are being forced to continually move through the building's lower level for fear of detonating motion-sensitive charges he has placed on them.

ENEMIES THE RIDDLER

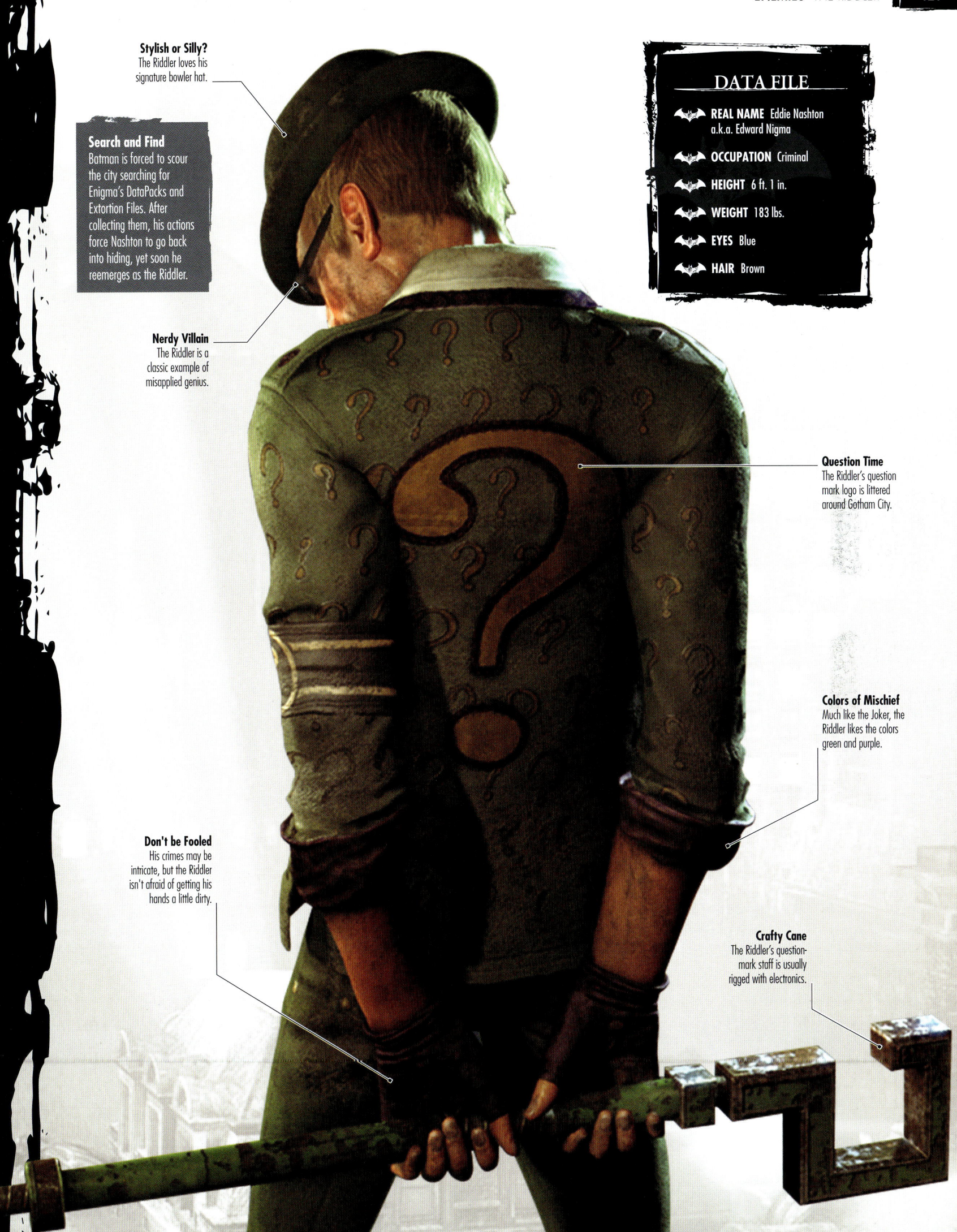

Stylish or Silly?
The Riddler loves his signature bowler hat.

Search and Find
Batman is forced to scour the city searching for Enigma's DataPacks and Extortion Files. After collecting them, his actions force Nashton to go back into hiding, yet soon he reemerges as the Riddler.

Nerdy Villain
The Riddler is a classic example of misapplied genius.

Don't be Fooled
His crimes may be intricate, but the Riddler isn't afraid of getting his hands a little dirty.

DATA FILE

- **REAL NAME** Eddie Nashton a.k.a. Edward Nigma
- **OCCUPATION** Criminal
- **HEIGHT** 6 ft. 1 in.
- **WEIGHT** 183 lbs.
- **EYES** Blue
- **HAIR** Brown

Question Time
The Riddler's question mark logo is littered around Gotham City.

Colors of Mischief
Much like the Joker, the Riddler likes the colors green and purple.

Crafty Cane
The Riddler's question-mark staff is usually rigged with electronics.

BLACK MASK

BLACK MASK IS ONE OF GOTHAM CITY'S MOST TERRIFYING MOB BOSSES AND HIS MASK'S SINISTER VISAGE ACCURATELY REFLECTS THE GANGSTER'S SOUL.

Roman Sionis was born into the lap of luxury. After his parents die in a suspicious fire, Roman inherits their company, but soon drives it into bankruptcy. Bruce Wayne bails him out, yet Sionis develops an extreme hatred towards Wayne. He adopts the identity of Black Mask, and like most of his ilk, his campaign for vengeance leads him down a dark road of crime and imprisonment.

THE MAN BEHIND THE MASK
One Christmas Eve, during Batman's early years in Gotham City, Black Mask places a bounty on the hero's head and eight deadly assassins answer his call. However, while ordering a hit on Batman isn't out of character for Sionis, the Dark Knight soon discovers that a new villain calling himself the Joker is impersonating Black Mask, and that it is this imposter who has hired the hit men. The Joker is eventually apprehended by Batman, but the real Black Mask escapes.

THE FACE OF JANUS
Despite apprehending the Joker on Christmas Eve, Batman's work is far from finished. Another of his tasks is to locate Black Mask's chemical stashes throughout the city. Labeled with the logo of Roman's company, Janus Cosmetics, the crates of chemicals are part of Black Mask's drug-trafficking operation, and Batman uses his Explosive Gel to destroy each one as he discovers them. After dealing with the seventh and final drug stash at the church in Park Row, Batman is attacked by Black Mask, and the Dark Knight has to take down the villain and his gang.

▲ **It Takes a Village**
Not naïve enough to attack the Batman alone, Black Mask has plenty of lackeys to help him attempt to overpower the Dark Knight.

"FIRST YOU FALL, THEN GOTHAM."
— Black Mask

MASKING HIS DEFEAT
In the final days of Arkham City, Nightwing comes across one of Black Mask's illegal operations. After taking out his thugs in a meat-packing facility, Nightwing pursues Black Mask onto a moving freight train. He is greeted by dozens of Black Mask's thugs and must fight them through a number of train cars before finally confronting and beating Black Mask himself.

No Jacket Required ▷
By the time Nightwing faces him, Black Mask has given up his signature white suit and appears a bit more casual and hands on.

ENEMIES BLACK MASK 123

DATA FILE

- **REAL NAME** Roman Sionis
- **OCCUPATION** Criminal
- **HEIGHT** 6 ft. 1 in.
- **WEIGHT** 195 lbs.
- **EYES** Brown
- **HAIR** Brown

Masked Menace
Black Mask's ebony mask is carved from his father's coffin.

Black Heart
Brutal and sadistic, Black Mask is a true gangster with no time for mercy, tolerance, or forgiveness. He harbors an especially deep hatred for the Joker after the villain impersonates him and murders his girlfriend.

Old Style Boss
A bit of a traditionalist, Black Mask often wears a suit for "work."

Sharp Dresser
Despite losing his family fortune, Black Mask has never lost his sense of style.

Old Habits Die Hard
Even though his identity is public knowledge, Black Mask still wears gloves during his crimes.

THE BOUNTY

THE GANG BOSS BLACK MASK USHERS IN CHRISTMAS EVE BY PLACING A BOUNTY ON THE DARK KNIGHT'S HEAD. BUT ALL IS NOT WHAT IT SEEMS…

When the Dark Knight learns that Black Mask has broken into Blackgate Prison and kidnapped Gotham City Police Commissioner Gillian B. Loeb, he immediately heads to the notorious penitentiary, only to tussle with Killer Croc and narrowly defeat the villain. Batman then learns that Black Mask's bounty has made the Dark Knight the most wanted man in Gotham City. Eight of the most dangerous villains in the world have decided to take up the contract and are attempting to take Batman down once and for all.

THE LAUGHING MASK

What Batman doesn't know is that Black Mask hasn't really been himself lately. A new player is in town. Calling himself the Joker, this criminal has broken into Black Mask's residence at Lacey Towers and killed Black Mask's girlfriend, as well as a decoy Black Mask that the wily villain sent in his place. The real Black Mask is now in hiding and the Joker has taken over his operation (and mask), and ordered the hit on Batman. It isn't long before the Joker lets Batman in on his "joke." Revealing the kidnapped Black Mask at Gotham Merchants Bank, the Joker

▲ **Bound and Gagged**
Batman confronts "Black Mask" at Gotham Merchants Bank, and discovers the true Black Mask, bound and gagged nearby.

manages to escape the Dark Knight's clutches and reconvenes with his henchmen at the Gotham Royal Hotel. Batman tracks him there and is attacked by another gangster, Bane. Battling Bane on one of the hotel's spacious balconies, the Dark Knight manages to triumph momentarily over his hulking, steroid-fueled opponent. When the police arrive, however, Bane makes his escape, firing a bazooka at the Joker who is attempting to flee the scene in his helicopter.

Although Batman is already aware of the Joker's criminal nature, he underlines his moral superiority to the Clown Prince of Crime by saving the villain from falling to his death.

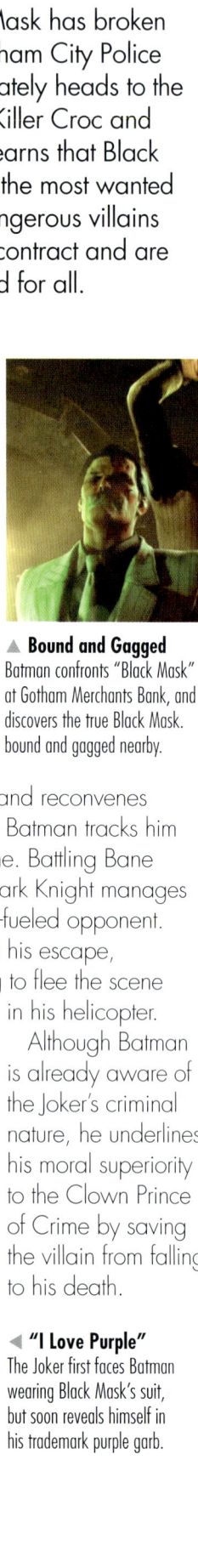

◀ **"I Love Purple"**
The Joker first faces Batman wearing Black Mask's suit, but soon reveals himself in his trademark purple garb.

BOUNTY HUNTERS

The assassins who take on the Joker's big-money challenge to finish Batman are an eclectic bunch. They range from natural-born brawlers, like Killer Croc and Bane, to stealthy assassins with well-honed fighting or killing skills, such as Deathstroke, Deadshot, Lady Shiva, and Copperhead. The Dark Knight is also threatened by other bizarre foes who rely on special, high-tech devices to amplify their killing abilities, such as Firefly and the Electrocutioner.

| Killer Croc | Deadshot | Deathstroke | Firefly |
| Bane | Copperhead | Lady Shiva | Electrocutioner |

Mister Big Shot
Roman Sionis, also known as Black Mask, is a major underworld player during the early days of Batman's career.

KILLER CROC

BORN WITH A SKIN CONDITION THAT ONLY SEEMS TO WORSEN WITH AGE, WAYLON JONES BECOMES KILLER CROC, ONE OF BATMAN'S MOST SAVAGE AND ANIMALISTIC OPPONENTS.

Waylon Jones seems to be devolving, every day becoming more like his namesake. Born with scaly green skin, he spent some time as a circus sideshow performer before deciding that his grotesque form was more fitting for a life of crime. Continuing to embrace his bestial side, Croc is a hulking behemoth more than willing to kill, and even eat, anyone who gets in his way.

SEE YOU LATER, ALLIGATOR

While Batman knows better than to think he's seen the last of Killer Croc after their battle in the sewers of Arkham Island, he is nonetheless surprised when he comes across the villain under the streets of Arkham City. Batman is separated from Croc by the metal bars of a sewer grate, when the villain catches his scent. With his animal-like senses, Croc can detect the Joker's poisoned blood circulating through Batman's veins. On this occasion Croc swims away, satisfied that Batman is as good as dead.

▲ **Brutal Battle**
In Batman's early years Killer Croc is less animalistic and slightly easier to beat.

CROCODILE HUNTER

Batman's first major battle with Killer Croc happens when the beast is hired as one of the assassins contracted to kill Batman one Christmas Eve. Croc faces the Dark Knight on the rooftop of Blackgate Prison. Croc puts up a strong fight against the Dark Knight as Black Mask makes his getaway. Eventually, Batman fells the giant, and after interrogating him, discovers the bounty that has been placed on his own head.

> "YOU ARE NOT WELCOME HERE."
> — Killer Croc

SEWER SAVAGE

By the time he is imprisoned in Arkham Asylum, Croc has lost much of his humanity. He appears to have grown bulkier, and has embraced his wild side. Batman is forced to fight Croc when attempting to collect plant spores in the sewers beneath Arkham Island in order to create an antidote to the Titan strain that the Joker has been developing. The Dark Knight barely escapes with his life, but manages to knock Croc into a lower part of the sewer system.

Killer Instinct ▶
In a fit of rage, Croc is unable to tell ally from enemy. Before his confrontation with Batman in the sewers, Croc attacks fellow villain Scarecrow.

ENEMIES KILLER CROC   127

Animal Eyes
Croc's eyes glow a sickly yellow hue.

Bone Crusher
Razor-sharp teeth line Croc's extremely strong jaw.

Man-Eater
Killer Croc has earned his reputation as a lethal opponent. He even bit the hand off Arkham guard and later police officer, Aaron Cash.

Useless Restraints
Arkham Asylum has always found it difficult to contain Croc's strength.

Death Grip
Croc is incredibly strong, and often drags his foes into the depths.

DATA FILE

- **REAL NAME** Waylon Jones
- **OCCUPATION** Criminal
- **HEIGHT** 9 ft
- **WEIGHT** 310 lbs.
- **EYES** Yellow
- **HAIR** None

COPPERHEAD

ONE OF THE MANY ASSASSINS SUPPOSEDLY HIRED BY BLACK MASK TO EXTERMINATE BATMAN, COPPERHEAD IS THE HUMAN EQUIVALENT OF A DEADLY SNAKE IN THE GRASS.

An escape artist thought to be of Central American origin, Copperhead is a master of poisons and contortion. Like the viper she is named after, Copperhead has many snake-like features such as a forked tongue and yellow, reptilian eyes. She also has an abnormal physiology that allows her to attack her foes in bizarre and unexpected ways, making her as deadly as her namesake.

SNAKEBITE

Copperhead first makes herself known to the Dark Knight when she interrupts his interrogation of Black Mask. Although he recognizes her from her file and her snake-like movements, Batman is unprepared for Copperhead's poison-tipped fingernails. As Batman staggers about the room, Copperhead brags that he is already dead even though his body doesn't realize it yet. Fighting through the pain, Batman scans the room for the poison hoping to send information about the compound to Alfred so he can try to concoct a cure.

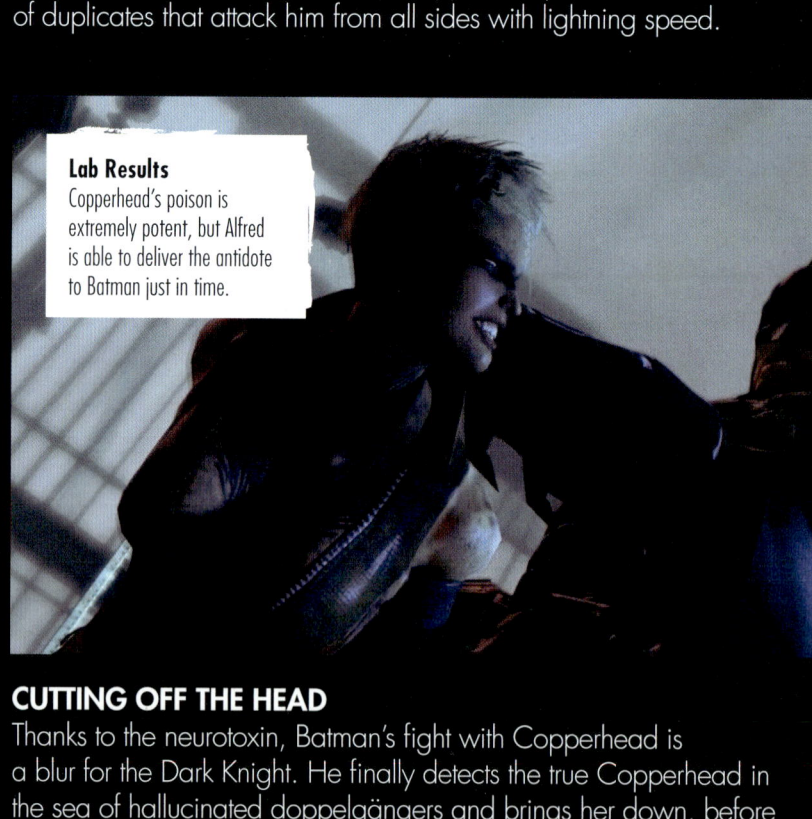

Three's a Crowd
It's hard enough to fight Copperhead without the effects of the poison causing Batman to see numerous versions of his opponent.

THAT GIRL IS POISON

Although on the verge of death from Copperhead's neurotoxin, Batman makes his way to higher levels of the building to receive a Batwing airdrop of the antitoxin that Alfred is manufacturing. On the way, he suffers hallucinations, ranging from a disapproving Alfred, to the dying Commissioner Loeb. Batman can't reach the drop point without confronting Copperhead once again. Adversely affected by the poison, the Dark Knight sees his opponent split off into a number of duplicates that attack him from all sides with lightning speed.

Lab Results
Copperhead's poison is extremely potent, but Alfred is able to deliver the antidote to Batman just in time.

CUTTING OFF THE HEAD

Thanks to the neurotoxin, Batman's fight with Copperhead is a blur for the Dark Knight. He finally detects the true Copperhead in the sea of hallucinated doppelgängers and brings her down, before dosing himself with Alfred's antidote. With his senses regained, Batman finishes off Copperhead and traps her in a shipping container for the G.C.P.D. to find.

> "I BET YOU NEVER EXPECTED THE END TO COME LIKE THIS."
> — Copperhead

ENEMIES COPPERHEAD 129

DATA FILE

- **REAL NAME** Unknown
- **OCCUPATION** Contract Killer
- **HEIGHT** 5 ft. 10 in.
- **WEIGHT** 160 lbs.
- **EYES** Yellow
- **HAIR** Blonde

No Identity
Wearing more makeup than mask, Copperhead nevertheless has kept her identity a secret.

Snake in the Grass
Perhaps only one of many assassins to call themselves Copperhead, this particular hired killer certainly looks the part of her namesake.

Vested Interest
Not one to ignore her own theme, Copperhead's vest appears to be made of snakeskin.

Inked and Dangerous
Copperhead's markings identify her gang affiliations.

Next to Godliness
Keeping clean doesn't appear to be one of Copperhead's priorities.

It's a Mystery
Copperhead wears fingerless gloves, yet her prints yield no information to the authorities.

Bent Double
Copperhead is able to contort herself into seemingly impossible shapes.

Clawed Killer
Metal claws help Copperhead inject her poison into her victims.

DEATHSTROKE

ALSO NICKNAMED "THE TERMINATOR," SLADE WILSON IS A MERCENARY FOR HIRE, ONE WHOSE SKILLS CHALLENGE EVEN THOSE OF BATMAN.

An accomplished member of the military's Special Forces, Slade Wilson agreed to undergo a program that dramatically altered his physical and mental abilities. He now operates at peak human capacity, if not better, with enhanced reflexes, speed, and stamina. These, combined with his master-level fighting expertise, make him one of the toughest hand-to-hand combatants Batman faces.

MEETING DEATH
Batman first tests his skills against those of Deathstroke when he is interrogating the Penguin aboard the villain's cargo ship. Contracted to kill Batman, Slade interrupts the Dark Knight Detective's impromptu meeting with the Penguin to savagely attack him. Although Batman eventually defeats Slade, who is then imprisoned in Blackgate Prison, the assassin gives him quite a run for his money in an epic fight.

Spoils of Victory
Known to switch out his arsenal as often as Deathstroke varies his uniform, Batman gained his Remote Claw after a battle with the mercenary.

WILSON'S WARDROBE
Deathstroke often changes his uniform based on what is needed for each particular fight. Everything about Wilson's armor is utilitarian—the villain is nothing if not practical. While he usually retains the navy/orange color split on his various masks, his armor fluctuates from slim- and form-fitting to bulky and solid. Deathstroke's arsenal rarely varies, however, as he favors a sword and his trusty collapsible metal staff.

> **"TODAY'S NOT A GOOD DAY FOR ROOKIES."**
> — Deathstroke

Souped-up Soldier
Deathstroke is a formidable opponent—physically he is more than a match for Batman.

LOCKDOWN
In the days before the construction of Arkham City, Deathstroke is again hired to take down Batman. Luring the Dark Knight to the Gotham Steel Mill, Deathstroke employs a group of thugs to wear Batman down and act as bait. When Batman beats those opponents, Deathstroke shoots one of them to coax the Dark Knight into hand-to-hand combat. Batman willingly runs headfirst into Deathstroke's trap, and brings the killer to justice.

Every Trick in the Book
To beat Deathstroke, Batman uses smoke pellets, electrified gauntlets, and even calls down a swarm of bats.

ENEMIES DEATHSTROKE 131

DATA FILE

- **REAL NAME** Slade Wilson
- **OCCUPATION** Mercenary
- **HEIGHT** 6 ft. 5 in.
- **WEIGHT** 225 lbs.
- **EYES** Blue
- **HAIR** Gray

An Eye for an Eye
Deathstroke's armored mask hides his missing eye.

Ammo
Deathstroke's suit holds plenty of ammunition for his weapons.

Advanced Armor
Deathstroke's armor is a mixture of composite plates and scales.

Gauntlets
Deathstroke's gauntlets are armored to help him block attacks.

Fists of Fury
Slade is an expert hand-to-hand combatant.

Handy Tools
An assassin who often kills close-in, Deathstroke must have his weapons within reach at any time.

Suicide Mission
A true professional, Deathstroke gets recruited into the government's Suicide Squad program.

Touch of Death
The hired assassin known as Deathstroke is one of the most evenly matched villains to ever take on the Dark Knight. An enhanced super-soldier, Deathstroke is known in some circles as the "Terminator" and has been offered jobs by mafia heads as well as government officials. Though blinded in one eye, Deathstroke is a consummate professional, with Batman being one of the only targets to escape his sights alive.

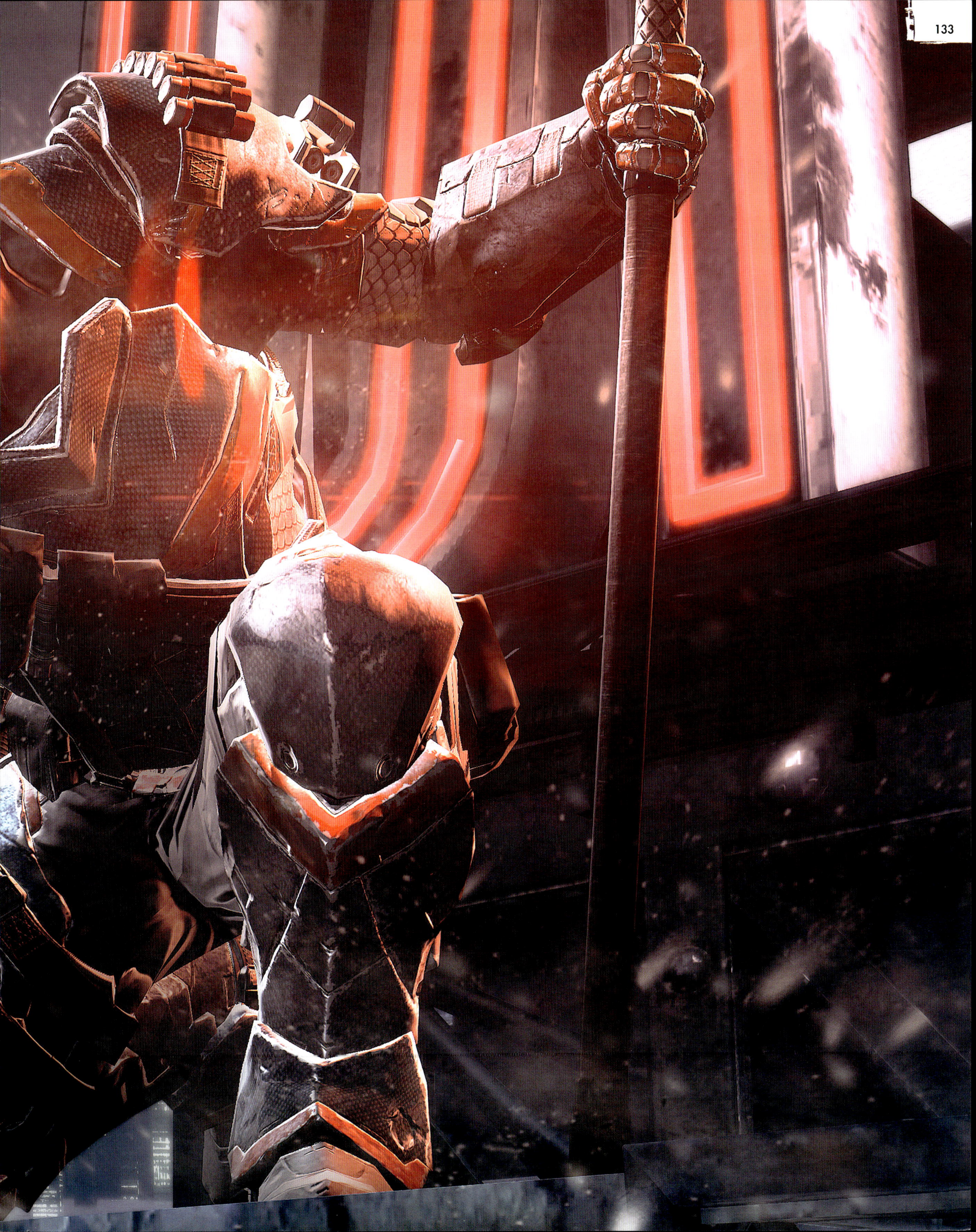

THE ELECTROCUTIONER

WHILE HIS SCARRED VISAGE IS INTIMIDATING, THE ELECTROCUTIONER PROVES TO BE THE ONE-TRICK PONY OF BATMAN VILLAINS.

The Electrocutioner, also known as Lester Buchinsky, has a flair for electronic engineering that would be impressive under any circumstances. Apart from that, however, Lester is just a glorified street tough out to make a name for himself. He earns his living as one of the Penguin's pit fighters, using electric gauntlets to beat his opponents. Ultimately, he is all bark, with very little bite.

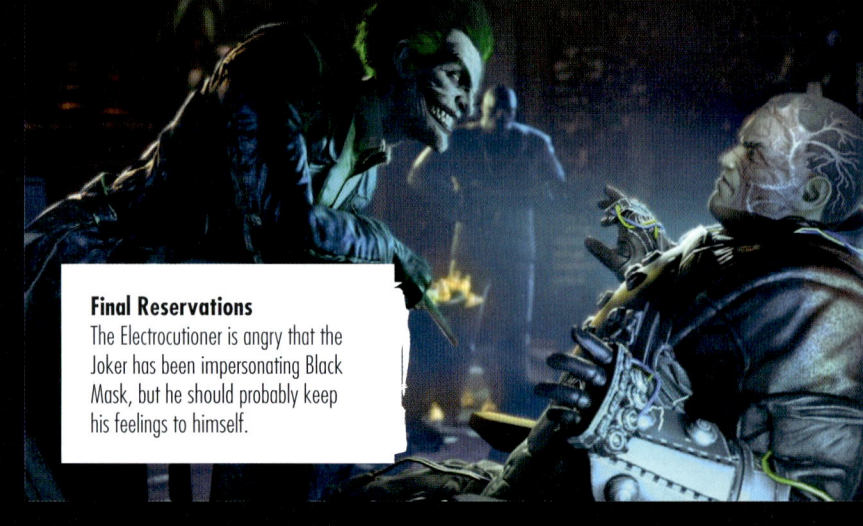

Final Reservations
The Electrocutioner is angry that the Joker has been impersonating Black Mask, but he should probably keep his feelings to himself.

A BEACON FOR BATMAN
While the Electrocutioner's lack of common sense has Batman doubting that he created his powerful Shock Gloves alone, the electrified weapons do make it easier for the Dark Knight to track down the villain. The Electrocutioner's gloves have a distinct electromagnetic signature that Batman follows. It leads him to a meeting with the remaining assassins and with Black Mask—who turns out to be the Joker. The Electrocutioner challenges the imposter, prompting the Clown Prince of Crime to kick his chair out of a high-rise window.

> "I'M-A KILL YOU... I'M-A JUMPSTART YOUR HEART —AND KILL YOU AGAIN!"
> —The Electrocutioner

AIN'T THAT A KICK IN THE HEAD
The Electrocutioner first crosses Batman's path when the Dark Knight is aboard the Penguin's cargo ship, attempting to apprehend the villain. Unfortunately for the Batman, that means fighting a host of the Penguin's goons, and some of his pit fighters, including the Electrocutioner. Although the Electrocutioner is eager to collect the bounty on Batman's head, the villain can't even stand up to one kick from the Dark Knight and the fight ends quickly.

Work Gloves
The Electrocutioner's Shock Gloves help Batman defeat criminals with greater ease, as well as charge up inert electronic equipment.

HAND-ME-DOWNS
After the Electrocutioner dies at the Joker's hands, the ever-pragmatic Batman decides not to let the villain's powerful gauntlets go to waste. He uses them for the rest of his campaign against the Joker, and also afterward on New Year's when tracking down Mr. Freeze. The gauntlets especially come in handy in combat situations, so much so that Batman later designs similar Powered Gauntlets, which he employs during a lockdown in Gotham City in the days before Arkham City's creation.

ENEMIES THE ELECTROCUTIONER   135

Put Up Or Shut Up
Not shy of boasting about his fighting prowess, the Electrocutioner fails to put his money where his mouth is when facing the Dark Knight.

Not a Bright Spark
The Electrocutioner is definitely not the craftiest of villains.

Scarface
The large scar on the Electrocutioner's face was most likely from a mishap with his own gauntlets.

Wired
The Electrocutioner wears a sophisticated harness that seems to work in tandem with his gloves.

DATA FILE

- **REAL NAME** Lester Buchinsky
- **OCCUPATION** Pit Fighter
- **HEIGHT** 6 ft. 4 in.
- **WEIGHT** 225 lbs.
- **EYES** Brown
- **HAIR** Brown

BANE

A VILLAIN WHO PROVES HE IS MUCH MORE THAN MEETS THE EYE, BANE IS BOTH BRAIN AND BRAWN, AND A TRUE MATCH FOR BATMAN.

The legends of Bane are many in the criminal underworld. Hailing from the island nation of Santa Prisca, many believe he was raised in its infamous prison, Peña Duro, a seemingly impossible feat of survival for a small boy. Perhaps due to his legendary status, Bane commands a fierce army of loyal mercenaries, including his right-hand man Bird, who would all lay down their lives for their leader.

BATTLE ROYAL

Bane possesses a larger-than-life physical presence and when Batman first encounters him, he towers over the Dark Knight. Although a master brawler and tactician, Bane does have one weakness—his reliance on the super-steroid known as Venom. When Batman first fights the villain at the Gotham Royal Hotel, Bane is using his Venom intermittently, to help boost his strength during the fight. Despite the performance-enhancing drugs, Batman seems to have the upper hand on the villain, until Bane escapes when police helicopters arrive.

▲ **Mindless Rampage**
Luckily for Batman, the TN-1 drastically affects the memory centers of Bane's brain, causing him to forget the Dark Knight's double identity.

TN-1

Batman's next battle with Bane is much tougher. Bane nearly kills Alfred in the Batcave after the villain discovers the Dark Knight's double identity, and Batman has a bone to pick with the mercenary. However, before they fight, Bane injects himself with TN-1, an experimental drug that changes the villain into a hulking brute—even larger than before. Physical force alone isn't an option, and so Batman is forced to use all his cunning to stop the villain.

▲ **Shocking End**
Batman is able to defeat Bane by luring the villain close to the electrified doors of Blackgate's prison cells, and then knocking him into the current.

"NOW DO ME A FAVOR... AND DIE!"
— Bane

FENDER BENDER

When the Joker takes over Arkham Asylum, his plan is to produce an experimental drug called Titan that is essentially a more powerful steroid than Bane's Venom. Without his permission, Bane is injected with Titan, and changes once more into a massive, near-mindless monster. While Batman does his best to take on this giant foe hand-to-hand, it takes the added help of the Batmobile's front fender to knock Bane out of the fight and into the bay.

Titan Hunt
After the battle at Arkham Asylum, Bane attempts to collect Titan samples for himself, even employing Batman's help until the Dark Knight turns the tables on him.

ENEMIES BANE   137

Mask
Bane's mask resembles that of a lucha libre wrestler.

DATA FILE

- **REAL NAME** Unknown
- **OCCUPATION** Fugitive/Criminal
- **HEIGHT** 5 ft. 6 in. (on Venom 6 ft. 8 in.)
- **WEIGHT** 140 lbs. (on Venom 350 lbs.)
- **EYES** Brown (on Venom: Green)
- **HAIR** Brown

The Baddest of Them All
Bane is obsessed with proving that he is the toughest, strongest, and cleverest act around. He views Batman as his greatest rival—hence his hatred for him.

Venom Tubes
Bane's body is often augmented by his Venom intake.

Work Clothes
Relying heavily on utilitarian clothing, Bane cares little for fashion.

Packing a Punch
Bane's fists grow larger with the Titan formula, making his punches even heavier.

Weaponized
Bane's original uniform is filled with small weapons, but his later look relies only on his brute strength.

BLACKGATE BREAK-IN

BATMAN HAS ALREADY FOUGHT THE JOKER AT THE GOTHAM ROYAL HOTEL. NOW HE MUST FACE HIM AGAIN WHEN THE VILLAIN TAKES OVER BLACKGATE PRISON—IT'S A LONG CHRISTMAS EVE FOR THE DARK KNIGHT.

Batman is exhausted from fighting eight deadly assassins during his first brush with the Joker, but there is no rest for the Dark Knight. After being incarcerated in Blackgate Prison, the Clown Prince of Crime manages to take over the penitentiary, inciting riots in the process, and Batman is forced to return there. Before he can take on the Joker, the Dark Knight must fight his way past many highly dangerous inmates—including the super-strong Bane.

◀ **Bad Omen**
The situation doesn't look good when Batman arrives at the prison, but he quickly puts the rioters down and makes his way through the penitentiary to Bane and the Joker.

THE BANE OF BLACKGATE

When Batman encounters Bane on the roof of the Gotham Royal Hotel, he has a difficult time besting the Venom-enhanced foe. As police helicopters arrive, Bane, having deduced Batman's double identity, escapes from the roof, heads straight to Wayne Manor, and attacks Alfred. Batman has to use his Shock Gloves to restart Alfred's heart and save his life.

The next time the Dark Knight confronts Bane, in Blackgate Prison, it is personal. Bane becomes even more powerful during this fight by injecting himself with TN-1, a super-steroid that gives him extraordinary strength. Now a hulking brute, Bane forces Batman to hide in the floor grates and ventilation shafts of Blackgate while he rampages through the prison, destroying anything in his way. To defeat this mammoth foe, Batman has to call on all his ingenuity and stealth, sneaking up on Bane and forcing him into the electrified doors of the prison cells. Despite Bane's vast strength, Batman is the victor.

Knowledge is Power ▶
Batman is pleased to discover that TN-1 erases memories. After their Blackgate battle, Bane has no knowledge of Batman's secret identity.

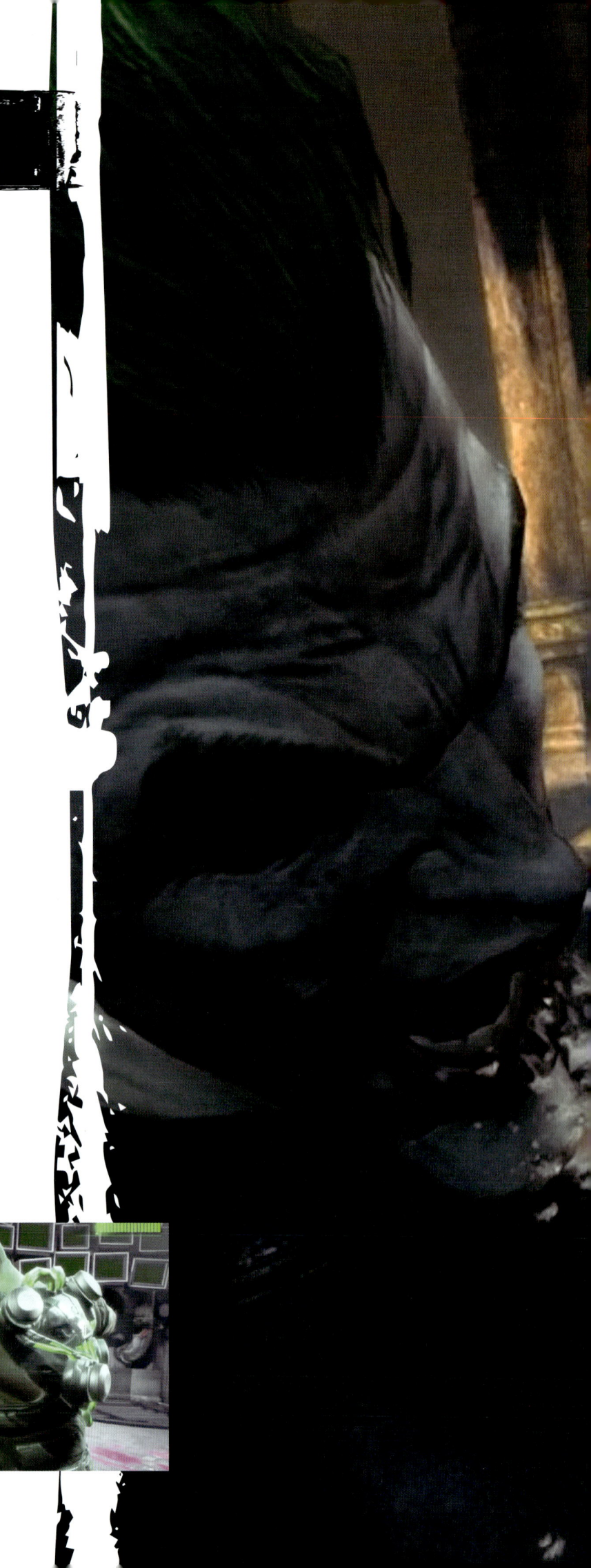

Butt of the Joke
After defeating Bane, Batman finds the Joker in the prison chapel. He takes his frustrations out on his new arch foe with a few well-placed punches and ends the Joker's first reign of terror.

FIREFLY

AN ASSASSIN WHO'S TAKEN THE CREATURE OF THE NIGHT MOTIF TO THE NEXT LEVEL, FIREFLY WANTS NOTHING MORE THAN TO SEE GOTHAM CITY BURN.

Garfield Lynns is a pyromaniac. For evidence of his obsession with fire, one has to look no further than Lynns' own bizarre appearance. His face and body are covered in severe burns from his experimentations with flammable materials. Presumably deriving twisted pleasure from being burned, Lynns refuses to seek treatment for his pain, desiring only to continue setting the world on fire.

THREE OUT OF FOUR
Firefly has a compulsive need to create fire, so when he can combine that with his day job, then that's just icing on the cake for the villain. As one of the assassins who attempts to collect the bounty on Batman's head one Christmas Eve, Firefly successfully draws out the Dark Knight when he places four bombs on Pioneer's Bridge. Batman manages to deactivate three of them, but without Captain Gordon's cooperation, the Dark Knight is unable to stop Firefly from detonating his final bomb.

IF YOU CAN'T STAND THE HEAT...
Despite the severe damage to Pioneer's Bridge, Batman is forced to continue his mission to take Firefly down. Unfortunately for the Dark Knight, the arsonist is just starting to enjoy himself. Surrounded by smoke and flame, Firefly battles Batman from the sky, raining fire from his flamethrower down on him, as well as tossing the occasional incendiary bomb. Clearly the underdog in this fight, Batman has to keep his wits about him and concentrates on using his Glue Grenades and Batarangs against the villain.

▲ **Calling Long Distance**
Batman is both a close-in and long-distance fighter, making it possible for him to fight back against Firefly despite the space between them.

A Hazardous Hobby
After causing Firefly to fall to the ground, Batman lets the villain know in no uncertain terms that he needs to rethink his hobby of choice.

UP IN THE AIR
After dodging Firefly's fiery onslaught, Batman is finally able to secure his Batclaw to the villain and pull him down to the bridge. A few punches later and Batman has fazed Lynns, forcing him to unleash an even heavier barrage of firepower. But when Firefly turns to flee, Batman uses his grapple to tag along with him into the sky, and eventually causes the villain to crash. Grounded, Firefly is no match for the Dark Knight in a fair fight.

> "FULLY FUELED AND READY TO MELT YOU DOWN!"
> — Firefly

What Goes Up...
Firefly's suit is powered by twin propulsion devices.

Hidden Horror
Firefly's flameproof helmet hides his hideous scars.

Winging It
Firefly has crafted wings for himself that allow flight.

Jet Blast
Firefly's winged jetpack emits a purple flame trail.

Boom!
Firefly's highly weaponized suit includes grenades.

Heat Resistant
Like the rest of his suit, Firefly's gloves are fully insulated to protect him from his flamethrower.

DATA FILE

- **REAL NAME** Garfield Lynns
- **OCCUPATION** Pyrotechnics Expert and Mercenary
- **HEIGHT** 5 ft. 11 in.
- **WEIGHT** 165 lbs.
- **EYES** Brown
- **HAIR** None (was Brown)

Hot Stuff
An extremely deadly flamethrower is Firefly's weapon of choice.

Bombs Away
Firefly's impressive pyrotechnic skills make building and using bombs an easy task. Batman must be careful — even the Dark Knight can't outrun an explosion.

Bulking Up
Firefly's suit is advanced, but it is also bulky and limits his mobility on the ground.

141

DEADSHOT

A TRAINED AND PRECISE MARKSMAN, DEADSHOT RARELY MISSES A SHOT, MAKING HIM ONE OF THE MOST FEARED HITMEN IN ALL OF GOTHAM CITY.

At first glance, it might appear that Deadshot is a man without a conscience, but he seems to harbor an almost suicidal hatred for himself, possibly due to all the heinous acts he's committed through the years. As one of the world's most deadly assassins, he employs 9mm wrist-mounted cannons, and even a sniper rifle on occasion, only missing his mark when confronted by Batman.

CHALLENGE ACCEPTED

Deadshot's appearance may change over years but his near perfect aim remains a constant. Responsible for felling a helicopter in Gotham City, Deadshot gets Batman's attention and challenges the Dark Knight to a battle at the Gotham Merchant's Bank. As crafty as he is deadly, Deadshot doesn't show up to his fight alone. Instead, he brings a heavily armed staff with him.

STRANGE BEDFELLOWS

After Hugo Strange has Arkham City built, he feels the need to silence some of his enemies as well as those who might reveal the corruption going on behind the scenes at the prison. Strange decides to hire Deadshot to assassinate some of these so-called political prisoners, with both Bruce Wayne and Batman on his list. After Batman discovers Deadshot's weapons store and his list of targets, he must rush to save reporter Jack Ryder before he becomes Deadshot's next victim.

▲ **Sweep the Leg**
Luckily, for Ryder, Batman arrives in time to save him from Deadshot. He imprisons the villain after surprising him with an attack from a grate beneath his feet.

SHOT IN THE DARK

Unlike other snipers in Gotham City, Deadshot's incredible marksmanship allows him to actually ricochet his shots in incredible ways. When his men are hunting Batman at the Gotham City Merchant's Bank, Deadshot keeps moving his sight from one thug to another, making it difficult for Batman to take down the killer's personal army. Batman still manages to bring Deadshot to justice, and soon the villain is serving time in Blackgate Prison. That is, until the mysterious Amanda Waller requests his services for her top-secret government program.

A Sight to Behold
Even after Batman takes out all of his men, Deadshot keeps ordering in more reinforcements to keep Batman in his sights.

> "I WAS EXPECTING SOMEONE A LITTLE MORE INTIMIDATING."
> — Deadshot

ENEMIES DEADSHOT 143

DATA FILE
- **REAL NAME** Floyd Lawton
- **OCCUPATION** Mercenary
- **HEIGHT** 6 ft. 1 in.
- **WEIGHT** 193 lbs.
- **EYES** Blue
- **HAIR** Brown

Second Sight
A gunsight is built directly into Deadshot's mask.

Money Talks
A true mercenary, Deadshot wants the bounty on the Dark Knight's head, and doesn't really care who is paying it!

Behind the Mask
The hitman's new mask reveals more of his face.

Seeing Red
Deadshot's costume has evolved into a duller shade of red over the years.

The Big Guns
Deadshot employs 9mm wrist-mounted guns for most of his dirty work.

Double Shot
Taking no chances, Deadshot wears a gun on each wrist.

MR. FREEZE

THE LITERALLY COLD-HEARTED VILLAIN NAMED MR. FREEZE HAS NO SYMPATHY FOR ANYONE ELSE BESIDES HIS DEEP-FROZEN WIFE, NORA.

Despite being forced to live in a protective, refrigerated suit, the scientist-turned-villain formely named Victor Fries spends little time worrying about his own bizarre physical condition. He spends most of his days obsessing over his wife, Nora, whom he has frozen to prevent her dying from the incurable condition Huntington's disease. Freeze will stop at nothing to find a cure for Nora, even if that means aligning himself with the worst type of criminal.

DOUBLE CROSSES TO BEAR
Batman first meets Mr. Freeze when Freeze crashes a New Year's party Bruce Wayne is hosting. After kidnapping Bruce's friend Ferris Boyle, Freeze then double-crosses his partner, the Penguin, freezing the mob boss in a block of ice. As the Dark Knight investigates the case, donning his special Extreme Environment suit to do so, he discovers that Freeze's condition has been caused by Boyle, when the wealthy businessman—and Fries' employer—attacked Fries during an argument in Fries' lab.

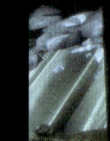

PUTTING FREEZE ON ICE
While Batman defeats Mr. Freeze, he does so with a heavy heart, realizing that Victor Fries has been motivated by trying to cure his wife. Ferris Boyle, Fries' boss at GothCorp, wants Freeze to focus his genius on weapons technology, despite an earlier agreement to the contrary. Batman is forced to take down Mr. Freeze when he seeks out Boyle for revenge. Freeze is later imprisoned in a special refrigerated cell in Arkham Asylum.

▲ The Cooler
Mr. Freeze's cryosuit is weaponized and gives the villain enhanced strength. When imprisoned in Arkham, Freeze is forced to live in a refrigerated cell without his suit.

"LEAVE MY WIFE OUT OF THIS, BATMAN!"
— Mr. Freeze

The Suit's Weak Spot
Mr. Freeze's suit gives him enhanced strength. To defeat him, Batman must smash the protective dome around his head.

FROZEN ASSET
Batman later clashes with Mr. Freeze inside Arkham City. Freeze has been hired by the Joker to find a cure for the Titan-based poison in the Clown Prince of Crime's blood, and Batman visits Freeze to obtain the cure for himself. After Batman saves the glacial villain from the Penguin's clutches, Freeze gives the Dark Knight valuable information to help find a cure. However, Freeze later turns on Batman, forcing the hero to defeat the powerful villain with his customary ingenuity.

ENEMIES MR. FREEZE

Reinforced Helmet
Freeze has learned to put more armor on his helmet since his first brush with the Batman.

Freeze Gun
Using advanced cryogenics, Freeze has weaponized his technology, despite never wanting to.

DATA FILE
- **REAL NAME** Dr. Victor Fries
- **OCCUPATION** Criminal
- **HEIGHT** 6 ft. 3 in.
- **WEIGHT** 190 lbs.
- **EYES** Blue
- **HAIR** None

Suit Up
Freeze's suit keeps his body temperature below freezing and gives him added strength and durability.

Snow Globe
Mr. Freeze has an affection for snow globes, as they remind him of the tragic fate of his wife, Nora.

Sub-Zero Origins
A mishap with cryogenic technology made scientist Victor Fries unable to survive in non-refrigerated temperatures. This forced him to devise his original Mr. Freeze suit.

Cold, Cold Heart
Willing to sacrifice everything for the sake of his frozen wife, Mr. Freeze is quite prepared to make Batman his enemy. After kidnapping Ferris Boyle, Mr. Freeze secures himself and his captive inside a seemingly inaccessible section of the GothCorp building.

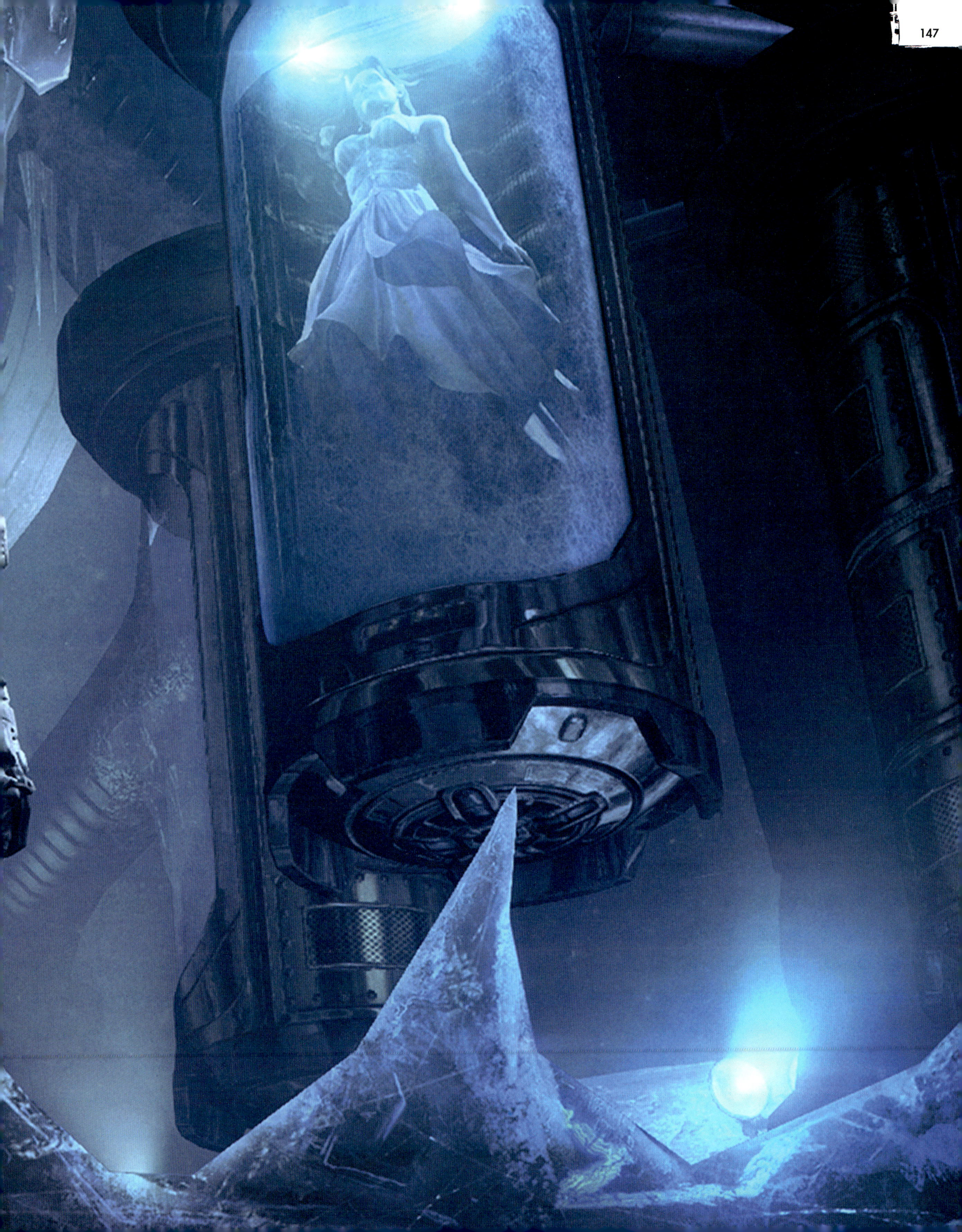

LADY SHIVA

A MASTER OF THE MARTIAL ARTS, LADY SHIVA IS CONSTANTLY TESTING HERSELF, SO IT IS ONLY A MATTER OF TIME BEFORE SHE TESTS BATMAN, TOO.

Unlike the rest of the assassins who attempt to cash in on the bounty offered by "Black Mask" on Christmas Eve in Gotham City, Shiva isn't interested in the money at all. Her real plan is to test the Dark Knight, to see if he is worthy of her master, Rā's al Ghūl, and his mysterious dark plans for Gotham City.

PREYING ON THE INNOCENT

Lady Shiva does her research before heading to Gotham City to challenge the Batman. She knows he spends his time defending Gotham City's innocents, so she plants an empty baby carriage alone in the city, complete with the recorded sound of a baby crying. Batman hears the child and comes to its rescue, only to meet Lady Shiva face-to-face. Shiva informs Batman that if he doesn't participate in her "test," an innocent man will be killed.

Cuts Like a Knife ▶
Bladed weapons are very difficult for Batman to defend himself against, making Shiva and her henchmen extremely dangerous opponents.

LADY OF THE LEAGUE

After discovering one of Shiva's murder victims, Batman saves another of her captives, despite having to fight his way through her ninja assistants. As it turns out, Shiva works for the League of Assassins, and has a very real agenda when it comes to Batman. While she never states it outright, Batman later realizes that Shiva is following the orders of the notorious Rā's al Ghūl, who plans to destroy all of Gotham City.

> "I ADMIRE YOUR PASSION, THOUGH YOUR CAUSE IS FLAWED."
> — Lady Shiva

Whatever It Takes
Shiva seems willing to do anything to test Batman, whether it's creating the illusion of a baby in harm or stringing up a man over electrified water.

PASSING THE TEST

Lady Shiva finally succeeds in luring the Dark Knight back to the lobby of Wonder Tower, the future site of another of Batman's showdowns with the League of Assassins. There she observes his technique as she and many of her highly trained ninjas attack the hero. In the end, Batman is able to hold his own against Shiva, earning a reprieve from her. She disappears in a puff of smoke before he can arrest her for murder, however.

ENEMIES LADY SHIVA

DATA FILE

- **REAL NAME** Unknown
- **OCCUPATION** Assassin
- **HEIGHT** 5 ft. 7 in.
- **WEIGHT** 135 lbs.
- **EYES** Brown
- **HAIR** Black

A Short Cut
Shiva keeps her hair short so her opponents cannot use it against her.

Icy Stare
Lady Shiva's intense gaze is heavy with purpose.

Heartless Smile
Shiva enjoys what she does, even when it involves murder.

Combat Attire
Always functional, Lady Shiva's wardrobe combines traditional styles with modern aesthetics.

Difference of Opinion
Lady Shiva thinks Batman is wrong to try to save Gotham City. To her mind, the city should be destroyed and rebuilt.

ANARKY

THE FACE OF A MISGUIDED REVOLUTION, ANARKY IS ALL TOO QUICK TO TURN TO VIOLENCE, EVEN WHEN FACING ONE OF HIS HEROES, BATMAN.

While he considers himself a voice of the people, Anarky is actually more dangerous than the corruption he seems to be opposing. With an obsessive hatred for corporations and government, Anarky is not averse to putting innocents in jeopardy to make a controversial statement for the city's oppressed. However, it's his charismatic nature and strong youth following that makes him a true force to be reckoned with.

RACE AGAINST THE MACHINE
Anarky first proves to be a real threat to the safety of the citizens of Gotham City when he begins placing bombs in strategic locations throughout the metropolis. Forced to jump through the vigilante's hoops, Batman must to race to each location and deactivate every bomb before its timer goes off. This is made even more difficult for the hero due to the large number of Anarky followers guarding each explosive device.

YOUTH IN REVOLT
With so many devoted followers, Anarky's influence is quickly growing throughout Gotham City. In fact, the villain and his lackeys have planted hidden Anarky symbols all around town, in various hard to reach places. Batman isn't sure if there is any significance to the Anarky tag locations, but just in case he seeks them all out and scans them into his Batcomputer via his cowl.

Tagging the Tags
Batman can only see Anarky's tags with the help of his Detective Vision. They are invisible to the naked eye.

COURTROOM DRAMA
While his planted bombs seem like a test of sorts for the Dark Knight, the real challenge Anarky presents is in the Solomon Wayne Courthouse. Batman finally meets the villain face to face there, and must fight through a host of Anarky devotees in order to bring the dangerous criminal to justice. Even in defeat, Anarky continues to rant his political manifesto, now considering Batman to be as bad as the police and other authority figures in Gotham City.

Force of the People
Anarky puts up quite a fight against the Dark Knight, using Molotov cocktails and even an electric baton against him.

> "YOU THINK YOU'RE A HERO, BUT YOU'RE REALLY JUST A SYMBOL OF HOW LOW THIS CITY'S FALLEN."
> — Anarky

ENEMIES ANARKY 151

DATA FILE

- **REAL NAME** Unknown
- **OCCUPATION** Political Activist
- **HEIGHT** 5 ft. 6 in.
- **WEIGHT** 145 lbs.
- **EYES** Unknown
- **HAIR** Unknown

Hooded Youth
Anarky's hood and overall fashion sense is an indication of his age.

Anonymous
Anarky's mask betrays no emotion.

Symbol of the Revolution
The traditional anarchy symbol adorns the criminal's winter jacket.

Rebel with a Cause?
Anarky's jacket bears a multitude of political pins.

Practicing Politics
Anarky's goal is to remain faceless and start a political upheaval in Gotham City. Fortunately, Batman cuts his career short.

Criminal Gear
Anarky's gloves leave no incriminating fingerprints behind.

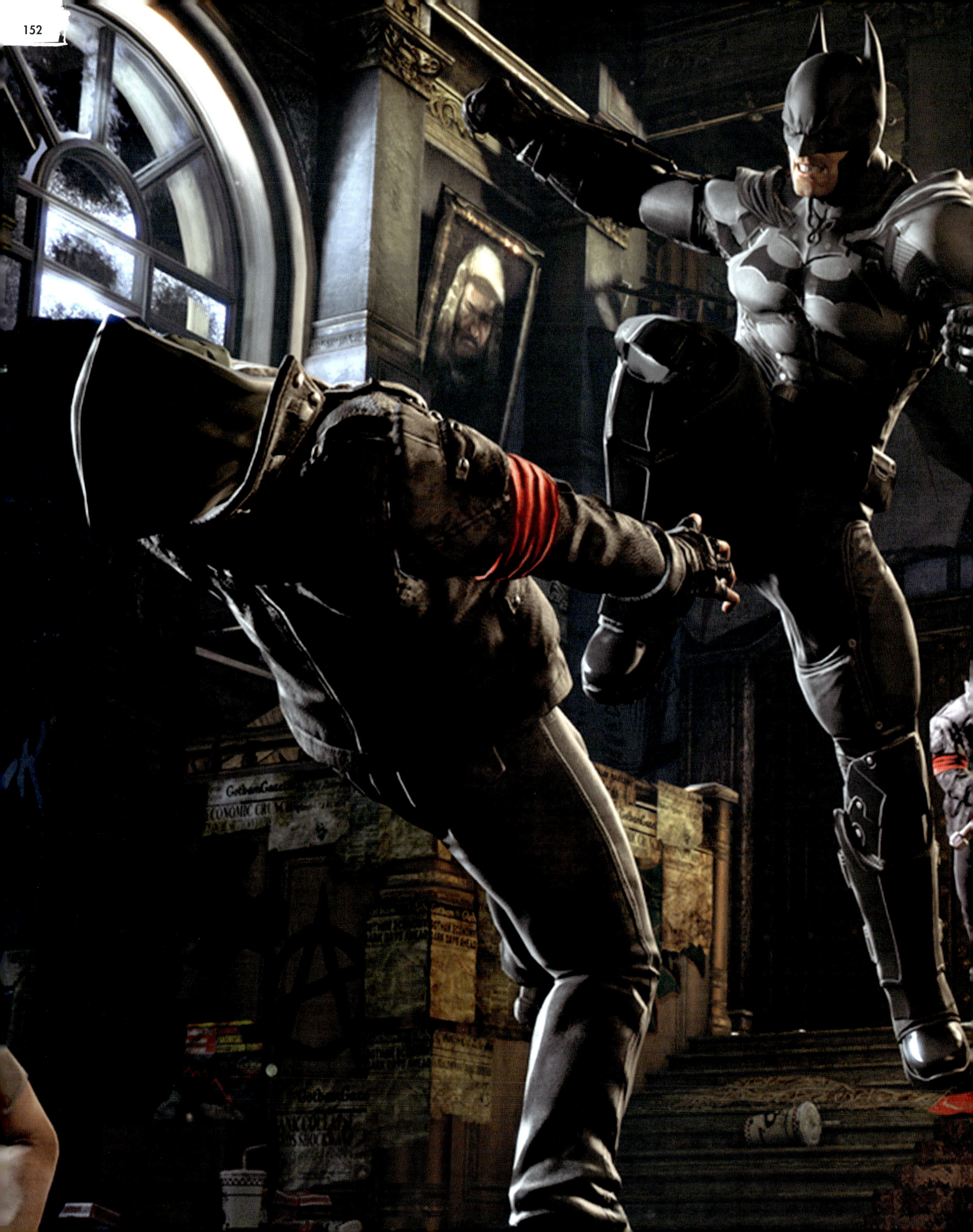

Complete Anarky
Batman combats the cult leader known as Anarky in the Solomon Wayne Courthouse, a formerly prestigious building that is vandalized and tagged with Anarky's appropriated anarchy symbol. Despite his youth, the young political activist causes quite a problem for Batman when the hero is just starting out in his career.

THE MAD HATTER

MAD AS A HATTER AND MUCH MORE MENACING THAN THE CLASSIC CHILDREN'S BOOK CHARACTER, THE MAD HATTER DOESN'T RELY ON SIZE AND STRENGTH—HIS THREAT COMES FROM HIS WARPED MIND.

Jervis Tetch is a man who suffers from several obsessions. Fascinated with the idea of *Alice's Adventures in Wonderland*, Tetch has based his entire criminal persona on Lewis Carroll's character of the Mad Hatter. Taking it one sage further, Tetch is also consumed with a bizarre love of hats. When combined with his technical genius and breakthrough work in the field of mind control, his madness may be dangerously contagious.

TEA FOR TWO
Batman's first encounter with the Mad Hatter involves rescuing a woman named Alice, whom the Mad Hatter has kidnapped. The Dark Knight will later face the Mad Hatter once more inside the walls of Arkham City when the villain again places the hero in a twisted fantasy world, this time through the use of an injection. It seems that after their first violent confrontation, the Mad Hatter has formed a strange obsession with Batman.

"MORE TEA BATMAN?"
The Mad Hatter

White Rabbits
The Mad Hatter's men wear masks that reference the White Rabbit from *Alice's Adventures in Wonderland*.

ACCEPTING THE INVITE
Batman meets Jervis Tetch, the Mad Hatter, after encountering some of his henchmen. Wearing bizarre masks, these lackeys sing an eerie tune while dancing, inviting Batman to a party. They are then electrocuted, and the Mad Hatter tells the Dark Knight via radio broadcast that he has an employment opportunity for him. In the background, Batman can hear the terrified voice of a woman that the Hatter calls Alice. He has no choice but to seek the villain out.

World of Wonder
Leaping through a seemingly wooded terrain and fighting thugs in bunny masks are just some of the challenges the Dark Knight faces under Tetch's influence.

THROUGH THE LOOKING GLASS
Using the ventilation shafts at the Hat Shop to spy on the Mad Hatter, Batman learns that the villain uses some sort of neural interface to control his henchmen. But when he confronts Tetch, the Dark Knight finds himself placed in some sort of hallucinatory trance thanks to the grandfather clock in the room. Battling through a seemingly real-life Wonderland, Batman is forced to discern reality from fiction as he makes his way through a maze of Carroll-inspired madness.

ENEMIES THE MAD HATTER   155

DATA FILE

- **REAL NAME:** Jervis Tetch
- **OCCUPATION:** Criminal, former clothing retailer
- **HEIGHT:** 4 ft. 11 in.
- **WEIGHT:** 115 lbs.
- **EYES:** Blue
- **HAIR:** Red

Price Tag
The Mad Hatter tries to match his look to classic depictions of his namesake.

High-Tech Hat
Oftentimes, the Mad Hatter's mind control stems from a device built into his own hat.

Small Stature
Despite being one of Batman's smallest foes, the Mad Hatter cannot be underestimated.

Distorting Reality
During the time of Arkham City, Batman unwittingly injects himself with a serum created by the Mad Hatter. Waking up at a macabre tea party, Batman faces up to other disturbing hallucinations while wearing a weird bunny mask.

SCARECROW

ONLY HAPPY WHEN FILLING OTHERS WITH FEAR, SCARECROW TAKES EVERY OPPORTUNITY TO LIVE UP TO HIS FRIGHTENING NAME.

Jonathan Crane has been fascinated by the emotion of fear for most of his life. A college professor fired from his job after experimenting on human subjects, Crane soon turned to a life of crime. Indulging his desire to terrify others, Crane began calling himself Scarecrow. He also developed a highly potent fear gas specially formulated to show his victims their worst nightmares.

LURKING IN THE SHADOWS

A creature of the shadows, much like the Dark Knight himself, Scarecrow realizes the value in waiting for the right moment to strike. After terrorizing Batman during the Joker's takeover of Arkham Asylum, Scarecrow keeps his activities hidden during the days of the Arkham City prison. While Batman manages to uncover a secret chamber in a ship floating between Amusement Mile and the Industrial District, hinting at Scarecrow's upcoming plan, he has no conception of the true horrors that await him.

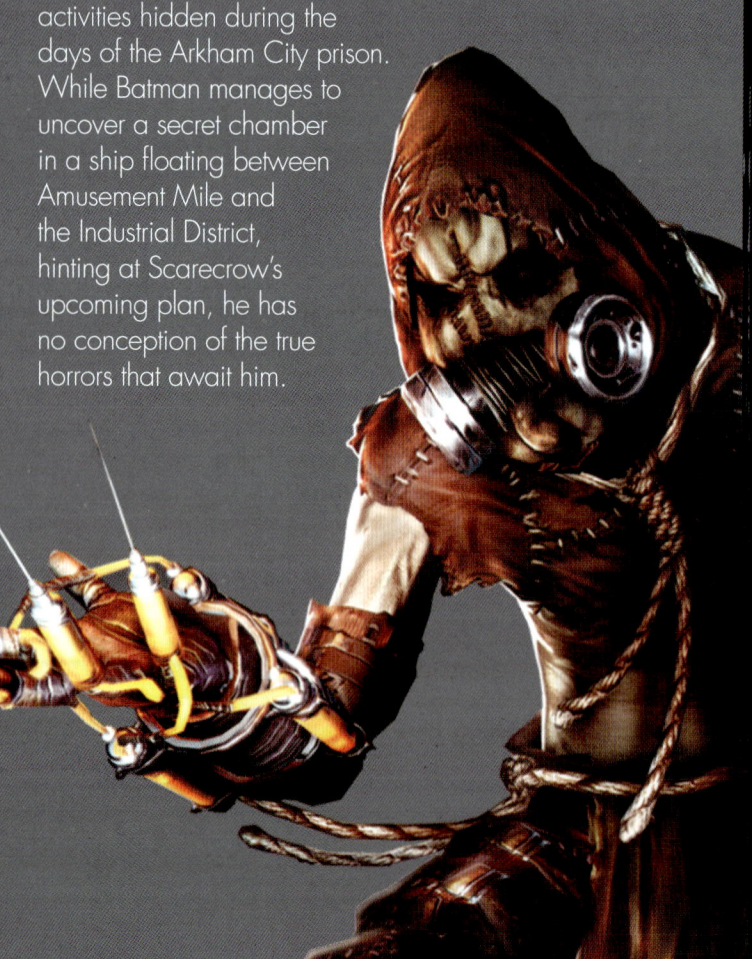

The Bright Knight
Batman is able to overcome the fear toxin in his system and shine a bit of light on Scarecrow's darkness.

SCAREBEAST

In order to confront Scarecrow in Arkham Asylum, Batman has to first fight through the fear-induced hallucinations that the villain's fear gas causes. In Batman's visions, Scarecrow appears as a hulking giant, towering over the ruins of a stone tower. The Dark Knight has to stay in the shadows and avoid discovery as he creeps up behind the behemoth, striking from the darkness and thereby giving Scarecrow something to fear himself.

DARKER ASYLUM

When trying to curb the Joker's takeover of Arkham Asylum, Batman experiences several hallucinations caused by Scarecrow's fear gas. From reliving his parents' death, to discovering their dead bodies coming back to life and haunting him, the fears prey on the Dark Knight. He even hallucinates the death of Commissioner Gordon. As one of Batman's only friends in the world, Gordon's supposed death almost causes Batman to give up all hope.

▲ **Fear Monger**
Scarecrow thrives on chaos, so he seems to enjoy the Joker's takeover of Arkham Island—until Batman catches up with him.

"YOU'RE ALL PART OF MY EXPERIMENT NOW!"
Scarecrow

ENEMIES SCARECROW

Fright Mask
Scarecrow's mask transforms a bookworm into a super-villain.

Hooded Figure
Scarecrow's hood helps to cast shadows onto his face, adding to his sinister air of mystery.

DATA FILE

- **REAL NAME:** Jonathan Crane
- **OCCUPATION:** Criminal
- **HEIGHT:** 6 ft.
- **WEIGHT:** 140 lbs.
- **EYES:** Blue
- **HAIR:** Brown

Fear Toxin
Scarecrow is always equipped with his fear toxin, and always concocting new types of this potent formula.

The Face of Terror
Scarecrow alters his appearance when he partners with the Arkham Knight, taking on an even more frightening guise.

Hidden Threat
Scarecrow's gloves contain sharp needles for injecting his fear toxin.

ACE IN THE HOLE

THE ARKHAM KNIGHT'S FIRST APPEARANCE COINCIDES PERFECTLY WITH SCARECROW'S LATEST TERROR ATTACK ON GOTHAM CITY. BATMAN SOON LEARNS THAT THAT'S NO COINCIDENCE.

After years of dealing with the madman, Batman is used to Scarecrow's tactics. So when the majority of Gotham City's populace flees when Scarecrow threatens to unleash a new strain of his fear toxin, Batman calmly begins to track the unique chemical compounds that Scarecrow is utilizing to manufacture it. With Oracle's help, Batman discovers that Scarecrow's noxious ingredients all originate from one location: Ace Chemicals.

TWO AGAINST ONE

Outside the Ace Chemicals plant, Batman meets the Arkham Knight for the first time. The Knight seems to have a personal vendetta against Batman, but the Dark Knight only views him as a new enemy standing in the way of his objective. Batman manages to corner the Arkham Knight, but the new foe makes his getaway, avoiding an attack from the Batmobile. With the threat of the Knight ended for the time being, Batman confronts Scarecrow, only to be doused with the nightmarish villain's fear toxin.

Private Army
Unlike Batman, the Arkham Knight does not embark on missions alone—he possesses a Militia of henchmen. Fortunately none are a match for the Dark Knight.

Shock to the System
Getting the drop on unsuspecting Militia, Batman makes a dramatic, high-voltage entrance.

CATWOMAN

A CREATURE OF THE ROOFTOPS EVERY BIT AS MUCH AS BATMAN, CATWOMAN IS A THIEF AT HEART WITH A SOFT SPOT FOR A CERTAIN DARK KNIGHT.

Selina Kyle turns her hard life on the streets into an even harder life on the lam when she becomes the costumed pilferer known as Catwoman. While she and Batman share a mutual attraction and countless flirtations, their very different moral codes always come between them, with Selina more often than not ending up on the wrong side of the law.

WE'LL ALWAYS HAVE BLACKGATE

Catwoman's first meeting with Batman is early on in his career, and results in her being apprehended by the police. Little does Batman know that that's exactly what Selina wants. Imprisoned in Blackgate Prison, Catwoman instigates a riot that sees several of Blackgate's worst offenders divvy up the penitentiary into territories. Always with a motive of her own, Catwoman sets up this elaborate scheme to free Bane from his cell for her employer, top-secret government agent Amanda Waller.

◀ **Complex Kitty**
A better person than she admits, Catwoman abandons her stolen goods in order to save Batman when she discovers that the Dark Knight is in danger.

QUIET AS A CAT

Catwoman is very active during the days of Arkham City, seeing a city full of criminals as nothing but a city of opportunity for a world-class thief like herself. She sets her sights on the TYGER confiscated goods vault, knowing that Hugo Strange's private security force has acquired many rare and valuable items. After convincing Poison Ivy to use her plant-based powers to make an entryway for her, Catwoman maneuvers into the vault, and makes off with the loot.

THE CAT CAME BACK

When Catwoman returns to her apartment after saving Batman's life, she barely escapes an explosion set by Two-Face. The villain has stolen some of Selina's things, preventing her from packing up and leaving Arkham City as she planned. Before she can hit the road, Catwoman must first head to the museum and take on Two-Face and his men, and retrieve her things from the split-personality villain.

▲ **Double Cross**
Two-Face had it in for Catwoman mainly because she had stolen a key card from him that helped unlock the TYGER vault.

> **"ANYONE EVER TELL YOU THAT YOU'RE FULL OF SURPRISES?"**
> — Catwoman

ENEMIES CATWOMAN

Cat's Eyes
Catwoman's goggles give her a form of night vision.

Ear to the Ground
Some parts of Catwoman's costume appear to be heavily influenced by Batman's.

DATA FILE

- **REAL NAME** Selina Kyle
- **OCCUPATION** Thief
- **HEIGHT** 5 ft. 7 in.
- **WEIGHT** 125 lbs.
- **EYES** Green
- **HAIR** Black

Tough but Flexible
Catwoman's suit is durable leather with padding underneath to soften the blows of combat.

A Nasty Scratch
Catwoman's gloves come equipped with razor-sharp claws.

Whiplashed
The weapon of choice for the feline fatale, Catwoman uses her whip to attack and climb.

Why Gotham?
Although she gave up on Arkham City, Catwoman has never given up on Gotham City. Unfortunately, that leads to her being taken captive by the Riddler.

POISON IVY

SEDUCTIVE AND BEAUTIFUL, POISON IVY HAS A WAY OF LURING PEOPLE IN WITH HER CHARMS, BUT HER TOUCH IS AS DEADLY AS HER NAME.

Born Pamela Lillian Isley, Poison Ivy was a botanist whose life was turned upside down by an experiment that transformed her into a plant/human hybrid. Able to control plant life and create toxins from her own blood, Poinson Ivy has a distinct tendency to side with plants over humans. She is also able to manipulate others with her pheromones, making men, especially, her slaves.

THE GREEN MILE
When the Joker takes over Arkham Island, Batman encounters Poison Ivy while walking past her cell. Oddly enough, she is one of the only inmates not freed by the Clown Prince of Crime. Batman refuses to let her run free, no matter how much she pleads. Luckily for Ivy, Harley Quinn later wanders by her cell and decides that there's no harm in letting her old friend out into the fresh air.

A KILLER GREEN THUMB
When the Joker injects Poison Ivy with the Titan strain, he hopes that she will become a rather amusing, monstrous plant, but physically Poison Ivy changes very little. She does become exceptionally powerful, however, and causes Arkham Island to be rapidly covered in deadly, mutated plants. In an effort to curb her growth, Batman battles Ivy in the Elizabeth Arkham Glasshouse, fighting off her lethal spores before ending her reign of plant-based terror.

▲ **Spore Subject**
Not only does she use a giant plant to shoot deadly spores at Batman, Ivy causes many more killer plants to sprout up all over Arkham Island.

> "I'LL ENJOY WATCHING YOU SQUIRM."
> — Poison Ivy

GIRL POWER
Poison Ivy and Catwoman have a bit of history, so when Catwoman invades Poison Ivy's home at the Baudelaire shop during the days of Arkham City, Ivy isn't exactly happy to see her fellow femme fatale. In fact, she uses her plant life to attack the female cat burglar, before Catwoman convinces her that they should pool their resources for their mutual benefit. Ivy has chosen to stay out of most of the fighting in Arkham City, but she agrees to help Catwoman break into the TYGER vault in order to retrieve a plant that is "imprisoned" there.

▶ **What's In a Name?**
Poison Ivy creates her base at the Baudelaire plant shop in Arkham City, a fitting location as Charles Pierre Baudelaire was an author who wrote *The Flowers of Evil*.

ENEMIES POISON IVY 163

DATA FILE

- **REAL NAME** Pamela Lillian Isley
- **OCCUPATION** Criminal
- **HEIGHT** 5 ft. 8 in.
- **WEIGHT** 115 lbs.
- **EYES** Green
- **HAIR** Red

Danger Red
Ivy's red hair is in stark contrast to her green complexion.

Green-Eyed Monster?
Ivy's glowing green eyes only add to her seductive control over men.

Healthy Glow
Chlorophyll in Ivy's skin has mutated it to a bright green color.

Free Spirit
Comfortable wearing little or nothing, Poison Ivy would rather embrace her natural beauty.

Planting Ideas
Plants obey Ivy's every command, and she often uses them as decoration.

Clearing the Air
When plant life in Gotham City is threatened by Scarecrow, Poison Ivy teams with Batman in order to purify the city's air.

PROFESSOR HUGO STRANGE

Evidence of Atrocity ▶
Strange conceals all his incriminating patient files in a secret, sealed-off room within Quincy Sharp's office.

A DOCTOR WITH A TWISTED MORAL CODE, HUGO STRANGE'S QUEST FOR KNOWLEDGE MAKES ANY EXPERIMENT WORTHWHILE TO HIM, NO MATTER HOW CRUEL THE PROCEDURE IS TO THE PATIENT.

One of the Dark Knight's worst enemies, Hugo Strange, disappears from the public eye, only to reappear as Mayor Quincy Sharp's personal psychiatrist right before the construction of Arkham City. Strange is intrigued by the criminal mind, but downright obsessed with Batman's. He has a personal interest in discovering the Dark Knight's secret identity—a feat he manages to accomplish where others have failed.

STRANGE HISTORY

While he has spent the majority of his life convincing the world that he's a trained medical professional and even holding self-help seminars on occasion, Professor Hugo Strange suffers from schizophrenic episodes that leave him unable to tell his fantasies from reality. When exploring Arkham Asylum during the Joker's takeover, Batman learns more about the sinister doctor when he stumbles across numerous folders labeled "Strange Files," and discovers the doctor's plans to erect Arkham City hidden in Warden Quincy Sharp's office.

▲ **Under the Influence**
Although he appears to be the man in control, Quincy Sharp is just a pawn in Hugo Strange's twisted game.

THE PUPPET MASTER

When he becomes Mayor Quincy Sharp's personal psychiatrist, Hugo Strange is finally in a position of true power. Using hypnotism and pressure to bend Sharp to his will, Strange is the main force behind the creation of the mega prison called Arkham City that takes up half of Gotham City's real estate. When Arkham City finally opens, Sharp goes public with his association with Strange, but by that point, Strange's past criminal record has been wiped clean.

Following Protocol
Protocol 10 is the order to wipe out the inmates of Arkham City by launching missile strikes on the entire facility from Wonder Tower.

CITY PLANNER

Strange runs Arkham City with an iron fist. He hires his own privatized security force called TYGER to patrol and maintain the prison's security. He has his enemies imprisoned in Arkham City, including Bruce Wayne who speaks out against the prison publicly. Strange's worst offense, however, is activating the mysterious Protocol 10, the order for missiles to be fired at Arkham City in an attempt to wipe it, and Gotham City, off the map. Luckily Batman confronts Strange and puts an end to his insane mission just in time.

> **"ARKHAM CITY HAS BECOME YOUR TOMB, WAYNE."**
> Professor Hugo Strange

VILLAINS PROFESSOR HUGO STRANGE

DATA FILE

- **REAL NAME** Hugo Strange
- **OCCUPATION** Psychiatrist
- **HEIGHT** 5 ft. 10 in.
- **WEIGHT** 180 lbs.
- **EYES** Gray
- **HAIR** Gray

Men of Shadows
Hugo Strange remains a mysterious man until his death at the hands of an even more mysterious figure — Rā's al Ghūl.

Signature Style
Strange always wears his trademark circular lenses.

Symbol of Authority
Proud of his command of Arkham City, Strange is never seen without his Arkham uniform.

Really Doctor?
Strange's medical degree is a subject of controversy.

Sinister Attire
Strange wears black gloves — a bit odd for someone in the medical field.

◀ Eye of the TYGER
Hugo Strange surrounds himself with a private security force called TYGER, making it impossible for the G.C.P.D. to regulate Arkham City.

TYGER, TYGER
Privatized and reporting only to Hugo Strange, the TYGER guards are constantly at odds with both Batman and Catwoman.

PLAYING WITH PAWNS
When Professor Hugo Strange becomes aware of Arkham Asylum Warden Quincy Sharp's split personality and his secret identity as the Spirit of Arkham, he knows he has the perfect pawn to manipulate. Earlier, Sharp had been a huge factor in the reopening of Arkham Asylum, so Strange decided to use Sharp—now the mayor—to campaign for the opening of Arkham City.

ARKHAM CITY

It's a Sign
Arkham City has many signs and warnings, reminding prisoners that escape attempts will not be tolerated.

ONLY A POPULATION LIVING IN TERROR COULD AGREE TO TURNING HALF THEIR CITY INTO A PRISON. BUT GOTHAM CITY IS THAT AFRAID, AND ARKHAM CITY IS THE RESULT OF THAT FEAR.

Professor Hugo Strange has been plotting Arkham City for quite some time. With the help of his secret backer, the terrorist mastermind Rā's al Ghūl, and Strange's unwitting puppet, Mayor Quincy Sharp, Strange is able to manipulate Gotham City's citizens into believing his plan to turn most of Old Gotham into a prison complex is a good idea.

The Dark Knight's City
Despite the new walls erected around the city, Batman knows Old Gotham well, which allows him to find his way around Arkham City quite easily.

OUT WITH THE OLD
The once proud borough of Old Gotham is surrounded by Arkham City's guarded and patrolled walls. Criminals of all walks of life are thrown together, forcing the sane to fight for their lives against the insane. Political prisoners and enemies of Hugo Strange are tossed in with notorious villains who have set up shop in many of Gotham City's formerly famous landmarks.

Night Court ▷
The once prestigious Solomon Wayne Courthouse becomes the domain of the villain Two-Face who creates his own form of twisted justice.

Backing Arkham
Hugo Strange spares no expense when building his prison complex, utilizing the near-limitless bankroll of Rā's al Ghūl.

City of Lights
Security is paramount for Arkham City's TYGER staff. Precautions are taken to keep prisoners inside, and outsiders out.

Inside Man
When Bruce Wayne is arrested for speaking out against Arkham City, Batman is finally able to explore inside the prison's walls.

CITY OF CRIME
Despite being a prison, Arkham City operates very much like a conventional metropolis. Criminals establish their individual businesses, many of which are fueled by illegal shipments from outside the city walls. Gangs roam the streets, picking on journalists or political prisoners who also find themselves locked behind the city's walls. Above them all lurks Batman, patrolling a town full of his worst enemies.

STRANGE CITY

WHEN A LARGE PORTION OF GOTHAM CITY IS TURNED INTO A PRISON, THE LIVING NIGHTMARES OF ARKHAM ASYLUM ARE FINALLY LOOSE ON THE STREETS.

Quincy Sharp has a great deal of influence in Gotham City. His campaigning led to Arkham Asylum being reopened, and his wardenship of that very institution has fueled his rise to power as Gotham City's mayor. Known for his hard stance against crime, Sharp decides to take the next step in his bizarre plan to rid the city of criminal activity. He has walls built around Old Gotham, transforming the area into a huge prison complex, a no man's land soon dubbed Arkham City.

▲ **Freezing Cold Comfort**
Batman is poisoned with the Joker's infected Titan blood while in Arkham City, forcing him to go to Mr. Freeze for help.

A PROGRAM FOR CHAOS

Carefully observing the creation of Sharp's pet project, Bruce Wayne realizes that he needs to speak out publicly against the creation of Arkham City. Wayne's press conference is interrupted, however, by the TYGER guards, a privatized security force in charge of keeping the peace in Arkham City. Wayne is arrested and after meeting Professor Hugo Strange—the mastermind pulling Sharp's strings—is imprisoned inside Arkham City.

Being imprisoned by Hugo Strange isn't completely off Batman's itinerary. In fact, he wants to see the inside of Arkham City. After being interrogated by Hugo Strange, and learning that Strange is aware of Wayne's infamous alter ego, Bruce heads to a drop point, arranged with Alfred, to retrieve his Batsuit.

Despite conflicts with the likes of the Joker, Mr. Freeze, and the terrorist Rā's al Ghūl, Batman meets his greatest challenge inside Arkham City when Hugo Strange activates Protocol 10, a plan intended to raze Gotham City entirely. Batman defeats Strange and his employer, Rā's al Chūl, in a dramatic conflict that only Batman walks away from alive.

The Price of Defeat
After Batman defeats Strange, Rā's al Ghūl kills his employee, disappointed by Strange's failure. Rā's then commits suicide.

Special Delivery
After escaping from the Penguin's goons, Bruce Wayne climbs to the top of the Ace Chemicals building to don his Batsuit, sent via Batwing by Alfred.

RĀ'S AL GHŪL

RĀ'S AL GHŪL TRANSLATES AS "THE DEMON'S HEAD." NO NAME COULD BE MORE FITTING FOR ONE OF BATMAN'S GREATEST ENEMIES.

Like many of the world's most dangerous terrorists, Rā's al Ghūl is convinced that he is fighting for a just cause. Alongside his beautiful daughter, Talia, Rā's al Ghūl wants to save the planet, even if that requires killing most of humanity in the process. Knowing that he is not long for this world, Rā's al Ghūl is also hunting for an heir to continue his merciless mission, and Batman perfectly fits the bill.

TEMPTED BY THE DEMON

Batman and Rā's al Ghūl have a very complicated relationship going back some time. Rā's has lived for over 600 years, thanks to the regenerative properties of the mystical Lazarus Pits, but even with the Pits' restorative effects, Rā's knows that he needs to choose an heir. He sees Batman as the perfect candidate, but even though the Dark Knight is infatuated with Rā's daughter, he would never succumb to temptation and stoop to Rā's level.

Trial by Fire
Talia is worried that her beloved will not return from the Demon Trials, but Batman is determined to lure her ruthless father, Rā's al Ghūl, out into the open.

THE DEMON TRIALS

During the days of Arkham City, Batman's blood is poisoned by the Joker. Working with Mr. Freeze to obtain a cure, Batman lies to Talia al Ghūl, telling her that he wishes to join her father's League of Assassins. Talia believes her longtime love, and leads Batman to a chamber below Wonder City, an abandoned, futuristic metropolis built underneath Gotham City around a Lazarus Pit. There, Batman drinks from a chalice and begins the Demon Trials, a hallucinogenic journey that challenges the Dark Knight's skills to their limits.

> "WELCOME, DETECTIVE. IT IS TIME FOR YOUR FINAL CHALLENGE."
> — Rā's al Ghūl

▲ **Exorcising the Demon**
Rā's al Ghul wants Batman to kill him and take his place as the head of the League of Assassins. But Batman wants no part in Rā's vicious organization.

PASSING THE DEMON TEST

After Batman passes the Demon Trials, Rā's al Ghūl reveals himself to him. The Dark Knight informs his foe that he has no intention of joining him and only wants a blood sample from Rā's to help Mr. Freeze find a cure for his infected blood. Enraged, Rā's grabs his own daughter to use as a hostage. Though Batman has deep feelings for Talia, he doesn't lose sight of his objective and carefully uses a Remote Control Batarang to take out Rā's from behind.

ENEMIES RĀ'S AL GHŪL 171

Swordplay
Rā's is an excellent swordsman and hand-to-hand combatant.

DATA FILE

- **REAL NAME** Unknown
- **OCCUPATION** International Terrorist
- **HEIGHT** 6 ft.
- **WEIGHT** 201 lbs.
- **EYES** Green
- **HAIR** Gray with White Streaks

Inhuman Glare
Rā's eyes glow with insane rage after stepping from the Lazarus Pit.

Armored and Dangerous
The Lazarus Pit can heal his wounds, but Rā's wears armor for extra protection.

Dark Tattoos
For some reason, Rā's' tattoos do not disappear when he emerges from the Lazarus Pit.

The Good Old Days
Rā's often dresses in ceremonial garb, harkening back to his earliest days.

The Demon's Head
Rā's takes his nom de guerre very seriously and uses its imagery in his wardrobe.

A Dead Man's Clue
Rā's al Ghūl is a legend, with his own modern-day folklore. While exploring Arkham Island, Batman comes across a corpse—an answer to one of the Riddler's riddles—hinting that Rā's al Ghūl will one day return.

TALIA AL GHŪL

THE DAUGHTER OF THE DEMON AND PERHAPS THE DARK KNIGHT'S TRUE LOVE, TALIA AL GHŪL HAS A WAY OF GETTING INSIDE BATMAN'S HEAD.

Not even Catwoman has managed to steal Batman's affection the way Talia al Ghūl has over the years. Although second in command of Rā's al Ghūl's League of Assassins, Talia has strong feelings for the Dark Knight. Forced to constantly choose between her father and her "beloved," Talia is a conflicted woman, as dangerous as she is beautiful.

Loving the Bat
Talia has a soft spot for Batman, so when her assassins get the best of him in Wonder City, she calls them off.

LIKE A BLOODHOUND
When Batman wounds a member of Rā's al Ghūl's League of Assassins at the museum, he follows her blood trail, knowing she will lead him back to Rā's al Ghūl, the very man he wants to see. As he follows the gruesome trail, Batman contacts Oracle, telling her that the assassin is a member of Talia's elite guard. Hearing Talia's name, Oracle immediately warns Batman to stay focused, knowing that the Dark Knight often lets Talia get in the way of his true goals.

NINJA TRAP
Following his planted tracker, Batman explores Wonder City, an abandoned retro-futuristic metropolis located under Gotham City's Wonder Tower. Constructed around a Lazarus Pit, Wonder City is the obvious choice for Rā's al Ghūl's stronghold. As Batman approaches, he is forced to fight off Talia al Ghūl's elite ninja guard. Weakened and near death, thanks to the Joker's poison flowing through his veins, Batman has a hard enough time staying on his feet, let alone combating a host of skilled fighters.

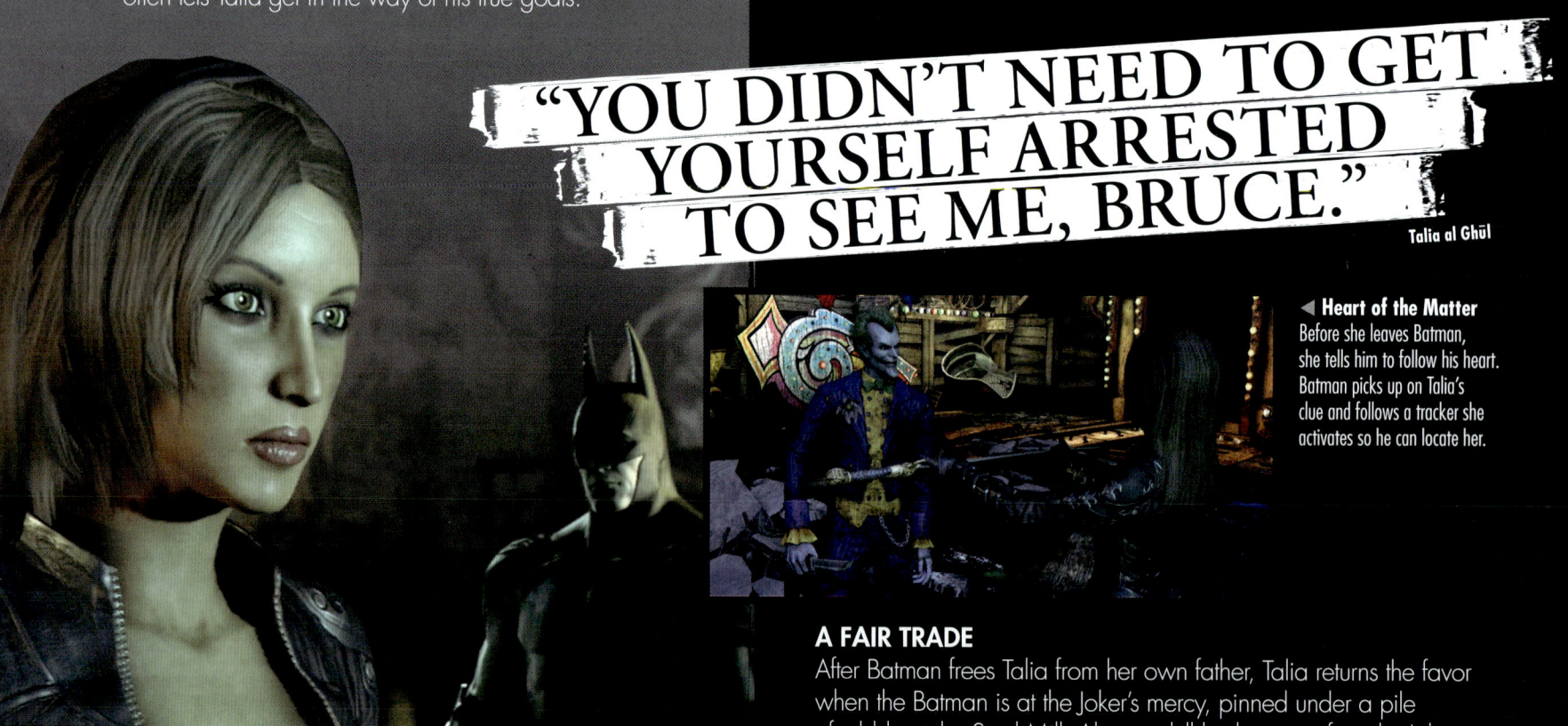

> "YOU DIDN'T NEED TO GET YOURSELF ARRESTED TO SEE ME, BRUCE."
> — Talia al Ghūl

◄ Heart of the Matter
Before she leaves Batman, she tells him to follow his heart. Batman picks up on Talia's clue and follows a tracker she activates so he can locate her.

A FAIR TRADE
After Batman frees Talia from her own father, Talia returns the favor when the Batman is at the Joker's mercy, pinned under a pile of rubble at the Steel Mill. About to kill his longtime foe, the Joker is interrupted by Talia who steps out of the shadows and offers herself in Batman's place. Aware of her knowledge of the Lazarus Pits and seeing the chance of immortality too good to pass up, the Joker takes Talia hostage instead, leaving Batman with a parting kick to the face.

ENEMIES TALIA AL GHŪL   173

Dangerous Mind
Talia is extremely intelligent, albeit conflicted.

Beguiling Charm
Beautiful and well spoken, Talia has a natural chemistry with Batman.

Mysterious Vigor?
Whether the Lazarus Pits have had anything to do with Talia's excellent health remains unknown.

Divided Loyalties
Talia and Batman's mutual attraction poses problems for both of them. She finds herself backing Batman against her father and other villains, while Batman can't let his feelings for her cloud his commitment to the whole of Gotham City.

DATA FILE

- **REAL NAME** Talia al Ghūl
- **OCCUPATION** Heir to the al Ghūl empire
- **HEIGHT** 5 ft. 7 in.
- **WEIGHT** 141 lbs.
- **EYES** Green
- **HAIR** Light Brown

TWO-FACE

THE DEFINITION OF A SPLIT PERSONALITY, TWO-FACE HAS A GOOD SIDE THAT IS CONSTANTLY AT WAR WITH HIS EVIL HALF. UNFORTUNATELY FOR GOTHAM CITY, THE BAD SIDE SEEMS TO WIN MORE OFTEN THAN NOT.

Harvey Dent is Gotham City's golden boy. A district attorney on the side of the angels, Dent's life changes when a gangster tosses a vial of acid in his face, scarring his near-perfect features. With half his face severely damaged, a sinister, darker side of Dent emerges. With the flip of a coin—also scarred on one half by the acid—Dent decides whether to indulge his good or evil half as the criminal Two-Face.

ONE MAN ODD COUPLE

It doesn't take long before Two-Face's crime sprees see him imprisoned in Arkham Asylum. Batman doesn't want to give up hope on his friend Harvey, but he rapidly realizes the depths of Two-Face's mental illness. Even Two-Face's cell in Arkham shows the villain's extraordinary obsession with the concept of duality. One half of the room is neat and organized, while the other half is dirty and vandalized.

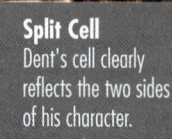

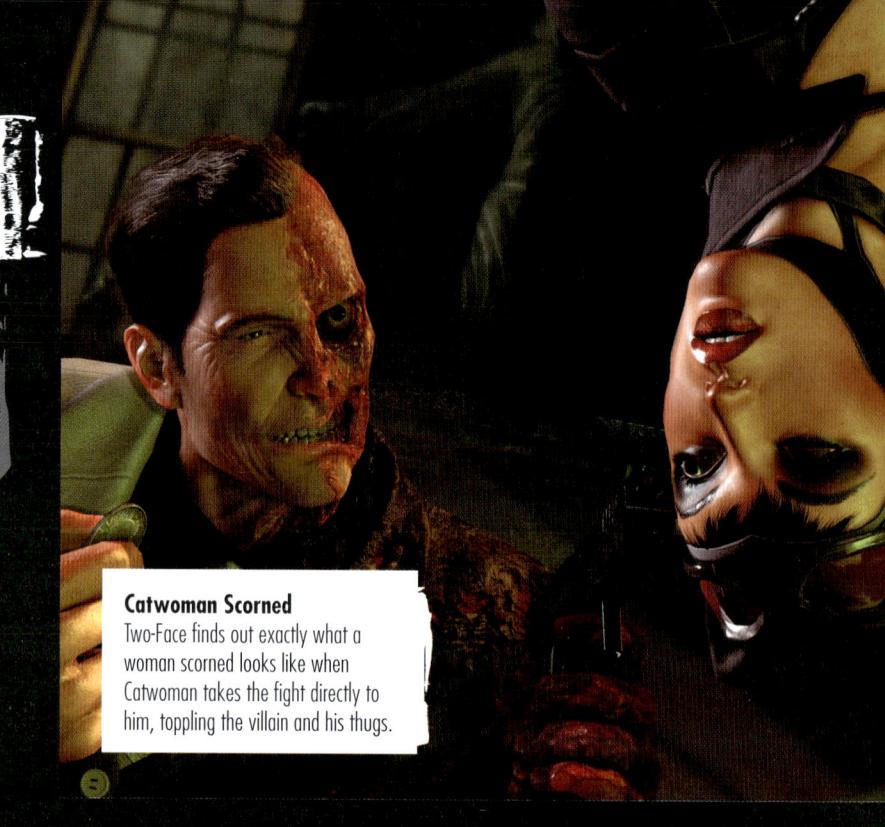

Split Cell
Dent's cell clearly reflects the two sides of his character.

Catwoman Scorned
Two-Face finds out exactly what a woman scorned looks like when Catwoman takes the fight directly to him, toppling the villain and his thugs.

TWO TO TANGO

During the time of Arkham City, Two-Face sets himself up as a crime boss in the Solomon Wayne Courthouse. But while Batman ends up foiling his plans and stopping his activities for a short while, the main thorn in Two-Face's side is Catwoman. Not only does Selina Kyle steal a valuable key card to the TYGER vault from the villain, she also takes him down in a violent confrontation after Two-Face steals items from Catwoman's apartment as revenge.

> ## "NO ONE STEALS FROM US!"
> —Two-Face

TWO-KNIGHT

Two-Face emerges once again to challenge Batman when the Dark Knight already has his hands full with the mysterious Arkham Knight. Although one of Gotham City's biggest crime bosses, Two-Face does a deal with the Penguin to help bulk up his gang's weaponry. Two-Face's appearance is slightly different; always clad in his two-toned suit, he seems to embrace his duality more than ever, and even shows off his scarred arm thanks to a frayed sleeve on his suit.

Robbery By Knight ▶
Up to his old tricks during the time of the Arkham Knight, Two-Face attempts to rob a bank, but fails, thanks to Batman's intervention.

ENEMIES TWO-FACE 175

DATA FILE

- **REAL NAME** Harvey Dent
- **OCCUPATION** Criminal, former District Attorney
- **HEIGHT** 6 ft.
- **WEIGHT** 182 lbs.
- **EYES** Brown/Gray
- **HAIR:** Black

Heads or Tails
To decide the fate of his victims, Two-Face uses his former good-luck charm — a "two-headed" trick silver dollar which is also scarred on one side from the acid.

Good Suit
The Harvey Dent side of Two-Face's trademark suit is white, tailored, and clean.

Bad Hair Day
Two-Face's hair was also a casualty of the acid thrown at him.

Eye on the Prize
Nearly all of Harvey's eye socket is exposed.

Half and Half
Two-Face's scarring creates an almost perfect line down the center of his face.

Bad Suit
The Two-Face side of his clothing is burnt and scarred, just like his face.

MR. ZSASZ

A SERIAL KILLER WHO SCARS HIS OWN SKIN AFTER EVERY FRESH MURDER, VICTOR ZSASZ WANTS NOTHING MORE THAN TO CREATE MORE OF HIS SICK TALLY MARKS.

Many of the problems in Victor Zsasz's life are of his own making. Zsasz grew up in a wealthy family, but he lost his money in a gambling incident at the Iceberg Lounge, and soon developed an obsession with murder. A true serial killer, Zsasz is always searching for new victims. After each murder he carves a deep gash into his own flesh as a grisly, permanent record of his kill.

ANSWERING THE CALL
When Batman is busy battling the Joker and trying to unravel the mystery of Arkham City, Zsasz takes the opportunity to strike again. Calling a variety of public phones until he reaches the Dark Knight, Zsasz threatens to kill an innocent if Batman doesn't answer a phone across town within the time limit set by the murderer. While the Dark Knight hates playing along with the killer's sick game, he complies for the sake of the innocent life at stake.

▲ **Calling Long Distance**
Each time he answers one of Zsasz' calls, Batman has to race across town and barely makes the twisted deadline.

Escape Artist ▶
Zsasz has spent much of his life behind bars, but seems to be able to escape with little trouble.

Unexpected Arrival
The only way to save the hostages is to use the element of surprise.

COLD CALLS
After Zsasz makes several phone calls taunting the Dark Knight, Batman is able to triangulate the killer's location. Tracking Zsasz back to his hideout, Batman then uses a variety of ventilation shafts, a makeshift raft, and a few steep ledges to creep up behind the villain and smash through the large glass window between them to take him by surprise. After knocking Zsasz unconscious, Batman cages the murderer, a fitting punishment for a feral animal.

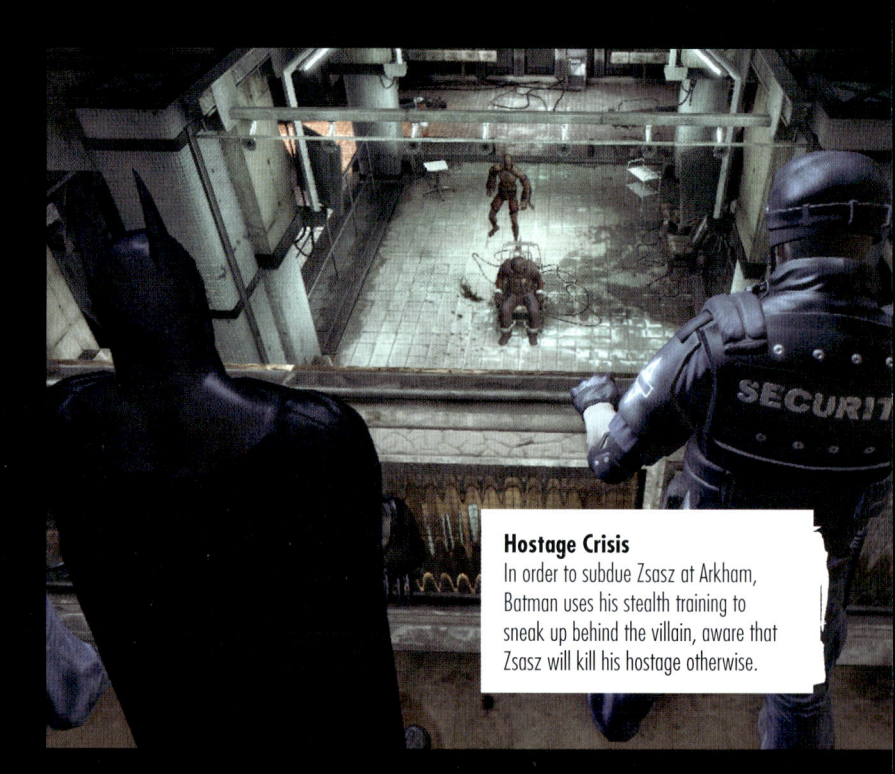

Hostage Crisis
In order to subdue Zsasz at Arkham, Batman uses his stealth training to sneak up behind the villain, aware that Zsasz will kill his hostage otherwise.

LETTING HIS GUARD DOWN
Zsasz kills whenever he has the opportunity, as the need to increase his personal body count is paramount to the murderer. So when the Joker takes over Arkham Asylum, Zsasz uses it as an opportunity to capture a hostage, a guard named Mike. Batman has to creep up on Zsasz for fear of the killer electrocuting the guard. He does this by swooping down from a nearby gargoyle, surprising the serial murderer with an aerial attack.

> "YOU CANNOT DENY ME THE MARK."
> — Mr. Zsasz

ENEMIES MR. ZSASZ 177

DATA FILE

- **REAL NAME** Victor Zsasz
- **OCCUPATION** Criminal
- **HEIGHT** 5 ft. 8 in.
- **WEIGHT** 150 lbs.
- **EYES** Blue
- **HAIR** None (formerly Blond)

Bald Evil
Zsasz has shaved his head in order to display more scars.

Unlocked
Despite Arkham Asylum's attempts to restrain him, Zsasz manages to escape time and time again.

Tally Man
Self-inflicted gashes cover Zsasz's body, one for each of his kills.

Serious Shackles
Arkham Asylum takes no chances when dealing with Mr. Zsasz.

Try, Try, Again
Zsasz is so determined to increase his body count that during the Joker's occupation of Arkham Island, he manages to free himself a second time. Batman is forced to save Dr. Penelope Young from the killer.

No Time to Change
Zsasz rarely changes out of his prison uniform, knowing he'll be back in jail in short order anyway.

SOLOMON GRUNDY

A POWERFUL, UNDEAD MONSTER THAT TOWERS OVER THE DARK KNIGHT, SOLOMON GRUNDY IS RAGE COME TO LIFE, A CREATURE WANTING NOTHING MORE THAN TO DESTROY BATMAN AND ANYONE ELSE IN HIS PATH.

"Solomon Grundy, born on a Monday, Christened on Tuesday, married on Wednesday, took ill on Thursday, grew worse on Friday, died on Saturday, buried on Sunday. That was the end of Solomon Grundy." The old rhyme inspires Cyrus Gold to adopt the name of Solomon Grundy when he dies and comes back to life as a powerful, undead swamp creature. What is more, the Grundy that haunts Gotham City cannot be killed.

SHOCK TREATMENT
Batman encounters Solomon Grundy when he goes to Blackgate Prison to stop a massive riot that enables the Joker, the Penguin, and Black Mask to each take over a different section of the prison. Black Mask overloads the penitentiary's generators hoping to wipe out his rivals, so Batman heads to the sewers below the prison to thwart his plan. It is there that Batman is attacked by Grundy but he manages to escape the villain by electrocuting him and then punching him in the head when he falls to his knees.

The Iceberg Lounge ▶
The Penguin attacks Batman from atop a literal iceberg, before shattering the floor to pit Batman against Grundy.

◀ Basement Terror
The Penguin brags that he found Grundy below the Lounge when he bought the place. He has kept him chained since then, waiting for the opportunity to use the monster's might.

SECRET WEAPON
The Penguin is a crafty adversary. He always seems to come prepared with a back-up plan, and when Batman breaks into the villain's Iceberg Lounge during the days of Arkham City, the Penguin is prepared for him. Apparently, Solomon Grundy has been roaming the sewers of Gotham City after his last brush with Batman, and manages to trap himself below the Lounge. When the Dark Knight gains the upper hand against the Penguin, the bird-themed crime boss quickly evens the odds and forces Batman to take on Grundy.

▲ Down But Not Out
After Batman's battle with Grundy at Blackgate, he tangles with the villain in the sewers once again while hunting down some of the Penguin's thugs.

Big Men
Grundy is one of the largest foes Batman faces, along with Clayface and the Joker (when injected with the Titan formula).

FORCE OF NATURE
Surprising Batman by blowing up the floor beneath his feet in the Iceberg Lounge, the Penguin grins from above as he sets Solomon Grundy free against the Dark Knight. A near mindless creature, Grundy has no qualms about attacking Batman with all his strength. With two iron balls attached to chains at his wrists, Grundy is a virtual one-man wrecking crew. Only by using his quickfire Explosive Gel and all his dexterity is the Caped Crusader able to triumph over the behemoth.

> **"SOLOMON GRUNDY. BORN ON A MONDAY."**
> — Solomon Grundy

ENEMIES SOLOMON GRUNDY 179

DATA FILE

- **REAL NAME** Cyrus Gold
- **OCCUPATION** None
- **HEIGHT** Varies
- **WEIGHT** Varies
- **EYES** Gray
- **HAIR** Gray

Empty-Headed
Grundy is almost completely mindless, especially when enraged.

Coat
Grundy's clothing is as worn and ragged as he is.

Mighty Grip
Grundy's hands are so large, he can literally toss Batman around.

Heartless Killer
Grundy can't be killed; in order to render him inert, Batman must rip out the villain's heart.

CLAYFACE

A SHAPE-SHIFTER AND BRILLIANT ACTOR, CLAYFACE CAN MOLD HIS MALLEABLE FORM IN ANY WAY HE DESIRES, AND CAN BLEND IN WITH ANY ENVIRONMENT.

Basil Karlo is an impressionist and actor known for his work in horror films. Karlo has always worried about his career and when he is replaced as the lead in a movie, he adopts the mask of the main character, Clayface, and becomes a killer. He injects himself with an unstable compound that gives him shape-changing abilities, a clay-like body, and plenty of muscle to stop Batman in his tracks.

HIS OWN CELLMATE

When Batman is searching for the kidnapped Warden Sharp in Arkham Asylum during Joker's takeover of Arkham Island, he comes across a cell that has muddy handprints all over it. The inhabitant of the cell is Aaron Cash, who asks to be set free. When the Dark Knight later returns to that same cell with the rescued warden, the inmate looks like Warden Sharp, and tells Batman that he has rescued the wrong warden. The inmate then transforms into Commissioner Gordon and Batman scans him with Detective Vision. The absence of a skeleton shows that he is actually Clayface.

CLAYFACE'S BIG JOKE

Thanks to Clayface's ability to change his appearance and look virtually identical to anyone he chooses, Batman later encounters the villain and doesn't realize it until much time has passed. When confronting the sickly Joker at the Steel Mill, Batman inspects what appears to be the villain's dead body, only to be pounced on by a very alive, and very healthy Joker. In reality, that healthy Joker is Clayface, who is impersonating his employer.

Blood Brothers ▶
Soon after the "healthy Joker" takes Batman by surprise, the real Clown Prince of Crime injects Batman with his own blood, in order to poison the Dark Knight.

Cold Shoulder
Extreme cold is one of Clayface's few weaknesses. It hardens his form and thus makes it very difficult for him to move.

TWO JOKERS FOR THE PRICE OF ONE

Despite not even being imprisoned in Arkham City, Clayface loves the idea of playing the part of the Joker, and agrees to help the twisted criminal. After Batman discovers that he is the Joker's doppelganger, Clayface attacks the hero with all his usual flair. He molds his arms into large clay hammers and blades, and even turns his entire form into a giant rolling boulder. He is only defeated by the Dark Knight when the hero utilizes his Freeze Blasts.

"THE ROLE OF A LIFETIME."
Clayface

ENEMIES CLAYFACE

DATA FILE
- **REAL NAME** Basil Karlo
- **OCCUPATION** None
- **HEIGHT** 8 ft. 2 in.
- **WEIGHT** 410 lbs.
- **EYES** Black
- **HAIR** None

Brain Power
Clayface has the mind of a brilliant actor and can capture subtle behavioral nuances of those he's impersonating.

Hard Clay
Clayface can harden his form at will, making him very dangerous.

Soft Body
Clayface's malleable body can take on any shape.

Slow Walker
Clayface isn't very fast on his feet, so he relies on extending his form for long-distance attacks.

No Bones About It
While Clayface looks just like the people he impersonates, when Batman scans him with Detective Vision, the absence of a skeleton reveals Clayface for who he truly is.

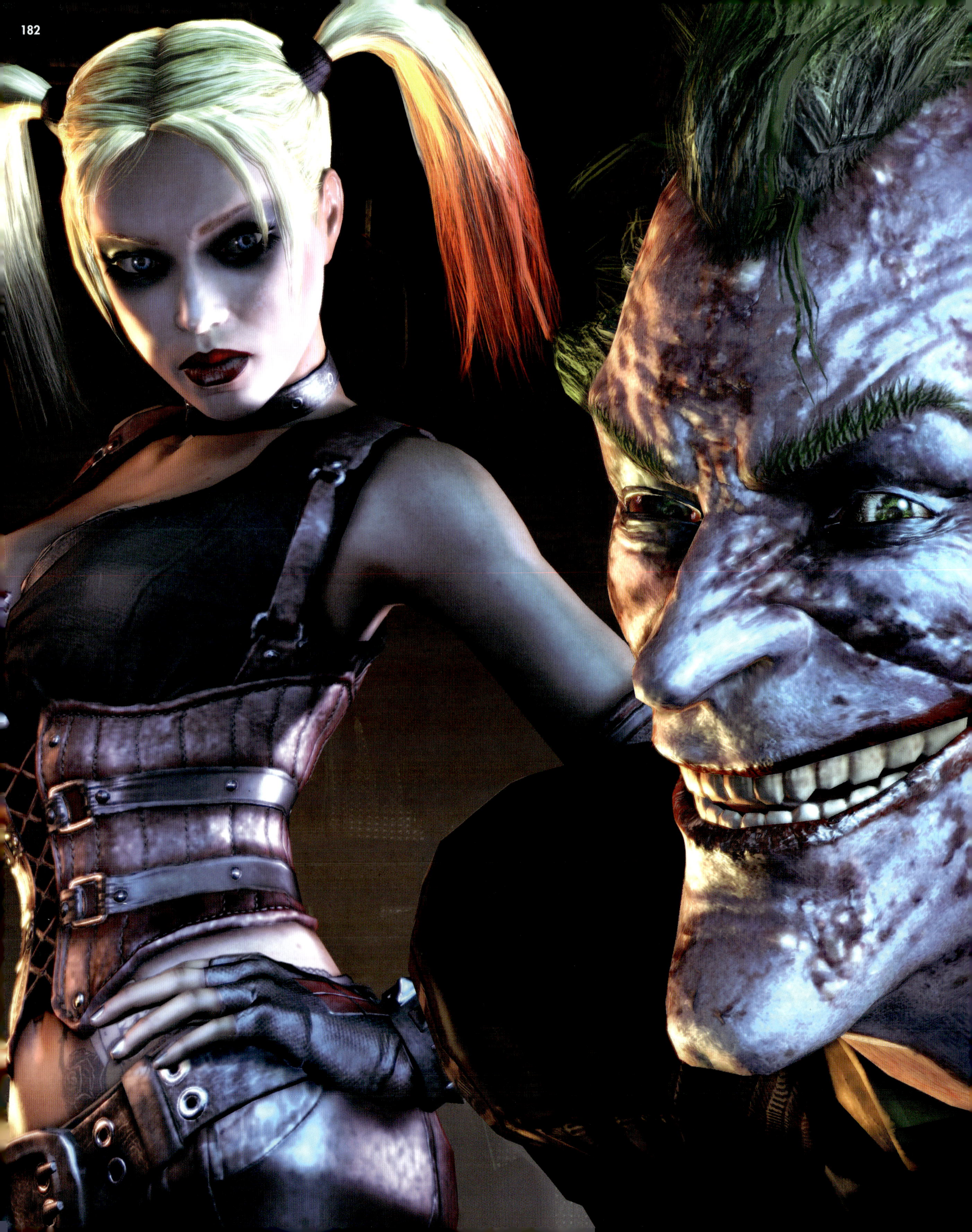

ENEMIES DEATH OF THE JOKER

DEATH OF THE JOKER

ARGUABLY THE GREATEST THREAT IN BATMAN'S ROGUES GALLERY, THE JOKER ALWAYS KNEW HE WAS LIVING ON BORROWED TIME. HE DECIDES TO GO OUT GRINNING.

During the final hours of Arkham City, the Joker is busy putting the finishing touches to what will become his final joke. His body is poisoned beyond hope of a cure owing to the Titan formula he injected when previously trying to take over Arkham Asylum. The Joker knows full well that he is dying, and he is determined to take Batman, his greatest foe, down with him. His body may be frail and rapidly getting weaker, but his mind remains as sharp—and as twisted—as ever.

BAD BLOOD
When Batman first encounters the Joker inside the walls of Arkham City, the villain gets the drop on him and injects him with his poisoned blood, forcing Batman to search for a cure. Batman embarks on a desperate quest that forces him to battle both Mr. Freeze and Rā's al Ghūl.

Things never go smoothly when dealing with the Joker, and Batman soon realizes that there is a twist in the villain's plot when he confronts the Joker at the Monarch Theatre, near the very same alley where Thomas and Martha Wayne were killed long ago. Talia al Ghūl stabs the Joker with her sword, revealing that Clayface has been impersonating the villain at the true Joker's instruction.

Despite trying to keep up appearances via Clayface's impersonation, the Joker is truly dying. After the defeat of Clayface, Batman saves himself by taking a cure for the Titan formula developed by Mr. Freeze. But before he can save the Joker, the Clown Prince of Crime shatters the vial containing his own salvation. The Joker dies as Batman looks on, his story ending in the same location as the Dark Knight's began.

▲ In His System
Batman was infected with the Joker's blood, a moment that would go on to haunt him long after Arkham City's destruction.

Tears for the Clown
Despite the Joker's terrible disease, Harley Quinn stays by his side, loyal to the end.

The End of an Era ▶
Batman carries the Joker's corpse out of the Monarch Theatre and out of Arkham City itself. The prison was no more, just like its most notorious inmate.

OTHER VILLAINS

THE JOKER, THE PENGUIN, AND THE RIDDLER AREN'T THE ONLY THREATS IN GOTHAM CITY. THOUGH NOT AS INFAMOUS, THERE ARE PLENTY OF OTHER VILLAINS WHO PRESENT A REAL DANGER TO THE DARK KNIGHT'S WORLD.

From a man obsessed with the days of the year to loyal lackeys simply following orders, Gotham City is full of dangerous men and women who have their own mad agendas. Left unchecked, these villains could be just as dangerous as any of the more notorious criminals, and each has required the Batman to take time out from his busy schedule to end their criminal campaigns.

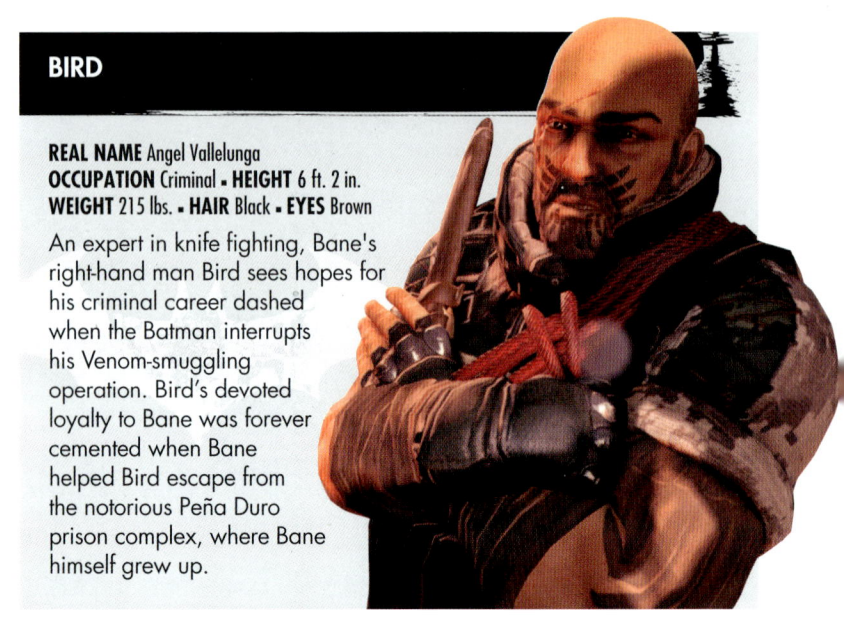

CALENDAR MAN

REAL NAME Julian Day • **OCCUPATION** Criminal • **HEIGHT** 5 ft. 9 in. **WEIGHT** 215 lbs. • **HAIR** None (formerly Brown) • **EYES** Blue

When he first apprehends Calendar Man and takes him to the police, Batman becomes more than just an urban legend. Gotham City realizes that their new protector is for real. Calendar Man doesn't pose much of a threat to the Dark Knight after that night, but he often gives Batman unsolicited advice, tainted by the villain's macabre obsession with the days of the year, and with holidays in particular.

BIRD

REAL NAME Angel Vallelunga **OCCUPATION** Criminal • **HEIGHT** 6 ft. 2 in. **WEIGHT** 215 lbs. • **HAIR** Black • **EYES** Brown

An expert in knife fighting, Bane's right-hand man Bird sees hopes for his criminal career dashed when the Batman interrupts his Venom-smuggling operation. Bird's devoted loyalty to Bane was forever cemented when Bane helped Bird escape from the notorious Peña Duro prison complex, where Bane himself grew up.

MAN-BAT

REAL NAME Dr. Kirk Langstrom **OCCUPATION** Scientist • **HEIGHT** 7 ft. 4 in. **WEIGHT** 315 lbs. • **HAIR** Brown • **EYES** Red

Dr. Kirk Langstrom is a scientist determined to find a cure for his hearing disabilities through studying the genetic makeup of bats. With noble goals, he develops an experimental serum that he applies to himself. The result is a dramatic mutation to his physical from, and he becomes a giant, hulking bat-like creature, a true physical match for Batman.

▲ **Day by Day**
Committed to Arkham for a time, Calendar Man's cell reflects his lifelong obsession with the days of the year.

ENEMIES OTHER VILLAINS

ALBERTO FALCONE

REAL NAME Alberto Falcone
OCCUPATION Criminal • **HEIGHT** 5 ft. 8 in.
WEIGHT 150 lbs. • **HAIR** Black • **EYES** Brown

The son of Gotham City crime boss Carmine Falcone, Alberto doesn't have his father's iron will nor his ability to command respect from those around him. In fact, early in Batman's career, he has to save Alberto from torture at the hands of rival mob boss the Penguin. The Falcone family remains a presence in Gotham City, but is nothing like the criminal dynasty it used to be.

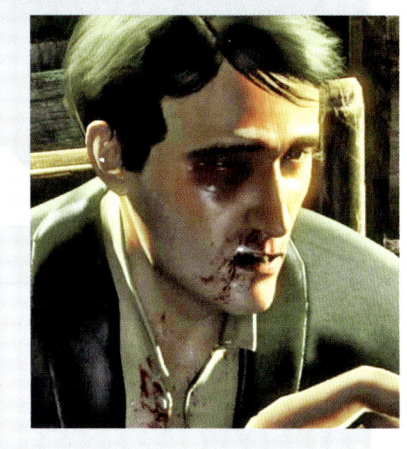

BRONZE TIGER

REAL NAME Ben Turner
OCCUPATION Criminal • **HEIGHT** 6 ft. 3 in.
WEIGHT 240 lbs. • **HAIR** Black • **EYES** Brown

A martial-arts expert with a penchant for using spiked weapons attached to his hands as claws, Bronze Tiger spends much of his time incarcerated in Blackgate Prison for a past crime. There he meets Batman, and decides to help the vigilante when the Penguin's thugs attack him during a prisoner rebellion. He is later recruited into the secret government program dubbed the Suicide Squad.

DEACON BLACKFIRE

REAL NAME Joseph Blackfire
OCCUPATION Criminal • **HEIGHT** Unknown • **WEIGHT** Unknown • **HAIR** White • **EYES** Blue

The leader of a bizarre cult of devoted followers, Deacon Blackfire is a relatively new thorn in Batman's side. Viewed as a powerful shaman by the many unfortunates who follow him without question, Blackfire is extremely charismatic, yet obviously a religious extremist. Batman discovers this first hand when he and Blackfire clash at the Lady of Gotham statue when Blackfire captures journalist Jack Ryder.

MR. HAMMER AND SICKLE

REAL NAME The Abramovici Twins
OCCUPATION Criminals
HEIGHT 6 ft. 10 in. (Mr. Hammer), 6 ft. 10 in. (Sickle) **WEIGHT** 290 lbs. (Mr. Hammer), 300 lbs. (Sickle) **HAIR** Green (Mr. Hammer), Black (Sickle) **EYES** Blue (Mr. Hammer), Brown (Sickle)

The Abramovici Twins were a conjoined sideshow act in a Russian circus when they attracted the interest of the Joker. He had the twins separated and kept one of them on his payroll who became Mr. Hammer, while the other joined the Penguin's gang as Sickle.

▲ **Hammered**
Mr. Hammer was employed by the Joker, who wanted a "right-hand man."

◀ **Cutting Ties**
The Abramovici twins were separated thanks to the surgical skills of Dr. Thomas Elliot (Hush). Sickle's bird tattoos reveal his allegiance to the Penguin.

HUSH

REAL NAME Thomas Elliot • **OCCUPATION** Criminal (former Surgeon) **HEIGHT** 6 ft. 3 in. • **WEIGHT** 225 lbs. • **HAIR** Reddish-Brown • **EYES** Blue (formerly Brown)

Thomas Elliot became obsessed with Bruce Wayne at an early age. Elliot had attempted to kill his parents and only failed due to the efforts of Bruce's father, Dr. Thomas Wayne. Years later Elliot, a gifted but unhinged surgeon, becomes a serial killer. He murders in order to piece together a new face—one that looks exactly like Bruce Wayne's.

▲ **Double Trouble**
Appearing almost identical to Bruce Wayne, Hush gains access to Wayne Enterprises and nearly kills Lucius Fox.

Hammering Home the Point

The Joker takes much joy when hiring Mr. Hammer as his right-hand man. Covered in tattoos that tell of his long and storied past, Mr. Hammer's lack of a left arm is certainly not a disability for the brutal criminal. In fact, he handles himself better than most of the Joker's other employees, posing a challenge for the Dark Knight Detective equal to that of Mr. Hammer's brother, Sickle.

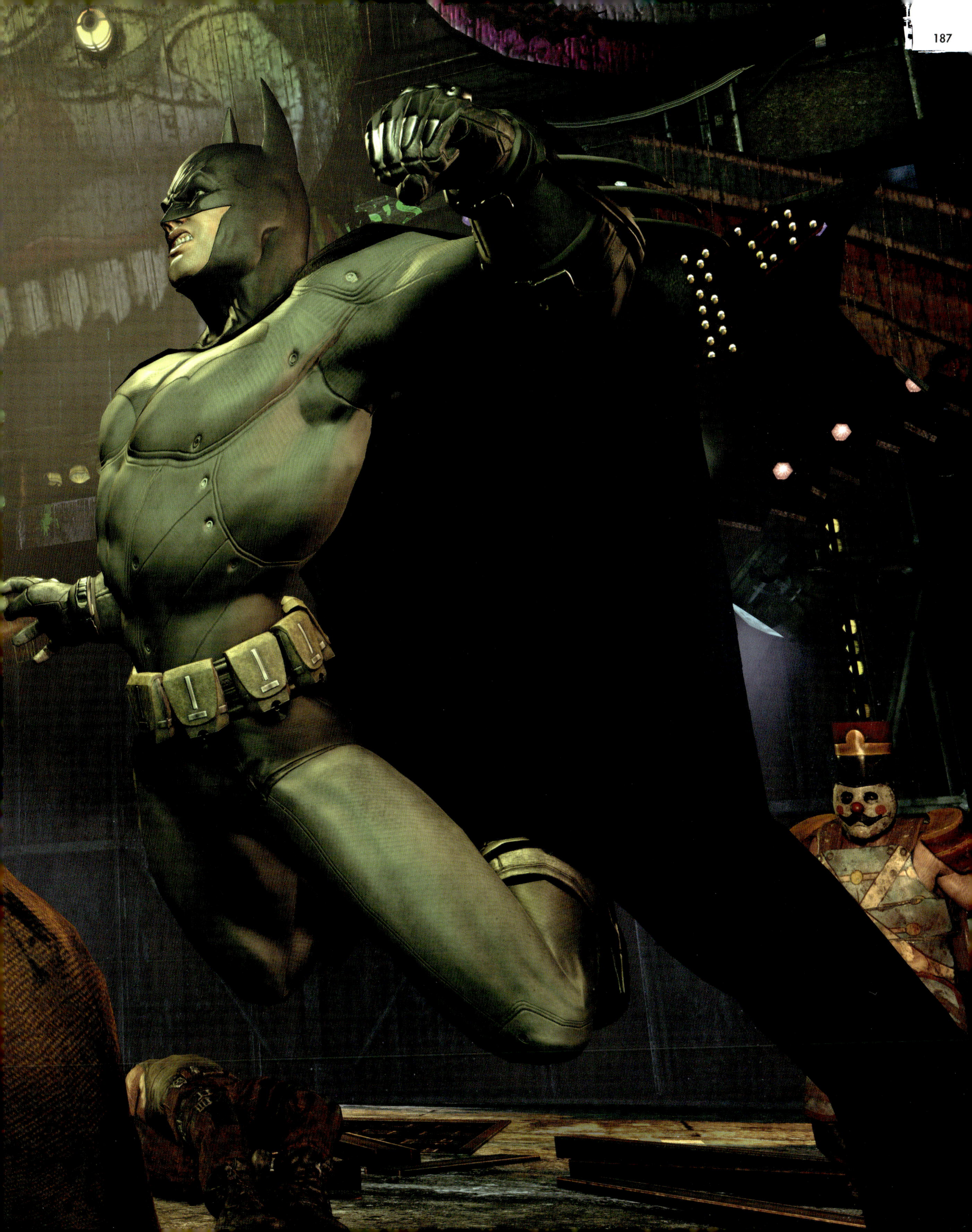

HENCHMEN

A CRIMINAL IN GOTHAM CITY IS ONLY AS GOOD AS THE MINDLESS DRONES HE SURROUNDS HIMSELF WITH. ANY SUPER VILLAIN KNOWS THAT YOU CAN'T HOPE TO TAKE DOWN THE FABLED DARK KNIGHT WITHOUT A SMALL ARMY AT YOUR SIDE.

Batman seems to spend the majority of his nightly patrols fighting through hundreds of disposable employees recruited by one criminal mastermind or another. The majority of the colorful faces in Batman's Rogues Gallery truly believe in the theory of strength in numbers, and the result has been a frequent headache for the Dark Knight, as he confronts a seemingly endless supply of sinister henchmen.

TRACEY BUXTON AND CANDY

The Penguin surrounds himself with beautiful assistants with a mean streak, and Tracey Buxton and Candy are certainly not exceptions to that rule. Despite their intelligence, both women seem to have no trace of a conscience, and quickly fall in league with the vicious crime boss.

◀ **Ruthless Accomplice**
Tracey Buxton met the Penguin while he was living abroad. She has no qualms about shooting someone for her boss.

RICKY "LOOSE LIPS" LEBLANC

An employee of the Penguin, Richard LeBlanc earned his street name from his inability to keep from revealing secrets when questioned by threatening figures like Batman. An arms dealer with connections all over the city, LeBlanc even fancies himself as a comedian.

BANE'S GANG

Perhaps no criminals are as loyal to their boss as those employed by the terrorist and assassin called Bane. His gang consists mostly of rebels from Santa Prisca, Bane's home country, and his men believe wholeheartedly in their leader's personal mission.

THE JOKER'S CLOWN THUGS

It seems the only criteria for becoming one of the Joker's thugs are a vicious streak, a criminal past, and a willingness to wear face paint. On one occasion, the Joker arranges for a mysterious fire to start at Blackgate Prison which causes all his men to be shipped to his side at Arkham Asylum while the penitentiary is rebuilt.

ENEMIES HENCHMEN

PENGUIN'S GOONS

Running the exclusive Iceberg Lounge and his many illegal operations, including an arms smuggling business, keeps the Penguin busy. So busy that he employs numerous thugs and criminals to keep his customers, and enemies, in line.

BLACKGATE PRISONERS

Whether Batman is fighting inmates after a breakout, as is the case early in his career, or encountering them after they are shipped in to Arkham Asylum due to the Joker's machinations, Blackgate prisoners always seem to make lots of trouble for Gotham City's Dark Knight.

TWO-FACE'S GOONS

The criminal Two-Face has an obsession with duality, and that theme is reflected in the attire of the men he employs. Half of them are allowed to show their faces, while the others are forced to hide behind disturbing masks.

HARLEY'S THUGS

After the Joker's death, Harley Quinn adopts mourning attire and sets up base in the Sionis Steel Mill. With the help of her red and black-wearing thugs, she even manages to kidnap Batman for a short time before the intervention of Robin.

HENRY ADAMS

When the Joker is dying from blood poisoned by the Titan formula, the malicious criminal "donates" his toxic blood to hospitals who are oblivious to its dangerous properties. Henry Adams is one of four people treated with the infected blood that slowly causes him to take on the twisted traits of the Joker.

ALBERT KING

Another of the victims infected by the Joker's toxic Titan blood is Albert King. He is a former champion boxer who was nicknamed the "Gotham Goliath," but in spite of his brutish stature, King is just as susceptible to the Joker's infectious personality as the other victims.

CHRISTINA BELL

The final innocent to be caught up in the Joker's poisoned blood transfusion scheme, Christina Bell is a CEO who ends up losing her organized mind, and develops quite an infatuation with Batman as an unwilling henchman of the Joker.

JOHNNY CHARISMA

A true showman by nature, Johnny Charisma has the Joker's tainted Titan formula flowing through his veins. He quickly devolves from a famous TV personality to a clone of the Clown Prince of Crime, displaying the Joker's zaniest qualities.

In the Crosshairs
Gotham City's rooftops often prove just as dangerous as its streets. Batman has stopped countless snipers perched atop buildings, especially during the days of Arkham City. Since a sniper's bullet can penetrate even Batman's armor, the Dark Knight has no choice but to take out snipers first.

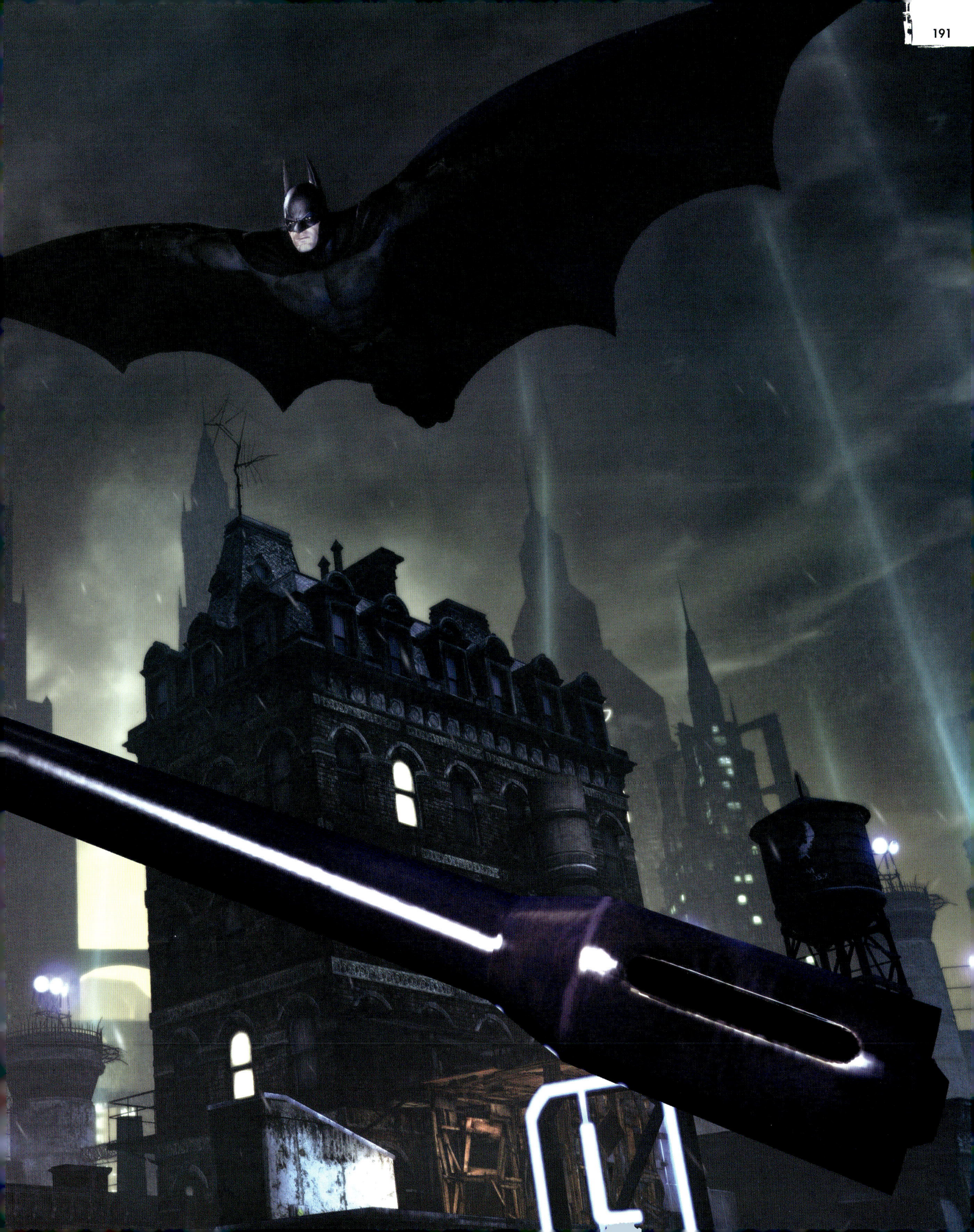

ARKHAM KNIGHT

WHEN BATMAN FIRST ENCOUNTERS THE MYSTERIOUS ARKHAM KNIGHT, HE HAS NO IDEA THAT THIS ARMORED FIGURE IS A LIVING EMBODIMENT OF HIS OWN GREATEST FAILURE.

During one of Scarecrow's plans to terrorize Gotham City, a heavily armored vigilante appears at the ACE Chemicals plant and shows that he is working with the fear-inducing villain. Batman already has his hands full dealing with Scarecrow and realizes that he might just be in over his head—especially when the bat-themed mystery man reveals that he knows many of the Dark Knight's most intimate secrets.

KNIGHT ERRANT
Although Batman doesn't know why at first, the Arkham Knight certainly has a vendetta against him. After revealing inside knowledge about the Batman's methods, the Arkham Knight manages to escape an onslaught from the Batmobile at ACE Chemicals. He later encounters Batman once again when the hero is facing Scarecrow on a zeppelin high above Gotham City.

A KNIGHT OF FEAR
The Arkham Knight is a pivotal player in Scarecrow's plan to release fear gas across Gotham City. The Knight uses a Commander Tank equipped with an experimental Cloudburst machine that causes Scarecrow's gas to blanket the metropolis. Avoiding the toxin, Batman pursues the Knight in the Batmobile, only to have his prized car destroyed by the Arkham Knight's excavator.

▲ **Mistaken Identity**
With the right lighting, the Arkham Knight can easily be mistaken for Batman by most Gotham City citizens.

"KEEP YOUR GUNS TRAINED ON HIM."
— Arkham Knight

QUESTIONS AFTER QUESTIONS
Everything about the Arkham Knight is a mystery to Batman. Why go by a name that pays tribute to the corrupt legacy of Arkham Asylum? Why wear a costume similar to Batman's own Batsuit? Why work with Scarecrow? And why does the villain have a desire to get revenge on the Dark Knight, when Batman has no idea who he is? The Batman encounters the Arkham Knight a few times before learning their shared history.

Darker Knight?
The Arkham Knight's armor has the Arkham Asylum's signature "A" on its chest, causing Batman to wonder what the Knight's connection is to the insane asylum.

ENEMIES ARKHAM KNIGHT 193

DATA FILE

- **REAL NAME** Unknown
- **OCCUPATION** Unknown
- **HEIGHT** Unknown
- **WEIGHT** Unknown
- **EYES** Unknown
- **HAIR** Unknown

Great Minds
The Arkham Knight is highly intelligent, as if trained by one of the world's greatest minds.

Head Gear
The Arkham Knight's helmet seems as sophisticated as Batman's own cowl.

Protected Chest
The Arkham Knight knows that Batman has a heavily armored chest plate, so he takes the same precaution.

Extreme Weapons
Similar to Batman, the Arkham Knight also carries a portable arsenal, although his tools tend to be far more lethal.

Armor
Segmented armor resembles Batman's suit in more than one way.

Gauntlets
Armored gauntlets help with close-in fighting.

Dark Reflection
The Arkham Knight commands an army of unmanned tanks, and possesses a fighting style very similar to that of the Batman.

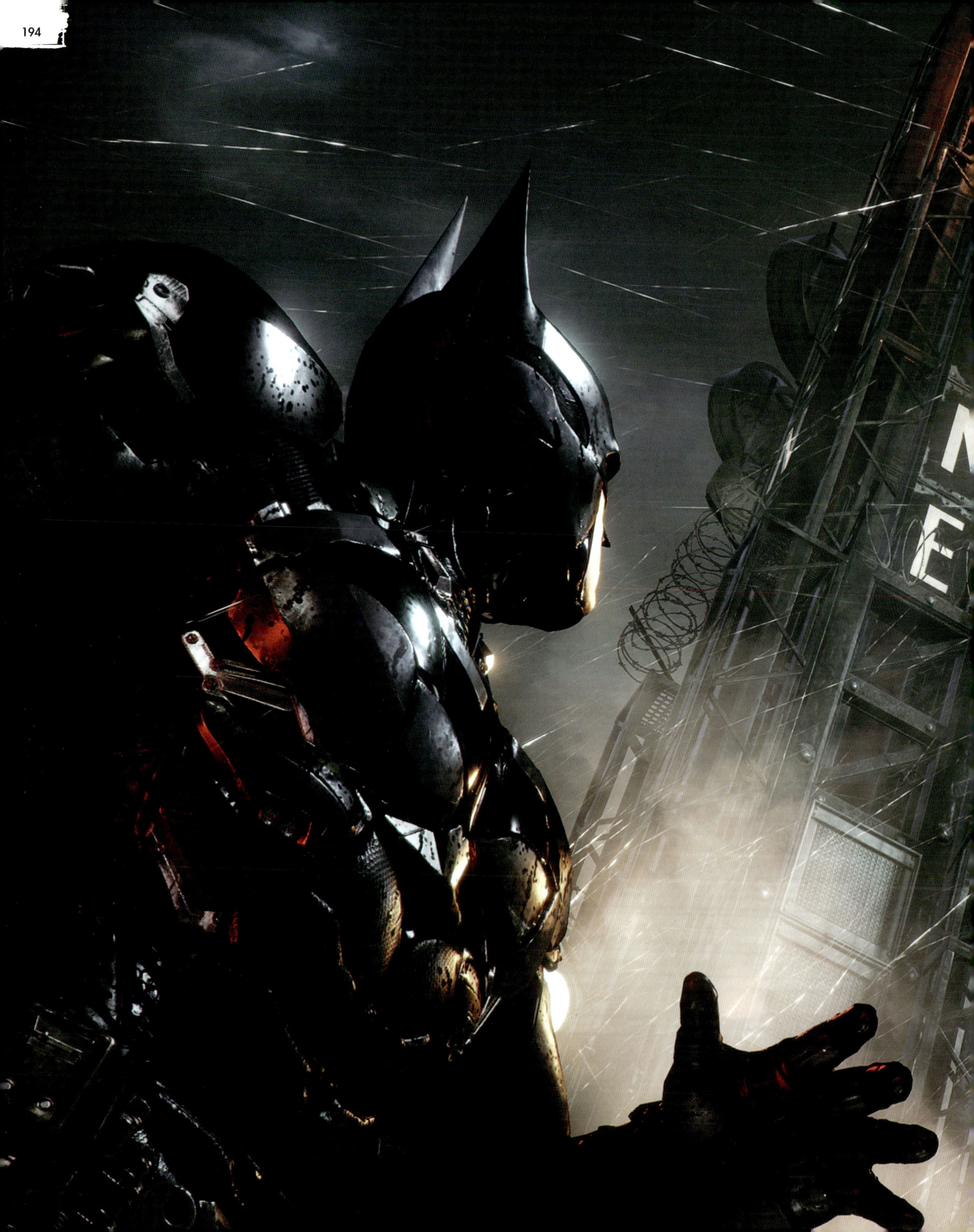

Knightmare
Batman has rarely let himself be ruled by his emotions. Catwoman seems to be able to manipulate Batman's feelings, as does the daughter of Rā's al Ghūl, Talia. But when Batman encounters the mysterious Arkham Knight, he ignores, perhaps deliberately, clues to the Knight's identity. For if the Arkham Knight is who Batman secretly suspects him to be, then that means he has truly failed someone he considers family.

INDEX

Page numbers in **bold** refer to main entries.

A

Abramovici Twins *see* Hammer, Mr.; Sickle
Ace Chemicals **72**, 110, 158–9, 169, 192
Adams, Henry **189**
al Ghūl, Ra's 16, 73, 168, **170–1**, 172, 183
  and Lady Shiva 148
  and Professor Hugo Strange 165, 166, 167, 168
  and Quincy Sharp 107
  suicide 168
al Ghūl, Talia 16, 17, 170, **172–3**, 195
  and the Joker 172, 183
  and Oracle 172
Alice 12, 154
Amusement Mile **71**, 156
Anarky 12, **150–3**
Animated Series, Batsuits 33
Anime, Batsuits 35
Arkham, Amadeus 100, 101, **106**, 107
Arkham, Elizabeth 100, 106
Arkham Asylum 15, 62, **98–107**
  Arkham family 100–1
  and Arkham Knight 192
  battle at 136
  the Joker's takeover 88, 102, 105, 107, 110, **116–17**, 120, 136, 156, 162, 176, 180
  Killer Croc in 126
  locations 102–5
  Mr. Freeze in 144
  Quincy Sharp and 168
  Scarecrow at 156
  staff 106–7
  Two-Face in 174
Arkham Asylum Armored Batsuit 31
Arkham Asylum Batsuit 31
Arkham Asylum Visitor Center 15
Arkham City 48, 62, 69, 70, 71, 73, 96, 104, 120, 122, 160, 162
  death of the Joker 183
  Professor Hugo Strange and 164, 166–8
  timeline 15, 16, 17
Arkham City Batsuit 31
Arkham family 100
Arkham Grounds **105**
Arkham Island 14, 15, 92, 102, 126, 162
Arkham Island Batcave 14, 100, **105**
Arkham Knight 17, 31, **34**, 40, 174, 192–5
  and Alfred 87
  identity of 195
  and James Gordon 88
  and Nightwing 84
  and Robin 82
  and Scarecrow 157, 158, 192
Arkham Knight Batsuit 31
Arkham Mansion 101, **104**
Arkham Origins Batsuit 30, 31
Azrael 15, 33, **96–7**

B

Ballroom (Wayne Manor) 26
Bane 61, **136–9**
  and Alfred 61, 86, 136
  and Bird 72, 184
  and the bounty 124, 125
  and Catwoman 160
  gang 67, **188**
  and the Joker 72
  timeline 12, 13, 14, 15
  and Vicki Vale 78
Bat-Signal 14, 70
Bat-Symbol 21, 60
Batarang 20, **50**, 53, 170
Batcave 13, 26, 27, **28–9**, 74
  Alfred in 86
  Arkham Island 14, 100, **105**
Batclaw **57**, 140
Batcomputer 29, 48, 64, 86, 150
Batgirl **92–3**
Batman **18–23**
  and Alberto Falcone 185
  and Alfred 86–7
  allies 80–97
  and Anarky 150–3
  and Arkham Asylum 100, 101
  and Arkham Knight 158, 192–5
  and Azrael 96–7
  and Bane 124, 125, 136–9
  Batcave 28–9
  Batmobile 40–7
  Batsuits 30–7
  Batwing 48–9
  and Bird 184
  and Black Mask 122–5
  and Blackgate prisoners 189
  and bounty hunters 124–5
  and Bronze Tiger 185
  and Calendar Man 184
  and Catwoman 160–1, 172, 195
  and Christina Bell 189
  and Clayface 180–1, 183
  cold cases 66–7
  and Copperhead 125, 128–9
  data file 21
  and Deacon Blackfire 185
  and Deadshot 125, 142–3
  and Deathstroke 125, 130–3
  and the Electrocutioner 134–5
  enemies 108–95
  fighting techniques 38–9
  and Firefly 125, 140–1
  and Gotham City P.D. 90–1
  and Harley Quinn 114–15, 189
  and Hush 185
  and Jim Gordon 88–9
  and the Joker 110–13, 116–17, 138, 139, 168, 170, 172, 180, 183
  and Killer Croc 125, 126–7
  and Lady Shiva 125, 148–9
  and Lucius Fox 79
  and the Mad Hatter 154–5
  and Man-Bat 184
  and Mr. Freeze 144–7, 168, 183
  and Mr. Hammer 186
  and Mr. Zsasz 176–7
  and Nightwing 84–5
  and Oracle 92–3
  and the Penguin 118–19
  and Poison Ivy 162–3
  and Professor Hugo Strange 164–8
  and Quincy Sharp 168
  and Ra's al Ghūl 168, 170–1, 183
  and the Riddler 120–1
  and Robin 82–3
  and Scarecrow 156–9, 192
  and Sickle 186
  and Solomon Grundy 178–9
  and Talia al Ghūl 170, 172–3, 195
  timeline 12–17
  and Two-Face 174–5
  and Warden Joseph 79
  Wayne Manor 26–7
  weapons 50–65
Batman Beyond Batsuit 34
Batman Incorporated Batsuit 35
Batmobile 10–11, 17, 28, **40–7**, 68, 192
  battle mode 45
  under the hood 44–5
  up close 42–3
Batsuit Chamber (Batcave) **29**, 30, 32
Batsuits 15, 20, 24, 28, **30–7**
Battle Armored Tech Batsuit 31
Batwing 28, **48–9**, 68
  attack mode 49
  drop points 15, 48, 68
  stealth mode 49
Baudelaire, Charles 72, 162
Baudelaire shop 15, **72**, 162
Bell, Christina **189**
Berks, Chucky 67
Beware the Batman Batsuit 37
Bird 13, 72, 136, **184**
Black Lantern Corps 35
Black Mask 53, 66, **122–5**, 128
  at Blackgate Prison 178
  and Bruce Wayne 122
  and Commissioner Loeb 124
  Gotham Church 71
  and the Joker 72, 122, 123, 124, 134
  Lacey Towers 72
  and Nightwing 84, 122
  timeline 12, 13, 14, 17
Blackest Night Batsuit 35
Blackfire, Deacon (Joseph) 17, 74, 78, **185**
Blackgate Prison **71**
  Bane's death at 136

break-in at 124, **138–9**
Bronze Tiger in 185
Catwoman in 160
Deadshot in 142
fire at 117, 188
Harley Quinn at 114
Killer Croc at 126
prisoners **189**
riot at 88, 178
timeline 12, 13, 14, 15
Blüdhaven 84
Bo staff, Robin's 83
Boles, Frank 14, **107**
and James Gordon 88, 107
and the Joker 107
bombs
Anarky 150
Firefly 140, 141
Botanical Gardens (Arkham Asylum) 14, 17, 102, 103
bounty hunters 125
Boyle, Ferris 13, 73, **79**
and Bruce Wayne 79
and Mr. Freeze 144, 147
Branden, Lieutenant Howard 12, **90**
Brightest Day Batsuit 36
Bristol district 75
Bronze Tiger 13, **185**
Buchinsky, Lester see Electrocutioner
Bullock, Detective Harvey **91**
Burnley hit and run 67
Buxton, Tracey 12, 118, **188**

C

Calendar Man 73, **184**
Caltrops 51
Candy 12, 118, **188**
Cane, Alex 67
cane, the Riddler's 121
cannons
Batmobile 43, 45
Deadshot's 142, 143
capes
Batman 30, 59
Robin 83
Carroll, Lewis 154
Carter, Andrew 67
Cash, Aaron 14, **107**, 127
Catwoman 13, 15, 16, 17, 74, **160–1**, 166, 172, 195
and Poison Ivy 160, 162

and Two-Face 160, 174
Charisma, Johnny **189**
Chase, Ian 67
Chen, Dr. 103
Christmas Eve 30, 66, 94, 122, 124, 126, 138, 140
Clayface 17, 54, 102, **180–1**, 183
impersonates the Joker 180, 183
Clock Tower 17, **74**
Cloudburst device 17, 79, 192
Clown Prince of Crime see the Joker
Clown thugs 188
Cobblepot, Oswald Chesterfield see the Penguin
Concussion Detonator **54**
Conroy, Kevin 7, 8
Copperhead 12, 125, **128–9**
Coventry 72
fire 67
Cowl 21, 24, 29, 30, 150
Detective Vision 64
the Riddler hacks into 120
Crane, Jonathan see Scarecrow
Crime Alley shootings 66, **67**
cryosuit, Mr. Freeze's 144, 145
Cryptographic Sequencer 56, **62**

D

Dark Knight see Batman
Dark Knight Returns Batsuit 33
Dark Knight Rises Batsuit 36
Dark Knight of the Round Table Batsuit 34
Day, Julian see Calendar Man
Deadshot 12, 13, 15, 66, 125, **142–3**
and Bruce Wayne 142
Deathstroke 12, 15, 57, 125, **130–3**
Remote Claw 12, 55
DeMarco, John 67
Demon Trials 16, 170
Dent, Harvey see Two-Face
Detective Mode **64–5**
Detective Vision 51, **64–5**, 83, 155, 180, 181
Diamond District 71, 73
Dini, Paul 7, 8
Disrupter 17, **56**, 84
Dixon Docks shooting 67
Dollotrons 75
Drake, Tim 82 see also Robin

E

Earth 2 Dark Knight Batsuit 37
Earth One Batsuit 37
electric baton, Anarky's 150
Electrocutioner, the 12, 125, **134–5**
and the Joker 134
Shock Gloves 12, 13, 61, 134
Elizabeth Arkham Asylum see Arkham Asylum
Elizabeth Arkham Glasshouse 15, 162
Elliot, Dr. Thomas see Hush
Enigma 12, 13, 62, 120
see also the Riddler
escrima sticks 84, 85
Explosive Gel **60**, 122, 178
Extreme Environment Batsuit 31, 50, 144, 147
Extreme Incarceration ward (Arkham Asylum) 102

F

Falcone, Alberto 12, **185**
Falcone, Carmine 185
Falcone Shipping Yard **74**
fighting techniques **38–9**
The Final Offer (cargo ship) 12
Firefly 12, 17, 71, 88, 125, **140–1**
Flag, Captain Rick 13
flamethrower, Firefly's 141
Flashpoint Batsuit 37
Fox, Lucius 16, 24, 44, 74, **79**
and Hush 185
Freeze Blast **54**, 180
freeze gun 145
Freeze, Mr. 13, 15, 16, 31, 54, 56, 63, 72, 73, 102, **144–7**, 170, 183
and the Joker 145
and the Penguin 144, 147
Fries, Nora 54, 144, 145
Fries, Victor see Freeze, Mr.

G

gauntlets
Arkham Knight 193
Azrael 97
Batman 30, 31, 33, 35, 37, 39, 42, 48, **61**
Deathstroke 131
the Electrocutioner 12, 13, 61, 134

Robin 83
Scarecrow 157
Glue Grenades **54**, 140
Gold, Cyrus see Grundy, Solomon
Gordon, Barbara 12, 14, 34, 82, 88, **92–3**, 140
and the Penguin 118
see also Oracle
Gordon, Commissioner James 12, 13, 14, 15, 88–9, 90, 91
and Arkham Knight 88
Batman hallucinates death of 156
Clayface impersonates 180
and Frank Boles 88, 107
and the Joker 88, 117
Gotham by Gaslight Batsuit 33
Gotham Casino 67
Gotham Church 15, 71, 78, 96, 122
Gotham City **68–79**
city society 78–9
locations 70–5
map 69
Wayne family investment in 77
Gotham City Police Department 70
Commissioner James Gordon **88–9**
personnel **90–1**
Gotham Merchants Bank 12, 67, 124, 142
Gotham Royal Hotel 12, **71**, 124, 136, 138
GothCorp 13, 144, 147
GothCorp Building **73**
Grand Hallway (Wayne Manor) 27
Grant, Owen 67
grapnel gun 51, 55, 57, 59
Grayson, Dick 82, 84, 85
see also Nightwing
grenades
Batman **54**
Firefly 141
Grundy, Solomon 13, 15, **178–9**
and the Penguin 178

H

Hamill, Mark 8
Hammer, Mr. 15, **185**, 186
Hanes, Robert 67
Hawkins, Martin "Mad Dog" 100, 101, 106
helicopter crash 66
Hideout, The **75**

Hill, Mayor 14
Hush 16, 79, **185**
   and Bruce Wayne 185
   and Lucius Fox 185

I

Iceberg Lounge 15, **73**, 178
Injustice Batsuit 37
Institute for Natural History 15, **73**, 118
Isley, Pamela Lillian *see* Poison Ivy

J

Jack Ryder Show 15, 117
Janus Cosmetics 122
Jezebel Plaza **71**
   fall at 67
Joker, the 38, 49, 61, 66, **110-13**
   and Ace Chemicals 72
   and Albert King 189
   and Arkham Asylum 102, 105, 107, 110, **116-17**, 120, 136, 156, 162, 176, 180
   at Blackgate Prison 178
   at Sionis Steel Mill 71
   and Black Mask 72, 122, 123, 124, 134
   and Blackgate Prison 138
   and Christina Bell 189
   Clayface impersonates 180, 183
   Clown thugs **188**
   death 17, 110, **183**
   defeat at Blackgate Prison 139
   and Dr. Penelope Young 106
   and the Electrocutioner 134
   and Frank Boles 107
   and Harley Quinn 110, 111, 117, 183
   and Henry Adams 189
   and James Gordon 88, 117
   and Johnny Charisma 189
   and Mr. Freeze 145
   and Mr. Hammer 185, 186
   and Oracle 92
   and Poison Ivy 162
   poisoned blood 15-16, 75, 168, 170, 180, 183, 189
   and Robin 82
   and Talia al Ghūl 172, 183
   thugs 39

   timeline 12, 13, 14, 15, 16, 17
Joker's Funhouse **72**, 110
Jones, Elvis 56
Jones, Waylon *see* Killer Croc
Joseph, Warden 12, 13, **79**
Justice League 3000 Batsuit 37

K

Kane, Bob 7
Karlo, Basil *see* Clayface
Kellerman, Dr. 103
Killer Croc 12, 14, 50, 105, 107, 124, 125, **126-7**
King, Albert **189**
Kirigi, Master 12, 51
Knightfall Batsuit 33
Krank Co. Toys 15
Kyle, Selina *see* Catwoman

L

Lacey Towers 12, **72**
Lady of Gotham Statue 17, 74, 185
Langstrom, Dr. Kirk *see* Man-Bat
Lawton, Floyd *see* Deadshot
Lazarus Pit 16, 73, 170, 172, 173
League of Assassins 16, 148, 170, 172
Leblanc, Ricky "Loose Lips" 12, **188**
Liberty Files Batsuit 35
Library (Wayne Manor) 27
Line Launcher 48, **55**
Loeb, Commissioner Gillian B. 12, 90, 91, 128
   and Black Mask 124
Long Halloween Batsuit 33
Lu, Qing 67
Lynns, Garfield *see* Firefly

M

Mad Hatter, the 12, 16, 32, **154-5**
Man-Bat **184**
Medical Facility (Arkham Asylum) **102**
Miagani Botanical Gardens **75**
Miagani Island district 75
Mike (Arkham guard) 176
Mine Detonator 56
missiles, Batmobile 45
Molotov cocktails 150
Monarch Theatre 17, 24, **71**, 183

Murphy, Bryan 67
My Alibi nightclub 13, 72

N

Nashton, Edward 12, 13, 62, 120
   see also the Riddler
New 52 Batsuit 36
New 52 metallic Batsuit 36
New 52 MK II Batsuit 36
New Gotham 69, 71
Nightwing 17, 24, 82, **84-5**
   and Arkham Knight 84
   and Black Mask 84, 122
   and the Penguin 84
ninjas 16, 148, 172
Noël Batsuit 36
North Refrigeration 17

O

Old Gotham 69, 71
   and Arkham City 166-7, 168
One Million Batsuit 34
Oracle 14, 16, 24, **92-3**
   Clock Tower 74
   and the Joker 92
   and the Penguin 92
   and Robin 82, 92
   and Scarecrow 158
   and Talia al Ghūl 172
Order of St. Dumas 96

P

Panessa Studios **75**
Park Row 68, 71, 72, 73, 96
Pauli's Diner 17, **74**
Peña Duro prison 136, 184
Penguin, the 38, 56, **118-19**
   and Alberto Falcone 185
   at Blackgate Prison 178
   and Barbara Gordon 118
   and Bruce Wayne 24
   and Candy 188
   and the Electrocutioner 134
   goons 169, 178, 185, 187
   Iceberg Lounge 73
   and Mr. Freeze 144, 147
   and Nightwing 84
   and Oracle 92
   and Ricky "Loose Lips" Leblanc 188
   and Sickle 185
   and Solomon Grundy 178

   timeline 12, 13, 14, 15, 17
   and Tracey Buxton 188
   and Two-Face 174
Penitentiary (Arkham Asylum) **102**
Pennyworth, Alfred 31, 66, **86-7**, 88, 128, 147
   and Arkham Knight 87
   and Bane 61, 86, 136, 138
   and Bruce Wayne 24, 86
   timeline 12, 13, 16
Pinkney, Cyrus 15, 77, **79**
Pinkney Orphanage **74**
Pioneers Bridge 13, **71**, 88, 140
Poison Ivy **162-3**
   Baudelaire 72
   Botanical Gardens 75, 103
   and Catwoman 160, 162
   and Harley Quinn 162
   and Scarecrow 163
   timeline 14, 15, 16, 17
Pretty Dolls Parlor **75**
Protocol 10 15, 16, 164, 168
Protocol 11 16
Pyg, Professor 75

Q

Quinn, Harley 33, 63, **114-15**
   and the Joker 110, 111, 117, 183
   and Poison Ivy 162
   Sionis Steel Mill 71
   thugs 189
   timeline 14, 15, 16, 17
Quinzel, Dr. Harleen 12, 114
   see also Quinn, Harley

R

Ramo, Nate 67
Red Hood 72, 82, 110
Red Son Batsuit 34
Remote Claw **55**, 130
Remote Electrical Charge **63**
Riddler, the 60, 62, **120-1**, 171
   DataPacks 57, 121
   Pinkney Orphanage 74
   timeline 14, 17
Riley, Horace 67
Riot Suppressor 45
Robin 17, 24, 60, 72, **82-3**
   and Arkham Knight 82
   and Harley Quinn 189
   and the Joker 82

and Oracle 82, 92
Rodriguez, Clarissa 67
Romano, Andrea 7
Ryder, Jack 15, 17, **78**
   and Deacon Blackfire 185
   and Deadshot 142

S

Santa Prisca 136, 188
Scarecrow 10, 32, **156–9**, 192
   and Arkham Knight 157, 158, 192
   fear toxin 10, 14, 17, 156, 157, 158, 174
   and Killer Croc 126
   and Oracle 158
   Pauli's Diner 174
   and Poison Ivy 163
   and Robin 82
   and Simon Stagg 79
   timeline 14, 17
sewers (Arkham Asylum) **105**, 126, 178
shark (the Penguin's pet) 15, 118
Sharp, Quincy **78**, **107**, 168
   Arkham Mansion 104
   Clayface impersonates 180
   and Professor Hugo Strange 78, 107, 164, 166, 168
   and Rā's al Ghūl 107
   timeline 14, 15, 16
Shiva, Lady 12, 125, **148–9**
   and Rā's al Ghūl 148
Shock Gloves 30, 31, **61**, 63, 134, 138
Sickle 15, **185**, 186
Sinestro Corps Batsuit 35
Sionis, Roman see Black Mask
Sionis Steel Mill 12, 15, 16, 17, 63, **71**, 110, 130, 172, 180, 189
Smoke Pellets **51**
snipers 190
snow globe 145
Solomon Wayne Courthouse 12, **73**, 96, 150, 153, 167, 174
Sonic Batarang 50
Sonic Shock 50
Spirit of Arkham 100, 101, 107, 166
Stagg, Simon 17, 75, **79**
Stagg Industires 75
Strange, Professor Hugo 48, **164–5**

   and Arkham City 142, 164, 166–8
   and Bruce Wayne 24, 168
   and Deadshot 142
   death 165, 168
   and Quincy Sharp 78, 107, 164, 166, 168
   and Rā's al Ghūl 165, 166, 167, 168
   timeline 15, 16
   Wonder Tower 73
Study (Wayne Manor) 27
Suicide Squad program 131, 185

T

Tetch, Jervis see the Mad Hatter
thermal vision 65
Thrillkiller Batsuit 34
thugs
   Bane's 188
   Harley Quinn's 189
   the Joker's 188
   the Penguin's 189
   Two-Face's 189
Timm, Bruce 7
Titan strain 14–15, 103, 110, 113, 136, 162, 168, 183, 189
TN-1 13, 136, 138
Todd, Jason 82, 83
Training Console (Batcave) 29
TV series, Batsuits 32
Two-Face **174–5**
   and Catwoman 160, 174
   goons 189
   and the Penguin 174
   Solomon Wayne Courthouse 73, 167
   timeline 15, 17
TYGER 15, 16, 160, 162, 164, 166, 167, 168, 174

U

Ultra Batclaw 14, 15, 57, 117
umbrellas, the Penguin's 119
Utility Belt 20, 21, 29, 31, 51, 53

V

Vale, Vicki 12, 16, **78**
Vallelunga, Angel see Bird
Venom 110, 136, 137, 138
Vulcan Guns 45

W

Waller, Amanda 13
   and Catwoman 160
   and Deadshot 142
Wayne, Bruce **24–5**
   and Alfred 24, 86
   and Arkham City 168
   becomes Batman 20–1
   and Black Mask 122
   and Deadshot 142
   death of parents 20, 24, 27, 38, 67, 68, 70, 71, 86
   family investment in Gotham City 77
   and Ferris Boyle 79
   and Gotham City society 78
   and Hush 185
   imprisoned 15, 24, 48
   New Year's party 144, 147
   and Owen Grant 67
   and the Penguin 24
   Pinkney Orphanage 74
   press conference 15
   and Professor Hugo Strange 24, 168
   training 12, 24
   Wayne Enterprises 74
Wayne, Martha 26, 68, 71, 79, 87, 103, 183
Wayne, Solomon 73, 77, 79
Wayne, Thomas 26, 68, 71, 79, 87, 103, 183
   and Hush 185
Wayne Enterprises 24, 29, 44, 48, 74, 185
Wayne Manor 13, 26–7, 74, 138
Wayne Tower 74
WayneTech 20, 62
   isolation chamber 17
weapons
   Anarky's electric baton 150
   Batarang 20, **50**, 53
   Batclaw **57**
   Batmobile 43, 45, 46
   Batmobile cannons 43, 45
   Batmobile missiles 45
   bombs 140, 141, 150
   Catwoman's whip 161
   Cryptographic Sequencer 56, **62**
   Deadshot's cannons 142, 143

   Detective Mode **64–5**
   Disruptor 17, **56**
   Explosive Gel **60**
   Firefly's flamethrower 141
   freeze gun 145
   grapnel gun 51, 55, 57, 59
   grenades **54**, 141
   Line Launcher 48, 55
   Molotov cocktails 150
   Nightwing's escrima sticks 84, 85
   Nightwing's wrist darts 84
   the Penguin's umbrellas 119
   Remote Claw 12, **55**
   Remote Electrical Charge 63
   Robin's Bo staff 83
   Shock Gloves 30, 31, **61**
   Smoke Pellets **51**
   Vulcan Guns 45

W

White Lantern 36
White Rabbits 154
Wilson, Slade see Deathstroke
Wine Cellar (Wayne Manor) 27
Wine-tasting Room (Wayne Manor) 27
Wonder City 16, **73**, 170, 172
Wonder Tower 12, 16, **73**, 148, 164, 172
Wonderland 154
Workshop (Batcave) 29
wrist darts 84

Y

Year One Batsuit 33
Young, Dr. Penelope 14, 103, 104, **106**
   and the Joker 106
   and Mr. Zsasz 177

Z

Zsasz, Mr. (Victor) 14, 15, 176–7
   and Dr. Penelope Young 177
Zur En Arrh Batsuit 32

ACKNOWLEDGMENTS

DK | Penguin Random House

Senior Editor Alastair Dougall
Senior Art Editor Robert Perry
Project Art Editor Owen Bennett
Senior Pre-Production Producer Jennifer Murray
Producer David Appleyard
Managing Editor Sadie Smith
Managing Art Editor Ron Stobbart
Art Director Lisa Lanzarini
Publisher Julie Ferris
Publishing Director Simon Beecroft

First American Edition, 2015
Published in the United States by DK Publishing
345 Hudson Street, New York, New York 10014
15 16 17 18 19 10 9 8 7 6 5 4 3 2 1
001-255741-Aug/2015

Copyright © 2015 DC Comics
BATMAN and all related characters and elements
are trademarks of and © DC Comics.
WB SHIELD: TM & © Warner Bros Entertainment Inc.
(s15)

Batman created by Bob Kane

DORL31385

Page design copyright © 2015 Dorling Kindersley Limited
A Penguin Random House Company

All rights reserved.
Without limiting the rights under the copyright reserved above, no part of
this publication may be reproduced, stored in or introduced into a retrieval system,
or transmitted, in any form, or by any means (electronic, mechanical, photocopying,
recording, or otherwise), without the prior written permission of the copyright owner.
Published in Great Britain by Dorling Kindersley Limited.

A catalog record for this book is available
from the Library of Congress.

ISBN: 978-1-4654-2827-1

DK books are available at special discounts when purchased in bulk for sales
promotions, premiums, fund-raising, or educational use. For details, contact:
DK Publishing Special Markets, 345 Hudson Street, New York, New York 10014
SpecialSales@dk.com

Printed and bound in China

The publishers would like to thank the following for their help: Elizabeth Seminario, Matthew Mizutani,
Ames Kirshen, Craig Mitchell, and Ernest Zamora from Warner Bros. Interactive Entertainment,
and the team at Rocksteady.

A WORLD OF IDEAS:
SEE ALL THERE IS TO KNOW
www.dk.com

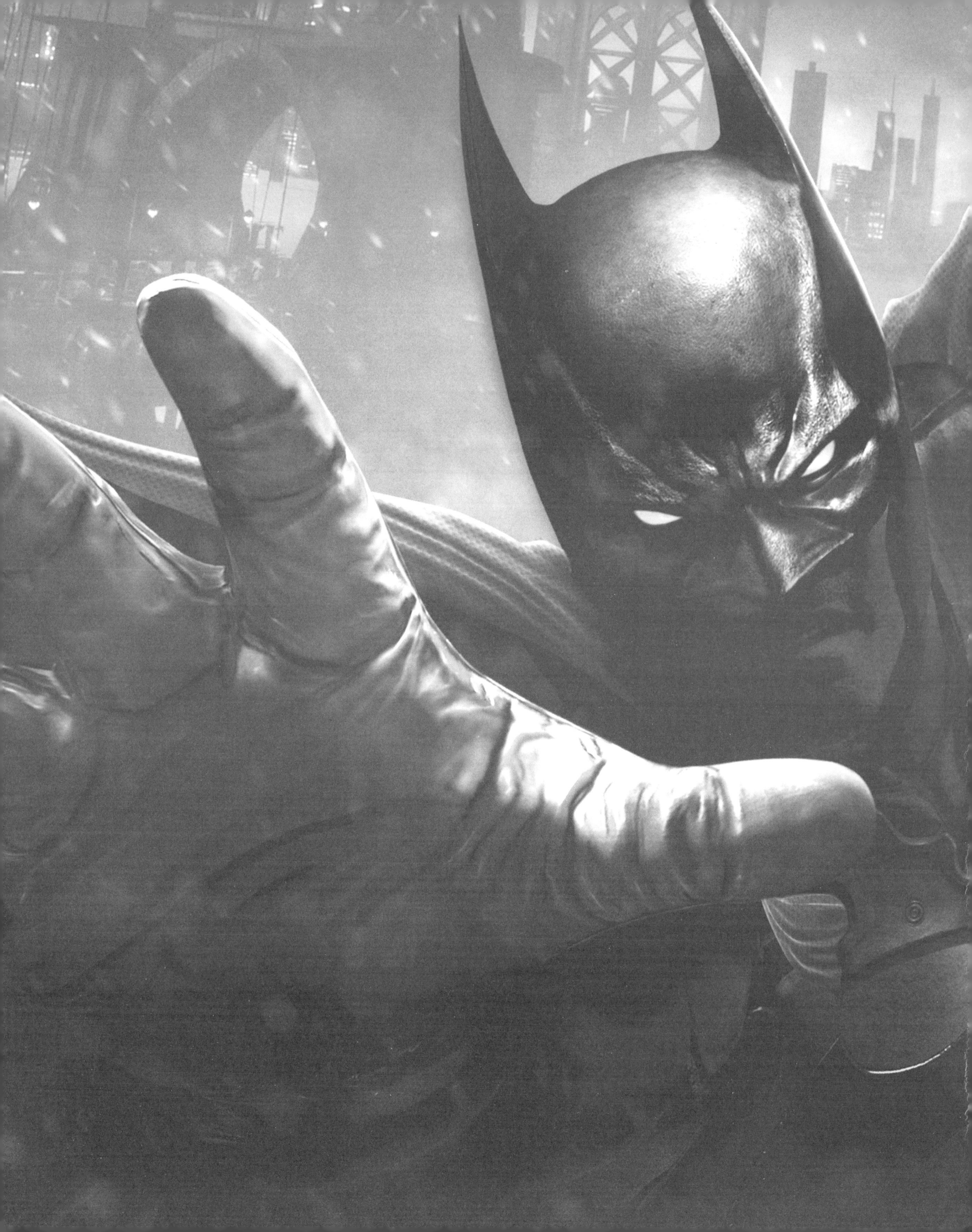